Lecture Notes in Computer Science 7011

Commenced Publication in 1973
Founding and Former Series Editors:
Gerhard Goos, Juris Hartmanis, and Jan van Leeuwen

Marc Joye   Debdeep Mukhopadhyay
Michael Tunstall (Eds.)

Security Aspects
in Information Technology

First International Conference
InfoSecHiComNet 2011
Haldia, India, October 19-22, 2011
Proceedings

 Springer

Volume Editors

Marc Joye
Technicolor, Security and Content Protection Labs
1 avenue de Belle Fontaine, 35576 Cesson-Sévigné Cedex, France
E-mail: marc.joye@technicolor.com

Debdeep Mukhopadhyay
Indian Institute of Technology
Department of Computer Science and Engineering
Kharagpur 721302, West Bengal, India
E-mail: debdeep@cse.iitkgp.ernet.in

Michael Tunstall
University of Bristol
Department of Computer Science
Merchant Venturers Building
Woodland Road
Bristol BS8 1UB, UK
E-mail: tunstall@cs.bris.ac.uk

ISSN 0302-9743   e-ISSN 1611-3349
ISBN 978-3-642-24585-5   e-ISBN 978-3-642-24586-2
DOI 10.1007/978-3-642-24586-2
Springer Heidelberg Dordrecht London New York

Library of Congress Control Number: 2011937700

CR Subject Classification (1998): E.3, C.2, K.6.5, D.4.6, J.1, G.2.1

LNCS Sublibrary: SL 4 – Security and Cryptology

Typesetting: Camera-ready by author, data conversion by Scientific Publishing Services, Chennai, India

Printed on acid-free paper

Springer is part of Springer Science+Business Media (www.springer.com)

Message from the General Chairs

We are happy to host the first International Conference on Security Aspects in Information Technology, High-Performance Computing and Networking, InfoSecHiComNet 2011, at Haldia Institute of Technology, Haldia, India, 19–22 October, 2011. This conference is being organized in cooperation with the International Association for Cryptographic Research (IACR) and in association with the Cryptology Research Society of India (CRSI).

As we are aware, different aspects of security, such as development of encryption algorithms and analysis of secrecy systems using high performance computing infrastructure, are of paramount importance for securing information. It is not only important to secure conventional electronic communication but security of networks is also emerging as a major thrust area of research in this age of digital communication. In this context, the present conference, InfoSecHiComNet 2011, is a very important event where the research community can deliberate upon different aspects of theoretical as well as application oriented work in the area of cryptology and information security. The conference has been divided into three tracks — Cryptography, Security Aspects in High Performance Computing, and Security Aspects in Networks.

It is expected that this conference will emerge as a powerful forum for researchers to interact and share their thoughts and their work with others, stimulating the growth of information and network security and cryptology research in the world, more specifically in India. The overwhelming response in quality submissions to the conference and transparent open review mechanism helped in keeping the standards high and also in encouraging researchers to participate in the conference and take up serious interest in pursuing research and development in this area. The presence of a large number of students indicates the growing interest in this area where achieving security and efficiency simultaneously in a network is a challenge.

The complete InfoSecHiComNet 2011 event spans over four days from 19 to 22 October 2011. The first day is totally dedicated to tutorials conducted by Michael Tunstall from the University of Bristol, UK and C. Pandurangan from IIT Madras, India. The main conference is held on the remaining three days with invited talks by experts from different parts of the world. Out of the 112 submitted papers, 14 papers have been selected through a transparent open review process and presented by the authors. The tutorials delivered by eminent speakers on areas covering recent developments in information security and cryptography provided insight to young researchers and also stimulated the thinking of others. We are thankful to all invited speakers who delivered stimulating talks and interesting tutorials on the subject.

A conference of this kind would not have been possible to organize without full support from different people across different committees. While all logistic and general organizational aspects were looked after by the Organizing Committee teams headed by Prof. Debasis Giri, the coordination and selection of technical papers required dedicated and time-bound efforts by the Program Chairs. We are thankful to Marc Joye, Michael Tunstall, and Debdeep Mukhopadhyay for their efforts in bringing out such an excellent technical program for the participants. We are also thankful to all the Technical Program Committee members for thoroughly reviewing the papers submitted to the conference and sending constructive suggestions and comments within the deadlines.

We are indebted to our fellow Organizing Chair, Prof. Debasis Giri, and his team, who worked hard in making the stay of the participants comfortable and the event enjoyable. Thanks are also due to the Chairman and Director of Haldia Institute of Technology for providing the venue and infrastructure and agreeing to host the conference.

We express our heartfelt thanks to Intel, Neucleodyne, the Defence Research and Development Organization (DRDO), the Ministry of Communication and Information Technology (MCIT), and the Department of Science and Technology (DST) for sponsoring the event.

Last but not least, we extend our sincere thanks to all those who contributed to InfoSecHiComNet 2011 and especially to the researchers who are now authors in this prestigious LNCS series of conference proceedings, which has been brought out so nicely.

October 2011   P.K. Saxena
                                                           P.D. Srivastava

Preface

We are glad to present the proceedings of the first International Conference on Security Aspects in Information Technology, High-Performance Computing and Networking (InfoSecHiComNet 2011), held October 19–22, 2011 in Haldia, West Bengal, India.

In response to the call for papers, 112 papers were submitted to the conference. These papers were evaluated on the basis of their significance, novelty, and technical quality. Each paper was reviewed by at least three members of the Program Committee. The Program Committee was aided by 13 sub-reviewers. Reviewing was double-blind, meaning that the Program Committee was not able to see the names and affiliations of the authors, and the authors were not told which committee members reviewed which papers. The Program Committee meeting was held electronically, with intensive discussions over a period of almost ten days. Of the papers submitted, 14 papers were selected for presentation at the conference. The program was completed with two instructive tutorials by C. Pandurangan (IIT Madras, India) and Michael Tunstall (University of Bristol, UK). Further, we had six invited talks by Ingrid Verbauwhede (Katholieke Universiteit Leuven, Belgium), Jörn-Marc Schmidt (IAIK, TUGraz, Austria), C.E. Venimadhavan (IISc, Bangalore,India), Benedikt Gierlichs (K.U.Leuven, Belgium), Palash Sarkar (ISI Kolkata,India), and Sanjay Burman (CAIR, India).

This conference was sponsored by Intel, Neucleodyne, the Defence Research and Development Organization, the Ministry of Communication and Information Technology, and the Department of Science and Technology, India. We would like to thank these organizations for their support, which helped us to reduce registration fees and make the conference a success.

InfoSecHiComNet 2011 was also organized in cooperation with the International Association for Cryptologic Research (IACR) and the Cryptology Research Society of India (CRSI). Their support has significantly contributed to raising the profile of the conference, which is reflected in the high quality of the submissions we received.

There is also a long list of people who volunteered their time and energy to put together the conference and who deserve acknowledgment. Thanks to all the members of the Program Committee, and the external reviewers, for all their hard work in the evaluation of the submitted papers. Our hearty thanks to the makers of EasyChair for allowing us to use the conference management system, which was largely instrumental in the timely and smooth operation needed in hosting such an international event. We also thank Springer for agreeing to publish the proceedings as a volume in the Lecture Notes in Computer Science series.

We are also very grateful to all the people who gave their assistance and ensured a smooth organization process: the local Organizing Committee of Haldia Institute of Technology. Special thanks to Dr. Debasis Giri, our Organizing Chair, for all his hard work, help and advice in initiating and making the conference a reality.

Last, but certainly not least, our thanks go to all the authors who submitted papers and all the attendees. We hope you find the program stimulating.

August 2011

Marc Joye
Debdeep Mukhopadhyay
Michael Tunstall

InfoSecHiComNet 2011

First International Conference on Security Aspects in Information Technology, High-Performance Computing and Networking

Haldia, India
October 19–22, 2011

Patron

Lakshman Seth   Haldia Institute of Technology, India

Honorary Chair

C. Chang   Feng Chia University, Taiwan

Publication and Organizing Chair

Debasis Giri   Haldia Institute of Technology, India

Program Chairs

Marc Joye   Technicolor, France
Debdeep Mukhopadhyay   IIT Kharagpur, India
Michael Tunstall   University of Bristol, UK

Program Committee

Anirban Banerjee   Indian Institute of Science, Education and
                               Research – Kolkata, India
Ranieri Baraglia   ISTI-CNR, Italy
S.S. Bedi   SAG, Delhi, India
Sanjukta Bhowmick   University of Nebraska at Omaha, USA
Swarup Bhunia   Case Western Reserve Univ., USA
Santosh Biswas   IIT Guwahati, India
Bezawada Bruhadeshwar   IIIT Hyderabad, India
Sanjay Burman   CAIR Bangalore, India
Junwei Cao   Tsinghua University, China
Amlan Chakrabarti   Calcutta University, India
R.S. Chakraborty   IIT Kharagpur, India
C. Chang   Feng Chia University, Taiwan
Amit Chattopadhyay   Rijksuniversity of Groningen, The Netherlands

Tzungshi Chen	National University of Tainan, Taiwan
Peter Chong	Nanyang Technological University, Singapore
Abhijit Das	IIT Kharagpur, India
Ashok Kumar Das	IIIT, Hyderabad, India
Sajal Das	University of Texas at Arlington, USA
Ratna Dutta	IIT Kharagpur, India
Niloy Ganguly	IIT Kharagpur, India
Praveen Gauravaram	Technical University of Denmark, Denmark
S.K. Ghosh	IIT Kharagpur, India
Debasis Giri	Haldia Institute of Technology, India
Tiong Goh	Victoria University of Wellington, New Zealand
Guangjie Han	Hohai University, China
Jing He	Georgia State University, USA
Honggang Hu	University of Waterloo, Canada
Shaoquan Jiang	University of Electronic Science and Technology of China, China
Xiaohong Jiang	Tohoku University, Japan
Willem Jonker	EIT ICT Labs, The Netherlands
Marc Joye	Technicolor, France
Ramesh Karri	Polytechnic University, NY, USA
Chun-Ta Li	Tainan University of Technology, Taiwan
Jie Li	University of Tsukuba, Japan
Constandinos Mavromoustakis	University of Nicosia, Cyprus
Bivas Mitra	French National Centre for Scientific Research(CNRS), Paris
Animesh Mukherjee	ISI Foundation, Italy
Debdeep Mukhopadhyay	IIT Kharagpur, India
Sourav Mukhopadhyay	IIT Kharagpur, India
Sukumar Nandi	IIT Guwahati, India
Saibal Pal	SAG, Delhi, India
Subrat Panda	IBM, India
C. Pandu Rangan	Indian Institute of Technology, Madras, India
Goutam Paul	Jadavpur University, India
Rajesh Pillai	SAG, Delhi, India
Vincent Rijmen	IAIK, Graz University of Technology, Austria
Bimal Roy	Indian Statistical Institute, Kolkata, India
Romit Roychoudhury	Duke University, USA
Dipanwita Roychowdhury	IIT Kharagpur, India
Kouichi Sakurai	Kyushu University, Japan
Areejit Samal	Univ. Paris-Sud, France and Max Planck Institute for Mathematics in the Sciences, Germany
P. Saxena	SAG, India
Peter Schwabe	Academia Sinica, Institute of Information Science, Taiwan
Indranil Sengupta	IIT Kharagpur, India

P. Srivastava	IIT Kharagpur, India
Shamik Sural	IIT Kharagpur, India
Willy Susilo	University of Wollongong, Australia
Junko Takahashi	NTT Information Sharing Platform Laboratories, Japan
Sabu Thampi	Indian Institute of Information Technology and Management, India
Michael Tunstall	University of Bristol, UK
Athanasios Vasilakos	University of Western Macedonia, Greece
Kamakoti Veezhinathan	IIT Madras, India
Ramarathnam Venkatesan	Microsoft Research, USA
Michal Wozniak	Wroclaw University of Technology, Poland
Naixue Xiong	Georgia State University, USA
Eiko Yoneki	University of Cambridge, UK
Amr Youssef	Concordia University, Canada

External Reviewers

Indivar Gupta	Rajesh Pillai
Arun Karthik Kanuparthi	Yizhi Ren
Aswin Krishna	Sharmila Deva Selvi
P.R. Mishra	Easter Selvan Suviseshamuthu
Seetharam Narasimhan	S.K. Tiwari
Ruchira Naskar	Mallapur Verraya Verraya
Takashi Nishide	Xinmu Wang

Local Organizing Committee

M.M. Bag	Sourav Mandal
Subhabrata Barman	Anjan Mishra
Nandan Bhattacharyya	Apratim Mitra
Debdas Ganguly	Anupam Pattanayak
Tarun Kumar Ghosh	Soumen Paul
Subhankar Joardar	Palash Ray
Shyamalendu Kandar	Soumen Saha
Asish Lahiri	Sk. Sahnawaj
A.B. Maity	Kabita Thaoroijam
Susmit Maity	

Table of Contents

Invited Talks

Engineering Trustworthy Systems 1
  Sanjay Burman

Secure Implementations for the Internet of Things 2
  Jörn-Marc Schmidt

Embedded Security

Model Based Hybrid Approach to Prevent SQL Injection Attacks in
PHP 3
  Kunal Sadalkar, Radhesh Mohandas, and Alwyn R. Pais

Security of Prime Field Pairing Cryptoprocessor against Differential
Power Attack 16
  Santosh Ghosh and Dipanwita Roychowdhury

Embedded Software Security through Key-Based Control Flow
Obfuscation 30
  *Rajat Subhra Chakraborty, Seetharam Narasimhan, and
  Swarup Bhunia*

Digital Rights Management

Reversible Watermarking Using *Priority Embedding* through Repeated
Application of *Integer Wavelet Transform* 45
  *Sambaran Bandyopadhyay, Ruchira Naskar, and
  Rajat Subhra Chakraborty*

Access Policy Based Key Management in Multi-level Multi-distributor
DRM Architecture 57
  Ratna Dutta, Dheerendra Mishra, and Sourav Mukhopadhyay

Access Polynomial Based Self-healing Key Distribution with Improved
Security and Performance 72
  Ratna Dutta

Cryptographic Protocols

An ID-Based Proxy Multi Signature Scheme without Bilinear
Pairings 83
  Namita Tiwari and Sahadeo Padhye

Distributed Signcryption Schemes with Formal Proof of Security   93
    Indivar Gupta and P.K. Saxena

Identity Based Online/Offline Encryption and Signcryption Schemes
Revisited   111
    S. Sharmila Deva Selvi, S. Sree Vivek, and C. Pandu Rangan

Cryptanalysis/Side Channel Attacks

"Rank Correction": A New Side-Channel Approach for Secret Key
Recovery.   128
    Maxime Nassar, Youssef Souissi, Sylvain Guilley, and
    Jean-Luc Danger

A Cache Trace Attack on CAMELLIA   144
    Rishabh Poddar, Amit Datta, and Chester Rebeiro

An Improvement of Linearization-Based Algebraic Attacks   157
    Satrajit Ghosh and Abhijit Das

Cipher Primitives

Generalized Avalanche Test for Stream Cipher Analysis   168
    P.R. Mishra, Indivar Gupta, and N.R. Pillai

On Applications of Singular Matrices over Finite Fields in
Cryptography   181
    Dhirendra Singh Yadav, Rajendra K. Sharma, and Wagish Shukla

Author Index   187

Engineering Trustworthy Systems

Sanjay Burman

Centre for Artificial Intelligence and Robotics,
C V Raman Nagar, Bangalore-560093, India
sb@cair.drdo.in

Abstract. Focus on building systems that are secure by design is being
driven by increasing number of security threats and the cost of system
compromise. The pervasive deployment of information technology in en-
tertainment to finance management to health care to critical infrastruc-
tures has lead to a situation where today - everything is a computing
device which can process and store information. These are networked for
communication.

There is increasing interdependence of all these networked computing
devices which have kinetic impact on the real world. The increased interdependence leads to a situation where a security failure at one point
can lead to a cascading domino effect leading to the ultimate failure of
critical infrastructure. Their failure can be disastrous to human life and
national security. Therefore, today the need for engineering secure systems is as necessary as the traditional engineering requirements such as
performance, energy-efficiency, cost, programmability and usability. This
emphasis on engineering security can drive the development of architectures and methodologies that are essential for achieving trustworthiness
in the realized systems. This talk will introduce the challenges in realization of systems that perform securely in the real world. An approach
to engineering the systems right from the architectural level to the final
implementation and security assessment of the systems to determine the
adequacy of robustness will be suggested.

M. Joye et al. (Eds.): InfoSecHiComNet 2011, LNCS 7011, p. 1, 2011.

Secure Implementations for the Internet of Things

Jörn-Marc Schmidt

Graz University of Technology
Institute for Applied Information Processing and Communications
Inffeldgasse 16a, 8010 Graz, Austria
joern-marc.schmidt@iaik.tugraz.at

Abstract. In the world envisioned by the Internet of Things (IoT), every object is able to communicate digitally. An important step towards this vision is the use of passive RFID tags. These devices are contactless powered by a reader field and hence do not require a dedicated power source. The corresponding counter-parts to these tags are already integrated in some modern mobile phones. The combination of mobile readers integrated in every-day objects like smart phones and low-cost tags could deliver basic building blocks for a lot of new applications. However, in order to get broad acceptance, the capabilities of such systems in the sense of usability are as important as their security to preserve the privacy of the users. No malicious user should benefit from information that is collected, transferred, or processed. Hence, the user must be able to rely on the protocol as well as on the implementation. In this talk, we discuss potential future developments of the Internet of Things and the requirements regarding security and privacy. Furthermore, we highlight the need for trustworthy implementations and show actual results in this context.

M. Joye et al. (Eds.): InfoSecHiComNet 2011, LNCS 7011, p. 2, 2011.
© Springer-Verlag Berlin Heidelberg 2011

Model Based Hybrid Approach to Prevent SQL Injection Attacks in PHP

Kunal Sadalkar, Radhesh Mohandas, and Alwyn R. Pais

Department of Computer Science and Engineering
National Institute of Technology Karnataka, Surathkal,India - 575025
kunalsadalkar@yahoo.co.in, {radhesh,alwyn.pais}@gmail.com

Abstract. SQL Injection vulnerability is ranked 1st in the OWASP[1] top 10 vulnerability list and has resulted in massive attacks on a number of websites in the past few years. Inspite of preventive measures like educating developers about safe coding practices, statistics shows that these vulnerabilities are still dominating the top. Various static and dynamic approaches have been proposed to mitigate this vulnerability. In this paper, we present a hybrid approach to prevent SQL injection attacks in PHP, a popular server side scripting language. This technique is more effective to prevent SQL injection attack in a dynamic web content environment without use of complex string analyzer logic. Initially, we construct a Query model for each hotspot by running the application in safe mode. In the production environment, dynamically generated queries are validated with it. The results and analysis shows the proposed approach is simple and effective to prevent common SQL injection vulnerabilities.

Keywords: SQL injection attack, static analysis, dynamic analysis, web vulnerabilities, unauthorized access, authentication bypass,input validation,database mapping.

1 Introduction

The industry is moving fast towards web based technologies. Ubiquity and cost effective remote services are the driving factors for the growth of the web based industries. Companies and organizations are adapting these upcoming technology to reduce cost and to satisfy their customers. Services like online shopping, e-banking, e-reservation, e-governance etc. have made daily life more productive. In a race to support more and more flexible solutions, web developers are skipping steps of best coding practices leading to serious web vulnerabilities. Lack of proper code review and increased complexity of configuring the security policies of web applications, enable malicious users to misuse these services and achieve monitory gains. Testing for these security vulnerabilities requires considerable time and resources and even known attacks are not addressed completely.

---

[1] Open Web Application Security Project.

M. Joye et al. (Eds.): InfoSecHiComNet 2011, LNCS 7011, pp. 3–15, 2011.
© Springer-Verlag Berlin Heidelberg 2011

Nowadays, PHP is well-known for server-side web development and widely used general-purpose scripting language on 75% of web servers. The overall proportion of PHP-related vulnerabilities on the database amount to: 20% in 2004, 28% in 2005, 43% in 2006, 36% in 2007, 35% in 2008, and 30% in 2009 [12,13]. According to SANS [14] statistics, the total numbers of vulnerabilities exploited in web applications are more than those of stand-alone system vulnerabilities. SQL Injection attacks continue to remain among the top three popular techniques used for compromising web sites. In SQL injection vulnerability the data from untrusted sources is used in a trusted manner and that allows execution of unintended queries.

Although the causes for SQL injection have been known for a long time and various solutions including defensive coding practices, static code reviews and runtime checks have been proposed, the problem persists for several reasons. Human code reviews are time consuming and expensive. Moreover the quality of code review strongly depends on the expertise of the reviewer. Defensive programming and input filtration prevents from malicious command to get executed, but this approach is fairly oblivious to new unanticipated patterns. Performance of runtime checks is sensitive to the size of the applications and also increases the false positive rates as the application logic gets updated. Finally any solution based on hybrid technique [1] to prevent SQL injection attacks suffers from the limitation of string analysis precision and execution performance penalty.

This paper addresses the comparative analysis of static and dynamic approach, highlights the inability of existing hybrid approaches[2] to prevent SQL injection attacks in PHP. Furthermore we propose a new alternative model based approach to counter the SQL injection attack in PHP. An empirical analysis shows that the proposed approach is extremely simple and does not need complex logic of static analysis based on a string analyzer.

2   Related Work

Our approach is a simple variant of the existing model based hybrid approach AMNeSIA [2]. This approach combines static analysis and runtime monitoring. In the static phase, it builds a query model for legitimate SQL with the help of java string analyzer (JSA)[8]. Query models are constructed as NDFA (Non Deterministic Finite Automata) whose nodes are SQL keywords and operators with special symbols for user input. During the run time, queries are intercepted with the instrumented code and crosschecked with the statically built query models. A limitation of AMNeSIA[2] tool is that it cannot be used for web applications other than those built on JSP. As the tool makes implicit use of JSA[8] library to build query model, the proposed approach does not work for PHP applications. Moreover this tool's success is dependent on the accuracy of the string analyzer.

Similarly JDBC checker[9] statically validates the correctness of dynamically generated queries. SQLDOM [7] and Safe Query Object [15] make use of encapsulation of database query in order to access the database safely. But in these cases, the developer has the overhead of learning a new programming paradigm. SQLrand [4] is another effective approach that based on query randomization. However the security of this approach totally depends on the key that had used for randomization.

Our mechanism provides SQL injection prevention for PHP web application based on the AMNeSIA logic, but with modifications to bypass the complex logic of static analysis and prevents the common SQL injection attacks.

3   Classifying SQL Injection Vulnerability

SQL injection is an attack technique that tricks the database to execute unintentional malicious code. SQL injection usually involves the combination of over elevated permissions, un-sanitized user input and/or true software vulnerabilities. This section briefly describes the vulnerability and its classification based on the methods of exploitation (see [11] for a detailed explanation of various types of SQL vulnerabilities).

Fig. 1. Generic Login page in PHP

To classify SQL injection let us consider a typical web application as shown in Fig. 1 with a login page written in PHP and connected to a MySQL database [Fig. 2]in the backend. When an user enters his credentials and presses the submit button, the data is sent to the server with well-known GET/POST command. On the server, the user input is embedded into a precrafted SQL statement and executed to retrieve the expected data. Let us assume that the query is of the form;

*SELECT * FROM Employee WHERE user_name = '$uname' and password = '$password';*

If user_name and password is provided from the user submitted form, query to be executed is form;

*SELECT * FROM Employee WHERE user_name = 'alice' and password = 'secret';*

```
2   ☐<?php
3     $username = $_POST['user'];
4     $pwd = $_POST['pass'];
5     $acct_num = $_POST['acct_num'];
6     $host = "localhost"; //database location
7     $user = "web"; //database username
8     $pass = ""; //database password
9     $db_name = "test"; //database name
10
11    //database connection
12    $link = mysql_connect($host, $user, $pass);
13    mysql_select_db($db_name);
14    if ($username)
15    $result  = mysql_query("select * from user where username ='".$username."' and pwd ='".$pwd."'");
16    else
17    $result  = mysql_query("select * from user where Acct_Number =".$acct_num." and pwd ='".$pwd."'");
18    ?>
```

Fig. 2. Backend logic to connect database and execute SQL command

Now, one of the root causes for SQL injection is to accept the user input without proper validation. Many programmers are simply not aware or do not care that the security of their application could be compromised through the entry of malicious input. Another reason could be the financial and time constraints imposed by management. Implementing functional requirementa quickly is the top of priority, while non-functional requirementa like security is often neglected. We classify SQL injection attack for the given application as follows.

3.1   Attack Based on Tautology

In the example above, suppose the attacker inputs *'$password'* and enters the value a' OR '1' = '1', the corresponding query becomes;
*SELECT * FROM Employee WHERE user_name = 'alice' and password = 'a' OR '1' ='1';*
    In this case no matter what the password entered is, the query will always return true and will allow the attacker to bypass the authentication.

3.2   Attack Based on Union

In this case attacker executes a malicious query along with the predefined query. Suppose an attacker inputs password as a' UNION SELECT * from password, query becomes;
SELECT * FROM Employee WHERE user_name = 'alice' and password = 'a' UNION SELECT * from password;
    Here, the attacker performs unauthorize access to other table data that meant to be remain confidential.

3.3   Attack Based on Comments

The character "–" marks the beginning of a SQL comment and anything beyond that is ignored. Suppose an attacker inputs *'$uname'* as a' OR '1' = '1' – then final query is interpreted as;

*SELECT * FROM Employee WHERE user_name = 'a' OR '1' = '1' – and
password = 'anything';*

This is one of the classic type of SQL injection attack where attacker bypasses common authentication by inserting comments at the user input field.

4   Static vs Dynamic Approach

Several static and dynamic approaches have been proposed to detect SQLIA on web applications[16]. Both suffer from their own sets of limitations. Static code analyzing is mainly based on tainted information flow tracking which suffers from the precision problem which models semantics of input sanitization of routines. They manually need to write routines for each query or every bug and also they are not fully automated. Most of the dynamic analysis approaches do not involve the development team directly, and they lead to higher false alarms.

Only static source code review or dynamic checking is not sufficient to protect from SQLIA vulnerabilities. Thus an automated hybrid mechanism is proposed to prevent SQLIA effectively.

5   Basic AMNeSIA Model for JSP Web Application and Its Limitation

AMNeSIA is a model based solution to prevent SQLIA on JSP web applications. It works in two phases.

Static analysis: It uses static analysis to analyze web application code and automatically generate the SQL model.

Runtime analysis: This is the step that monitors all dynamically generated queries and checks them to be with compliance to the statically generated models. When this step detects that a query is violating the model, it classifies the input as an attack, logs the necessary information and throws an exception that the application can then deal with suitably.

5.1   Principles

- Identify the Hotspots:
    This step involves analyzing the web application code by simply scanning the code and identifying the hotspots which are the locations where the queries are sent for execution.
- Build the SQL query model:
    - The Application class files are given as input to JSA (Java String Analyzer)[8]. It outputs a NDFA (Non-Deterministic Finite Automata) with all character level possibilities of the strings.
    - It further analyzes the NDFA to create a query model and transforms it into semantically meaningful SQL keywords, operators and literal values.
- Instrument the Application:

- In this phase, AMNeSIA[2] creates a monitor function that checks for queries at runtime.
- It inserts the call to the monitor function before accessing the database at each place.
- The Monitor call is invoked with two parameters; the query that is to be submitted and the unique identifier to the hotspot.

– Runtime monitor:

- During runtime, the query is sent to the runtime monitor before accessing the database.
- The monitor parses the query string into a sequence of tokens.
- Runtime monitoring verifies for query acceptance test by traversing the sequence of tokens. Depending on test result, it allows/restrict the database access.

5.2   Limitations and Assumptions of AMNeSIA Model in JSP

At the time of evaluation this technique doesn't produces any false negatives or false positives. But there is a chance to get false positives and false negatives in some situations

– When the string analysis results in a SQL query model that is overly conservative and includes spurious queries (i.e. queries that could not be generated by the application) that happen to match an attack;
– When a legitimate query happens to have the same "SQL structure" of an attack. For example, if a developer adds conditions to a query from within a loop, an attacker who inserts an additional condition of the same type would generate a query that does not violate the SQL-query model.
– In some cases, as the analysis cannot distinguish a variable or a hard-coded SQL token, it raises false positives for a string model that is precise enough. In particular, if the hard-coded string is used in the application to construct a SQL token, the technique will generate an incomplete SQL-query model.
– AMNeSIA[2] tool makes use of Java String Analyzer (JSA)[8] library to statically analyze the source code and thereby get the query models. Thus it can't be used for web applications other than those built on JSP such as PHP or ASP.

6   Proposed Solution

AMNeSIA was developed exclusively for JSP web applications. We propose a variant of this approach for PHP web applications. We modified the program flow of basic AMNeSIA[2] model to make it applicable for PHP web applications without using the complex logic of static analysis.

Our mechanism is divided into a safe mode and a production mode environment. Initially a given web application is scanned for hotspot signatures.

Hotspots are the locations in a web application where the query gets executed (EX: functions like mysql_query(), db→ query() etc.). After identifying the hotspot, the application is instrumented with a special function. Then we run it under a safe mode environment that is defined with the valid set of inputs from the developer/tester. Because the application is instrumented with the special function at the hotspot, it changes the program flow and, helps to capture the particular query. The instrumented code calls the special function with arguments (*hotspot_id, query*). The captured query is then tokenized; The DFA is constructed and stored as a query model. During the production mode environment, queries with user input are intercepted with the instrumented call and are verified against the query models built in the safe mode. Queries those violate the model are prevented from getting executed.

The primary advantage of running the application in a safe mode environment is to bypass the complex logic of static analysis of source code that includes intermediate code generation, control flow generation, data flow generation and finally DFA construction.

6.1   Algorithms

Our algorithm has been divided into two distinct parts. First part of it focuses on identifying the hotspots and instrumenting an application for either safe or production environment mode. Query model validation and attack detection is in the second part of it. In the safe environment mode, proposed algorithm statically analyzes the source code and constructs standard query model by taking legitimate set of input parameters from the tester/developer. After obtaining query models, application is once again instrumented for the production mode environment. Detection algorithm in the production mode performs verification of dynamically generated query with the query model built in safe mode. It makes use of the graph traversal algorithm to validate with the query model.

6.2   Examples

Following examples illustrates the working of our proposed algorithm. We have considered two cases. First one is the input parameters without SQL injection, and the second one is with the SQL injection string. Before we test for these cases, let us once again consider a web application as shown in the Fig.1, with two text boxes which accepts (α, β) as input and a submit button. Then corresponding query model obtained after safe mode testing is represented as below.
SQL query:
*SELECT * FROM Employee WHERE user_name = 'α' and password = 'β';*
Query model:
SQL(H_id,α, β):
Where,
H_id: ID of the Hotspot
α is the value from the textbox user name
β is the value from the textbox password

Algorithm 1. Identify Hotspots and Instrument the source code

---

Inputs: PHP web application with safe input parameters.
Output: Instrumented Files

---

get_count_files(*path*): Returns total number of files for the specified application path
get_token_all(*file*):PHP inbuilt function that returns all tokens for the given input file.
signature_found(*token*):Matches token with predefined hotspot signatures.
get_hotspot_location(*hotspot_id*): Returns hotspot position in the file for given hotspot_id.
get_environment():Returns safe or production environment mode.
instrument_for_safe_mode(*hotspot_id,code,location*):Instruments the source file for safe environment mode with special function query_validate()
instrument_for_production_mode(*hotspot_id,code,location*):Instruments the source file for production environment mode with special function query_validate()

```
1:  for i = 0 TO get_count_files(path) do
2:      list_of_tokens ← get_token_all(file[i])
3:      hotspots ← {}
4:      hotspot_count ← 0
5:      for j = 0 TO get_count(list_of_tokens) do
6:          if signature_found(list_of_tokens[j]) = True then
7:              hotspots ← location_pointer
8:              hotspot_id ← hotspot_count
9:              hotspot_count ← hotspot_count + 1
10:         else
11:             continue
12:         end if
13:     end for
14: end for
15: for k = 0 TO hotspot_count do
16:     hotspot_id ← get_hotspot_id(hotspot[k])
17:     location ← get_hotspot_location(hotspot_id)
18:     if get_environment() = safe then
19:         instrumented_files[] ← instrument_for_safe_mode(hotspot_id, instr_code, location)
20:     else
21:         instrumented_files[] ← instrument_for_production_mode(hotspot_id, instr_code, location)
22:     end if
23: end for
24: return instrumented_files[]
```

Algorithm 2. Algorithm to detect SQL injection attack in the production mode environment

Inputs: PHP web application instrumented for production mode environment.
Output: Injection = True / False

read_query(): Captures dynamic generated query in the production mode.
parse_query(*query_string*):Parses query according to the SQL standard rules and returns corresponding tokens.
query_validate(*hotspot_id,query_tokens*): Uses the graph traversal algorithm to validate dynamically generated query with its static model.

1: *production_mode_query ← read_query()*
2: *query_tokens ← parse_query(production_mode_query)*
3: **if** *query_validate(hotspot_id, query_tokens) = FALSE* **then**
4:     **return** TRUE
5: **else**
6:     **return** FALSE
7: **end if**

CASE 1 Verifying with normal input parameters:
Let us assume that user had input $\alpha = abc$; $\beta = $ pwd123 in the production mode environment. SQL statement generated for the corresponding query at that hotspot becomes,
*SELECT * FROM Employee WHERE user_name ='abc' AND password='pwd123'*
As per our algorithm, initially above query is tokenized according to the SQL standard rules and further it passes to the query validation module. In the query validation module, get_safe_mode_query() returns query model which has already obtained in the safe mode environment. Each token obtained after tokenizing production mode query is validated with this query model (DFA). In this case as each token matches with expected query model, the *query_validate()* function returns true and ultimately allows execution of the query.
CASE 2 Verifying parameters with SQL injection string:
Let us assume that user had input $\alpha =$ a' OR 1 =1 - -; $\beta=$ pwd123 in the production mode environment. SQL statement generated for the corresponding query at that hotspot is interpreted as,
*SELECT * FROM Employee WHERE user_name ='a' OR 1=1 - - AND password='pwd123'*
As we can see that, the attacker has inserted malicious input which tries to change the semantic of the query.Here special characters like single quote (') and double dash (- -) along with the SQL keywords has been inserted in the input field. Because of these extra tokens, production mode query mismatches with the expected query model and *query_validate()* function returns false. As a result it forbids the database access and prevents from executing unintended malicious query.

7   Implementation

We implemented the proposed approach for PHP web applications. In this section we briefly explain the PHP tool and the mechanism to overcome the challenge of statically analyzing the PHP web application.

Fig.3 shows the different modules of the implemented tool. Initially the

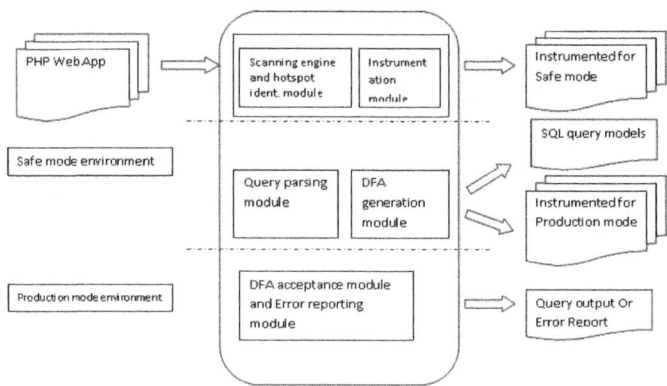

Fig. 3. Architecture of the Model Based Hybrid Approach to Prevent SQL injection Attack Tool

scanning engine scans PHP files from the web application. It uses the inbuilt PHP function get_token_all() to tokenize the given application and searches for hotspot signatures. Once it finds the hotspot signatures, the instrumentation module puts a special function call,*query_validate()*, just before it. This special function *query_validate()*, modifies the original program flow and collects the query run in the safe mode environment. The same function has been used in validation module where it validates the production run query with the query model built in safe mode. The validate module contains both DFA construction module and DFA acceptance module. We describe the functionality of each module as below.

1. *Hotspot identification module*: Accepts PHP files as an input and identifies hotspot for given hotspot signatures.
2. *Instrumentation module:* Patches extra instrumented code before every hotspot and includes file containing dynamic checking function at the beginning of every php file.
3. *Query parsing module*: Queries obtained at the hotspots are passed to the sql_parser module. The sql_parser module tokenizes the query according to the MySQL standards and the tokens are then passed to the DFA construction module.
4. *DFA construction module in Safe mode Environment*: A DFA (M) is defined as a 5-tuple, $(Q, \Sigma, \delta, q0, F)$, consisting of a finite set of states (Q),a finite set

of input symbols called the alphabet (Σ), a transition function ($\delta : Q \ \Sigma \rightarrow$ Q), a start state (q0 $\in$Q), a set of accept states (F $\subseteq$ Q)

The Tokenized query is given to the DFA construction module that converts it into above specified format.

5. *DFA verification module in Production mode Environment:* This module uses the graph based DFA traversal method to identify deviation in the production time environment query with the model obtained in safe environment mode.

6. *Error reporting module:* Depending on the result from DFA verification module this module either reports the injection activity or allows to accessing the database.

8   Experimental Setup

All tests were performed on a PC with Intel core 2 Duo processor (2.0 GHz) and 3 GB DDR3 memory.To validate our approach, we have taken a proof of concept perspective about making an application secure from users or insider SQL-injections. Our objective was to test the proposed mechanism thoroughly with respect to all kind of SQL injection attacks and for the applications with different complexities.We choose five well-known open source applications[17].This set of subjects was used in previous work by us and also other researchers.

As per our approach, for each application we had generated two sets of test inputs. First test set contained HTTP request statements with valid the input set. For each application, the test-bed had about 600 legitimate HTTP requests. They had been used during the safe mode environment in order obtain query models. The inputs were generated for the safe mode testing in a manner that they covered almost every hotspot in an application.

Also we assumed that the testing done for the safe mode environment is in-house testing, therefore developer must have knowledge about the number of the input that must be tested with respect to cover all the hotspots within an application. If the developer fails to test for certain valid input, then the semantics of the query may not get captured in the safe mode environment. As a result it may lead to the false alarm in the production mode environment.

Second test set contained request statements with the malicious SQL injection input. For each application, the production mode test set contained about 3000 malformed HTTP requests with SQL injection related strings. These malformed requests are constructed by surveying different exploits.

9   Result and Analysis

The applications chosen are vulnerable to SQL injection attacks and could be compromised with any one of the attacking technique described in section 3. Instrumentation overhead is computed as total percentage of extra code added into the original application. Table 1 show, instrumentation overhead is directly

Table 1. Empirical analysis of Model based Hybrid Technique to Prevent SQL Injection Attacks in sample open source PHP web applications

Web App	Line of Code (K)	Hotspots Instrumented	Detection Rate (%)	Instrumentation Size Overhead(%)	False Positive	AVG Query Overhead(%)
BookStore	6.8	75	100	13	15	2.43
Classifieds	3.7	55	100	10	11	1.89
EmpDir	1.8	35	100	7	13	1.70
Events	2.5	39	100	12	9	1.71
Portal	6.2	61	100	11	15	1.99

proportional to the number of hotspots found in the application. We have modified the testbed of attack vectors as per our requirements and collected the results. We believe that the attack vectors used covers almost all kind of SQL injection attacks. The effectiveness of the proposed approach determined by the ratio of the number of attacks prevented by the total number of attacks performed. Results shows that the proposed approach is 100% effective to prevent known SQL injection attacks. However, it also shows that proposed approach raises some false positives where it detects as SQL injection attack even if it doesn't exists. The reason for false positive is because the developer ran the test with a limited set of inputs in the safe mode. They can be eliminated by testing with complete set of valid input cases in safe environment mode. Finally the last column represents average time overhead to access database in the production mode environment.

10   Conclusion and Future Work

In this paper we presented an automatic technique to prevent SQL injection attack in PHP web applications. We made significant changes in the original approach to reduce the complexity and made it applicable to PHP. The technique utilizes the inherent nature of the program flow to construct query models and bypasses the complex logic of static analysis. Unlike other security analysis tools, our tool can be readily used on existing application or newly developed ones. This proposed approach seems to be more promising for preventing SQL injection attacks in normal PHP web applications with very little overhead.

In future, we will focus on reducing false alarm by applying machine learning algorithms in Safe Environment mode and hence improving the accuracy. Further, we shall apply the same approach to prevent SQL injection attacks in other scripting language such as PERL.

Acknowledgments. We acknowledge the financial support provided by MCIT-NewDelhi, GOI, by the sanction Order No: 12(10)/09ESD dated 08.01.2010.

References

1. Halfond, W.G., Orso, A.: Combining Static Analysis and Runtime Monitoring to Counter SQL-Injection Attacks. In: Proc. of the Third Intern. ICSE Workshop on Dynamic Analysis (WODA 2005), pp. 22–28 (May 2005)
2. Halfond, W., Orso, A.: AMNESIA: Analysis and Monitoring for NEutralizing SQL Injection Attacks. In: Proc. 20th IEEE and ACM Int'l Conf. Automated Software Eng., pp. 174–183 (2005)
3. Halfond, W.G., Orso, A.: Combining Static Analysis and Runtime Monitoring to Counter SQL-Injection Attacks. In: Proceedings of the Third International ICSE Workshop on Dynamic Analysis (WODA 2005), St. Louis, MO, USA, pp. 22–28 (May 2005)
4. Boyd, S.W., Keromytis, A.D.: SQLrand: Preventing SQL injection attacks. In: Jakobsson, M., Yung, M., Zhou, J. (eds.) ACNS 2004. LNCS, vol. 3089, pp. 292–302. Springer, Heidelberg (2004)
5. Buehrer, G.T., Weide, B.W., Sivilotti, P.A.G.: Using Parse Tree Validation to Prevent SQL Injection Attacks. In: International Workshop on Software Engineering and Middleware, SEM (2005)
6. Su, Z., Wassermann, G.: The Essence of Command Injection Attacks in Web Applications. In: The 33rd Annual Symposium on Principles of Programming Languages, POPL 2006 (January 2006)
7. McClure, R., Kruger, I.: SQL DOM: Compile Time Checking of Dynamic SQL Statements. In: Proceedings of the 27th International Conference on Software Engineering (ICSE 2005), pp. 88–96 (2005)
8. Christensen, A.S., Møller, A., Schwartzbach, M.I.: Precise Analysis of String Expressions. In: Cousot, R. (ed.) SAS 2003. LNCS, vol. 2694, pp. 1–18. Springer, Heidelberg (2003)
9. Gould, C., Su, Z., Devanbu, P.: JDBC Checker: A Static Analysis Tool for SQL/JDBC Applications. In: Proceedings of the 26th International Conference on Software Engineering (ICSE 2004) Formal Demos, pp. 697–698 (2004)
10. Monticelli, F.: PhD SQLPrevent thesis. University of British Columbia (UBC) Vancouver, Canada (2008)
11. Owasp, O. W.: Top ten most critical web application vulnerabilities (2010), http://www.owasp.org/index.php/Top_10_2010-Main
12. PHP usage statistics, http://www.php.net/usage.php
13. Wikipedia, http://en.wikipedia.org/wiki/PHP
14. System Administration, Networking, and Security Institute (SANS), http://www.sans.org/
15. Cook, W.R., Rai, S.: Safe Query Objects: Statically Typed Objects as Remotely Executable Queries. In: Proc. 27th Intl Conf. Software Eng., pp. 97–106 (May 2005)
16. Amirtahmasebi, K., et al.: A survey of SQL injection defense mechanisms. In: Int. Conf. for Internet Technology and Secured Trans., ICITST 2009, pp. 1–8 (November 2009)
17. PHP Open source web applications, http://www.goto.com

Security of Prime Field Pairing Cryptoprocessor against Differential Power Attack

Santosh Ghosh and Dipanwita Roychowdhury

Department of Computer Science and Engineering,
Indian Institute of Technology,
Kharagpur, India
{santosh,drc}@cse.iitkgp.ernet.in

Abstract. This paper deals with the differential power attack on a pairing cryptoprocessor. The cryptoprocessor is designed for pairing computations on elliptic curves defined over finite fields with large prime characteristic. The work pinpoints the vulnerabilities of such pairing computations against side-channel attacks. By exploiting the power consumptions, the paper experimentally demonstrates such vulnerability on FPGA platform. A suitable counteracting technique is also suggested to overcome such vulnerability.

Keywords: Pairing Based Cryptography, Side-channel Analysis, Power Analysis Attack, DPA Attack, Prime Fields.

1 Introduction

Bilinear pairing or pairing is a new and increasingly popular way of constructing cryptographic protocols. This has resulted in the development of pairing based schemes such as identity based encryption (IBE) which are ideally used in identity aware devices. The security of such devices leads to the security of pairing computations. In the last decade, an increasingly popular form of attack known as side-channel attack (SCA) [5,6], which exploits the weakness in implementations, have developed. SCA breaks a cryptosystems by analyzing the information that could be measured through some covert channel of a cryptoprocessor like : power consumption, time, electromagnetic radiation, fault, etc.

Pairing can be computed on different characteristic fields like binary ($\mathbb{F}_{2^m}$), trinary ($\mathbb{F}_{3^m}$), and large prime ($\mathbb{F}_p$). The security of pairing computations over first two fields against differential power analysis (DPA) attack have been described in [11] and [7], respectively. DPA on pairing in general is described in [3,4]. However, security analysis of pairing computations especially on prime fields against side-channel attack has not been considered before.

This paper explores the side-channel vulnerability of pairing computations on FPGA platform. One of the popular pairing friendly elliptic curves defined over $\mathbb{F}_p$ is the Barreto-Naehrig curve (BN curve) [13]. A dual-core pairing cryptoprocessor for BN curves has been developed on FPGA platform. The paper proposes an optimized parallel scheduling of underlying finite field operations

M. Joye et al. (Eds.): InfoSecHiComNet 2011, LNCS 7011, pp. 16–29, 2011.
© Springer-Verlag Berlin Heidelberg 2011

for Tate pairing computations by the cryptoprocessor. It further observes the mathematical formula of different steps of the pairing computation and pinpoints the vulnerability against side-channel attacks. The paper then describes a differential power analysis (DPA) technique based on such vulnerability. The actual DPA attack has been mounted on FPGA platforms which ascertains the secret parameter of pairing computation. The paper then proposes a suitable computation technique for counteracting the above vulnerability.

The paper is organized as follows: section 2 provides a mathematical background of pairing computation technique. The description of pairing cryptoprocessor over prime field is given in section 3. The vulnerability of pairing computation over prime fields is pointed out in section 4. The proposed DPA attack and its counteracting technique is described in section 5. The paper is concluded in section 6.

2   Mathematical Background

Pairing is a bilinear map which is performed on a pair of elements of a group (say $\mathbb{G}_1$) to an element of another group (say $\mathbb{G}_3$). Pairings for cryptographic applications use an additive group defined over elliptic or hyperelliptic curves as $\mathbb{G}_1$ and a multiplicative group defined over an integer field as $\mathbb{G}_2$ [9]. The mapping also follow two important properties called *bilinearity* and *non-degeneracy*. Sometimes the pairing is computed on two elements from two different additive groups (say $\mathbb{G}_1$ and $\mathbb{G}_2$) and it maps to an element of a multiplicative group $\mathbb{G}_3$. The groups $\mathbb{G}_1$ and $\mathbb{G}_2$ are in general formed by an elliptic curve over $\mathbb{F}_q$ and $\mathbb{F}_{q^k}$, where k is also known as embedding degree of the elliptic curve. The security of a pairing is based on the difficulty to solve the discrete logarithm problem in $\mathbb{G}_1$, $\mathbb{G}_2$, and $\mathbb{G}_3$.

The computation efficiency of such bilinear map is also an important factor for cryptographic applications. Cryptographic pairings are efficiently computed by Miller's algorithm [1,2] which is shown in Alg. 1. More specifically this algorithm shows the computation of Tate pairing. Several optimizations of this algorithm have been presented in [10]. The resulting algorithm proposed in [10] is called BKLS algorithm for Tate pairing computation. Other pairings like ate, R-ate are computed by similar way using different parameters other than r and by interchanging the input points [15].

The underlying elliptic curve plays an important role for achieving computation efficiency and security of a pairing computation. Active research is going on for finding out such a *pairing-friendly* elliptic curves. One of the most popular pairing-friendly elliptic curves is known as Barreto-Naehrig curves (BN curves) [13]. The BN curve is defined over a large prime field with embedding degree 12. Thus $\mathbb{G}_1$ and $\mathbb{G}_2$ in Alg. 1 are additive elliptic curve groups defined over $\mathbb{F}_p$ and $\mathbb{F}_{p^{12}}$, respectively. The pairing value $t_r(P,Q) = f \in \mathbb{G}_3$, where $\mathbb{G}_3$ is a multiplicative integer group defined over $\mathbb{F}_{p^{12}}$. For achieving 128-bit security the BN curve is defined over a 256-bit prime field.

The BN curves also admit a sextic twist [15], which means that the point Q in Alg. 1) is mapped on a point Q' defined over $\mathbb{F}_{p^2}$. Thus, the line functions $l_{T,T}(Q)$

Input: $P \in G_1$ and $Q \in G_2$.
Output: $t_r(P, Q)$.

Write r in binary : $r = \sum_{i=0}^{L-1} r_i 2^i$.
$T \leftarrow P$, $f \leftarrow 1$.
for i *from* $L - 2$ *downto* 0 **do**
   | $T \leftarrow 2T$.
   | $f \leftarrow f^2 \cdot l_{T,T}(Q)$.
   | **if** $r_i = 1$ *and* $i \neq 0$ **then**
   | | $T \leftarrow T + P$.
   | | $f \leftarrow f \cdot l_{T,P}(Q)$.
   | **end**
end
return $f^{(q^k - 1)/r}$.

Algorithm 1. Computing the Tate pairing

and $l_{T,P}(Q)$ is computed over $\mathbb{F}_{p^2}$ instead of $\mathbb{F}_{p^{12}}$. Value of the line functions are represented as : $l_0 + l_1 W^2 + l_2 W^3$, with $l_0 \in \mathbb{F}_p$, $l_1, l_2 \in \mathbb{F}_{p^2}$, and a quadratic non-residue W over $\mathbb{F}_{p^2}$. The Miller function f is computed over $\mathbb{F}_{p^{12}}$, which is represented as : $f_0 + f_1 W + f_2 W^2 + f_3 W^3 + f_4 W^4 + f_5 W^5$, with $f_i \in \mathbb{F}_{p^2}$. So in the Tate pairing computation f^2, $f^2 \cdot l_{T,T}(Q)$, and $f \cdot l_{T,P}(Q)$ are performed on $\mathbb{F}_{p^{12}}$. Whereas all other computations are performed on $\mathbb{F}_p$ and $\mathbb{F}_{p^2}$.

The detailed procedure of pairing computation including the final exponentiation on BN curve is described in [15] and [16]. Another efficient way of computing final exponentiation is described in [17]. We use Jacobian coordinate systems for performing elliptic curve operations, where a point (X, Y, Z) corresponds to the point (x, y) in affine coordinates with $x = X/Z^2$ and $y = Y/Z^3$.

3   Pairing Crytoprocessor (PCP)

The major operations for a pairing computation are point doubling (PD), point addition (PA), line computation $(l(Q))$, f^2, and $f \cdot l(Q)$. In case of Tate pairing on BN curve, the PA and PD are performed in $\mathbb{F}_p$. Similarly, the operation $l(Q)$ is performed in $\mathbb{F}_{p^2}$ while the other two operations are performed in $\mathbb{F}_{p^{12}}$. However, the operations in these extension fields consist of a set of operations in underlying $\mathbb{F}_p$.

The current work explores the side-channel vulnerabilities of a pairing cryptoprocessor (PCP). Therefore, instead of designing a new architecture from the scratch, we implement the pairing cryptoprocessor that was proposed in [18] on FPGA platform. The work first implement a programmable core for computing all necessary $\mathbb{F}_p$ operations. Based on this programmable core we design a cryptoprocessor for pairing computation on FPGA platform. The proposed design consists two programmable cores which exploit the parallelism of Miller's algorithm. Each of the programmable cores can perform operations on $\mathbb{F}_p$ and $\mathbb{F}_{p^2}$.

We follow the formula and algorithms for the computation of asymmetric Tate pairing that are given in [15]. The major steps in pairing algorithm (Alg. 1) are *the Miller function* and *the final exponentiation*. The Miller function consists of two major steps, namely : *doubling step* and *addition step*. Here, we discuss the computation of above steps for Tate pairing over BN curve on our dual-core PCP.

The Tate pairing (t_r) over BN curve takes input points P and Q over $\mathbb{F}_p$ and $\mathbb{F}_{p^2}$, respectively. The parameter r is a 256-bit prime of Hamming weight 91. Thus, the Miller algorithm runs for 255 iterations having 255 doubling steps and 90 addition steps. There are sufficient independent operations within the doubling and addition steps which can be performed in parallel. Our dual-core PCP consists of a fixed number of functional units. Therefore, an optimization can be done based on the available functional units and the operations. In the following subsections, we describe an optimized scheduling of above steps on proposed PCP.

3.1   Computation of Doubling Step

The doubling step consists of the following computations.

- The point doubling $(2T)$ operation.
- The computation of tangent line at point T $(l_{T,T}(Q))$.
- The squaring of Miller function (f^2).
- The multiplication of Miller function with line function $(f^2 \cdot l_{T,T}(Q))$.

The computation of $2T$, $l_{T,T}(Q)$, and f^2 are performed in parallel on our PCP. In Jacobian coordinates the formulae for doubling a point $T = (X, Y, Z)$ are $2T = (X_3, Y_3, Z_3)$ where $X_3 = 9X^4 - 8XY^2$, $Y_3 = (3X^2)(4XY^2 - X_3) - 8Y^4$ and $Z_3 = 2YZ$. The tangent line at T, after clearing denominators, is $l(x, y) = 3X^3 - 2Y^2 - 3X^2Z^2x + Z_3Z^2y$ [14].

In case of Tate pairing computation on BN curves, the parameters $\{x, y\} \in \mathbb{F}_{p^2}$ and $\{X, Y, Z, X_3, Y_3, Z_3\} \in \mathbb{F}_p$. Let us assume that x and y are represented as $x_0 + x_1\mathcal{U}$ and $y_0 + y_1\mathcal{U}$, where $\{x_0, x_1, y_0, y_1\} \in \mathbb{F}_p$ and $\mathcal{U}$ is an indeterminant. The above operations are performed by one of the programmable cores in the dual-core PCP by following way.

$$
\begin{aligned}
&1.\ t_0 \leftarrow X^2, \quad t_1 \leftarrow Y^2, \quad t_2 \leftarrow Y \cdot Z \\
&2.\ t_3 \leftarrow (t_0)^2, \quad t_4 \leftarrow X \cdot t_1, \quad t_5 \leftarrow (t_1)^2 \\
&3.\ t_4 \leftarrow 2t_4, \quad t_6 \leftarrow 2t_3, \quad Z_3 \leftarrow 2t_2 \\
&4.\ t_4 \leftarrow 2t_4, \quad t_6 \leftarrow 2t_6, \quad t_5 \leftarrow 2t_5 \\
&5.\ t_3 \leftarrow t_3 + t_6, \quad t_5 \leftarrow 2t_5 \\
&6.\ X_3 \leftarrow t_3 - t_2, \quad t_5 \leftarrow 2t_5 \\
&7.\ t_3 \leftarrow t_4 - X_3, \quad t_7 \leftarrow t_7 + t_0
\end{aligned}
$$

$$8.\ t_7 \leftarrow t_7 \cdot t_3, \quad t_4 \leftarrow Z^2, \quad t_2 \leftarrow X \cdot t_0$$
$$9.\ Y_3 \leftarrow t_7 - t_5, \quad t_1 \leftarrow 2t_1, \quad t_5 \leftarrow 2t_2$$
$$10.\ t_4 \leftarrow t_4 \cdot t_0, \quad t_0 \leftarrow t_4 \cdot Z_3$$
$$11.\ t_2 \leftarrow 2t_4, \quad t_5 \leftarrow t_2 + t_5$$
$$12.\ t_4 \leftarrow t_4 + t_2, \quad l_0 \leftarrow t_5 - t_1$$
$$13.\ l_{10} \leftarrow t_4 \cdot x_0, \quad l_{11} \leftarrow t_4 \cdot x_1$$
$$14.\ l_{20} \leftarrow t_0 \cdot y_0, \quad l_{21} \leftarrow t_0 \cdot y_1$$

In the above scheduling nonlinear $\mathbb{F}_p$ operations are performed in the instructions 1, 2, 8, 10, 13, and 14. If we assume that $\mathbb{F}_p$ squaring $(s) \approx \mathbb{F}_p$ multiplication (m) then the cost of above operations is $6m$ on a programmable core in our dual-core PCP. At the same time other core starts the computation of f^2. We represent the Miller function $f \in \mathbb{F}_{((p^2)^3)^2}$ as : $(f_{0,0} + f_{0,1}\mathcal{V} + f_{0,2}\mathcal{V}^2) + (f_{0,0} + f_{0,1}\mathcal{V} + f_{0,2}\mathcal{V}^2)\mathcal{W}$, where $f_{i,j} \in \mathbb{F}_{p^2}$. The equivalent representations of f are :

$$f = f_0 + f_1\mathcal{W}, \ \text{where} f_0, f_1 \in \mathbb{F}_{p^6}; f \in \mathbb{F}_{(p^6)^2}.$$
$$= (f_{0,0} + f_{0,1}\mathcal{V} + f_{0,2}\mathcal{V}^2) + (f_{1,0} + f_{1,1}\mathcal{V} + f_{1,2}\mathcal{V}^2)\mathcal{W},$$
$$\text{where} f_{i,j} \in \mathbb{F}_{p^2}; f \in \mathbb{F}_{((p^2)^3)^2}.$$
$$= f_{0,0} + f_{1,0}\mathcal{W} + f_{0,1}\mathcal{W}^2 + f_{1,1}\mathcal{W}^3 + f_{0,2}\mathcal{W}^4 + f_{1,2}\mathcal{W}^5$$
$$\text{where} f_{i,j} \in \mathbb{F}_{p^2}; f \in \mathbb{F}_{(p^2)^6}.$$

The computation of $c = f^2$ is performed in $\mathbb{F}_{p^{12}}$ using complex method by following way.

$$v = f_0 \cdot f_1,$$
$$c_0 = (f_0 + f_1)(f_0 + \beta f_1) - v - \beta v,$$
$$c_1 = 2v,$$

where v, c_0, c_1 are in $\mathbb{F}_{p^6}$ and β is a quadratic non-residue in $\mathbb{F}_{p^6}$. It requires two $\mathbb{F}_{p^6}$ multiplications. Now, one $\mathbb{F}_{p^6}$ multiplication is performed in the tower field $\mathbb{F}_{(p^2)^3}$ using Karatsuba technique by six multiplications in $\mathbb{F}_{p^2}$. Let us consider that an element $a_i \in \mathbb{F}_{p^2}$ is represented as : $a_{i0} + a_{i1}\mathcal{U}$, $a_{ij} \in \mathbb{F}_p$. The computation of $v = f_0 \cdot f_1$ on a programmable core is as follows:

$$1. \quad \tilde{v}_0 \leftarrow f_{00} \cdot f_{10}, \ \text{where} \ f_{00}, f_{10} \in \mathbb{F}_{p^2}$$
$$2. \quad \tilde{v}_1 \leftarrow f_{01} \cdot f_{11}, \ \text{where} \ f_{01}, f_{11} \in \mathbb{F}_{p^2}$$
$$3. \quad \tilde{v}_2 \leftarrow f_{02} \cdot f_{12}, \ \text{where} \ f_{02}, f_{12} \in \mathbb{F}_{p^2}$$
$$4. \quad t_{10} \leftarrow f_{010} + f_{020}, \quad t_{11} \leftarrow f_{011} + f_{021}$$
$$5. \quad t_{20} \leftarrow f_{110} + f_{120}, \quad t_{21} \leftarrow f_{111} + f_{121}$$
$$6. \quad t_3 \leftarrow t_1 \cdot t_2, \ \text{where} \ t_1, t_2 \in \mathbb{F}_{p^2}$$
$$7. \quad t_{10} \leftarrow \tilde{v}_{10} + \tilde{v}_{20}, \quad t_{11} \leftarrow \tilde{v}_{11} - \tilde{v}_{21}$$
$$8. \quad t_{30} \leftarrow t_{30} - t_{10}, \quad t_{31} \leftarrow t_{31} - t_{11}$$
$$9. \quad t_{31} \leftarrow t_{31} + t_{31}$$
$$10. \quad v_{00} \leftarrow \tilde{v}_{00} - t_{31}, \quad v_{01} \leftarrow \tilde{v}_{01} + t_{30}$$

11.	$t_{10} \leftarrow f_{000} + f_{010}, \quad t_{11} \leftarrow f_{001} + f_{011}$
12.	$t_{20} \leftarrow f_{100} + f_{110}, \quad t_{21} \leftarrow f_{101} + f_{111}.$
13.	$t_3 \leftarrow t_1 \cdot t_2, \text{ where } t_1, t_2 \in \mathbb{F}_{p^2}$
14.	$t_{10} \leftarrow \tilde{v}_{00} + \tilde{v}_{10}, \quad t_{11} \leftarrow \tilde{v}_{01} - \tilde{v}_{11}$
15.	$t_{20} \leftarrow \tilde{v}_{21} + \tilde{v}_{21}$
16.	$t_{10} \leftarrow t_{10} + t_{20}, \quad t_{11} \leftarrow \tilde{v}_{20} - t_{11}$
17.	$v_{10} \leftarrow t_{30} - t_{10}, \quad v_{11} \leftarrow t_{31} + t_{11}$
18.	$t_{10} \leftarrow f_{000} + f_{020}, \quad t_{11} \leftarrow f_{001} + f_{021}$
19.	$t_{20} \leftarrow f_{100} + f_{120}, \quad t_{21} \leftarrow f_{101} + f_{121}$
20.	$t_3 \leftarrow t_1 \cdot t_2, \text{ where } t_1, t_2 \in \mathbb{F}_{p^2}$
21.	$t_{10} \leftarrow \tilde{v}_{00} + \tilde{v}_{20}, \quad t_{11} \leftarrow \tilde{v}_{01} + \tilde{v}_{21}$
22.	$t_{10} \leftarrow \tilde{v}_{10} - t_{10}, \quad t_{11} \leftarrow \tilde{v}_{11} - t_{11}$
23.	$v_{20} \leftarrow t_{30} + t_{10}, \quad v_{21} \leftarrow t_{31} + t_{11}$

The result $v \in \mathbb{F}_{p^6}$ is represented as : $(v_{00}+v_{01}\mathcal{U})+(v_{10}+v_{11}\mathcal{U})\mathcal{V}+(v_{20}+v_{21}\mathcal{U})\mathcal{V}^2$, where $v_{ij} \in \mathbb{F}_p$. In the above computation, steps 1, 2, 3, 6, 13, 20 perform multiplications in $\mathbb{F}_{p^2}$. Thus the cost of $v = f_0 \cdot f_1$ is $6m$, which is computed in parallel with $2T$, $l_{T,T}(Q)$ by the proposed PCP.

The second $\mathbb{F}_{p^6}$ multiplication, *i.e.*, the computation of $(f_0 + f_1)(f_0 + \beta f_1)$ is performed by both the programmable cores, which costs only $3m$ in the PCP. Therefore, the total cost of computing $2T$, $l_{T,T}(Q)$, and f^2 by the PCP is $9m$.

The $l(Q)$ is represented as : $(l_0 + l_1\mathcal{V}) + (l_2\mathcal{V})\mathcal{W}$, where $l_0 \in \mathbb{F}_p$, $l_1, l_2 \in \mathbb{F}_{p^2}$, which is equivalent to $l_0 + l_1\mathcal{W}^2 + l_2\mathcal{W}^3$. The computation of $f \cdot l(Q)$ is performed in the tower field $\mathbb{F}_{((p^2)^3)^2}$ by following way.

$$\begin{aligned} f' &= f \cdot l(Q) \\ &= ((f_{0,0} + f_{0,1}\mathcal{V} + f_{0,2}\mathcal{V}^2) + (f_{1,0} + f_{1,1}\mathcal{V} + f_{1,2}\mathcal{V}^2)\mathcal{W}) \cdot \\ & \quad ((l_0 + l_1\mathcal{V}) + (l_2\mathcal{V})\mathcal{W}) \end{aligned}$$

The top most extension is quadratic. Thus the computation of $f \cdot l(Q)$ is done by three $\mathbb{F}_{p^6}$ multiplications, which are identified as :

$$\begin{aligned} t_1^1 &= (l_0 + l_1\mathcal{V}) \cdot (f_{0,0} + f_{0,1}\mathcal{V} + f_{0,2}\mathcal{V}^2) \\ t_2^1 &= (l_2\mathcal{V}) \cdot (f_{1,0} + f_{1,1}\mathcal{V} + f_{1,2}\mathcal{V}^2) \\ t_3^1 &= (l_0 + (l_1 + l_2)\mathcal{V}) \cdot (((f_{0,0} + f_{1,0}) + (f_{0,1} + f_{1,1})\mathcal{V} + \\ & \quad (f_{0,2} + f_{1,2})\mathcal{V}^2) \end{aligned}$$

One multiplication in $\mathbb{F}_{p^6}$ using Karatsuba method requires 18 $\mathbb{F}_p$ multiplications. However, due to the sparse representation of $l(Q)$ the cost of computing t_i^1, $1 \leq i \leq 3$ is lesser than the actual costs of three $\mathbb{F}_{p^6}$ multiplications. Both the equations for t_1^1 and t_3^1 require only 14 $\mathbb{F}_p$ multiplications. In our parallel cryptoprocessor the above two equations are computed in parallel on two programmable cores, which costs $5m$. The computation of t_2^1 requires only nine $\mathbb{F}_p$ multiplications, which is performed on both the cores and it costs only $2m$.

Therefore, the computation of $f \cdot l(Q)$ requires 37 $\mathbb{F}_p$ multiplications, which costs only $7m$ in our PCP. Therefore, the total cost for computing the doubling step (the computation of $2T, l_{T,T}(Q), f^2$, and $f \cdot l(Q)$) of the Miller algorithm for Tate pairing on BN curve is $9m + 7m = 16m$.

3.2   Computation of Addition Step

The addition step consists of the computations of $T + P$, $l_{T,P}(Q)$, and $f \cdot l_{T,P}(Q)$. The formulae for mixed Jacobian-affine addition are the following: if $T = (X_1, Y_1, Z_1)$ is in Jacobian coordinates and $P = (X_2, Y_2)$ is in affine coordinates, then $T + P = (X_3, Y_3, Z_3)$ where $X_3 = (Y_2 Z_1^3 - Y_1)^2 - (X_2 Z_1^2 - X_1)^2 (X_1 + X_2 Z_1^2)$, $Y_3 = (Y_2 Z_1^3 - Y_1)(X_1(X_2 Z_1^2 - X_1)^2 - X_3) - Y_1(X_2 Z_1^2 - X_1)^3$, $Z_3 = Z_1(X_2 Z_1^2 - X_1)$. The line through T and P is $l(x, y) = (X_2(Y_2 Z_1^3 - Y_1) - Y_2 Z_3) - (Y_2 Z_1^3 - Y_1)x + Z_3 \cdot y$. During the addition step of Miller algorithm we compute the above operations in parallel on both cores. There are limited independent operations in this step. Therefore, there are scopes for optimizing the scheduling of operations on $\mathbb{F}_p$ arithmetic units for reducing the additional registers and related wiring. The respective scheduling is shown here.

1. $t_0 \leftarrow Y_2 \cdot Z_1$, $t_0 \leftarrow (Z_1)^2$
2. $t_0 \leftarrow t_1 \cdot t_0$, $t_1 \leftarrow t_1 \cdot X_2$
3. $t_4 \leftarrow t_1 + X_1$, $t_0 \leftarrow t_0 - Y_1$, $t_5 \leftarrow t_1 - X_1$
4. $t_3 \leftarrow (t_0)^2$, $Z_3 \leftarrow t_5 \cdot Z_1$, $t_7 \leftarrow (t_5)^2; l_{10} \leftarrow t_0 \cdot x_0$,
    $l_{11} \leftarrow t_0 \cdot x_1$
5. $t_2 \leftarrow t_7 \cdot X_1$, $t_4 \leftarrow t_4 \cdot t_7$, $t_5 \leftarrow t_5 \cdot t_7; t_{10} \leftarrow t_0 \cdot X_2$
6. $X_3 \leftarrow t_3 - t_4$
7. $t_2 \leftarrow t_2 - X_3$
8. $t_2 \leftarrow t_2 \cdot t_0$, $t_4 \leftarrow Y_2 \cdot Z_3$, $t_5 \leftarrow t_5 \cdot Y_1; l_{20} \leftarrow Z_3 \cdot y_0$,
    $l_{21} \leftarrow Z_3 \cdot y_1$
9. $Y_3 \leftarrow t_2 - t_5; l_0 \leftarrow t_{10} - t_4$

In the above scheduling, the nonlinear operations (multiplication and squaring) in $\mathbb{F}_p$ are performed in steps 1, 2, 4, 5, and 8. Thus, the cost of computing $T + P$, $l_{T,P}(Q)$ is $5m$ in the PCP. This computation is followed by $f \cdot l(Q)$, which costs $7m$. Therefore, the cost for evaluating the addition step is $5m + 7m = 12m$ in the PCP.

3.3   Computation of Final Exponentiation

The final exponentiation is computed by following way. It follows the optimization to factor $(p^{12} - 1)/r$ into three parts [16] and compute $f^{(p^{12}-1)/r}$ as :

$$f^{\frac{p^{12}-1}{r}} = f^{(p^6-1) \times \frac{p^6+1}{p^4-p^2+1} \times \frac{p^4-p^2+1}{r}}$$
$$= \left((f^{p^6-1})^{p^2+1} \right)^{\frac{p^4-p^2+1}{r}}.$$

The computation is done by following way:

1. $f \leftarrow f^{p^6-1}$.
2. $f \leftarrow f^{p^2+1}$.
3. $a \leftarrow f^{-(6z+5)}$, $b \leftarrow a^p$, $b \leftarrow a \cdot b$.
4. Compute f^p, f^{p^2}, f^{p^3}.
5. $f \leftarrow f^{p^3} \cdot \left[b \cdot (f^p)^2 \cdot f^{p^2} \right]^{6z^2+1} \cdot b \cdot (f^p \cdot f)^9 \cdot a \cdot f^4$,

where z is a BN parameter and we choose $z = 6000000000001\text{F2D}$ (in hexadecimal). Table 1 lists the operation costs of final exponentiation on the PCP. The power of $(p^6 - 1)$ in $\mathbb{F}_{(p^6)^2}$ is an easy exponentiation, which is performed by a conjugation (Frobenius) and a division [17,12]. The operation $f^{p^6} = f_0 - f_1 \mathcal{W}$. Thus, f^{p^6-1} is performed by one inversion and one multiplication in $\mathbb{F}_{p^{12}}$, which costs $29m$ on our dual-core PCP.

Table 1. Operation costs for the final exponentiation on our PCP

Operation	cost on PCP
f^{p^6-1}	$29m$
f^{p^2+1}	$12m$
$f^{-(6z+5)}$	$480m$
a^p, $a \cdot b$, f^p, f^{p^2}, f^{p^3}	$21m$
$T \leftarrow b \cdot (f^p)^2 \cdot f^{p^2}$	$24m$
$T \leftarrow T^{6z^2+1}$	$951m$
$f^{p^3} \cdot T \cdot b \cdot (f^p \cdot f)^9 \cdot f^4$	$93m$

The exponentiations f^{6z+5}, T^z and $(T^z)^{6z}$ are performed by repeated square-and-multiply. Note that $6z + 5$ and $6z$ have bitlength 66 and Hamming weight 11, while z has bitlength 63 and Hamming weight 11.

3.4 Cost for Computing Tate Pairing

In case of BN curve, r has bitlength 256 and Hamming weight 91. Thus the total cost for evaluating iterative Miller function of the Tate pairing computation is $5176m$ on our PCP. The cost for computing the final exponentiation is $1610m$. Hence, the total cost for computing a Tate pairing over BN curves by our cryptoprocessor is $6786m$, which takes $1,764,360$ cycles. The cryptoprocessor finishes one Tate pairing computation over BN curve in $35.3ms$ on a Virtex-4 FPGA platform. It consumes $52k$ slices and runs at 50 MHz clock frequency.

4 Side-Channel Vulnerability

Page and Vercauteren [7] presented SPA and DPA attacks on the pairing computations performed by the Duursma-Lee algorithm [8] and the BLKS algorithm [10] over $\mathbb{F}_{3^m}$. The power consumption attack on η_T pairing computation over $\mathbb{F}_{2^m}$ is described by Kim *et al.* in [11]. However, the same in case of $\mathbb{F}_p$ has not been studied so far. This section investigates the security of pairing computations over $\mathbb{F}_p$ against power consumption attacks.

4.1   Weakness of Pairing Computations in $\mathbb{F}_p$

In the decryption step of identity-based encryption schemes, a dominant operation is $e(U, S_{ID})$, where S_{ID} is the fixed secret key, and U is a part of a ciphertext [19]. In this case side-channel attacks may try to extract the secret key from the pairing computation by repeatedly manipulating U. The Tate pairing over $\mathbb{F}_p$ consists of elliptic curve group operations (ECD and ECA), the line functions, and the Miller function [15]. The line functions as per the definition provided by Chatterjee *et al.* [14] use both the public point U and private point S_{ID}. The formula of line functions are based on the underlying $\mathbb{F}_p$ primitives.

During the addition step of Tate pairing computation the formula of the line function is $l(x, y) = (y - Y_2)Z_3 - (x - X_2)(Y_2 Z_1^3 - Y_1)$ [14]. In pairing based cryptographic schemes, the point $T = (X_1, Y_1, Z_1)$ is an intermediate resultant point of current point doubling operation, the point $U = (X_2, Y_2)$ is used as a public parameter (it could be the plain texts or messages), and $S_{ID} = (x, y)$ is used as the private key. The resultant point $(T+U)$ is represented by (X_3, Y_3, Z_3). Therefore, in such a scheme the operations $(x - X_2)$ and $(y - Y_2)$ could be exploited through side-channel attacks for finding out the x and y-coordinates of the secret point.

5   Proposed DPA Attack

In this section, we investigate differential power analysis (or DPA) attack against the subtraction $(x - X_2)$ used in the Tate pairing on elliptic curves in $\mathbb{F}_p$, where x is secret and X_2 is public and known to, or even chosen by, the attacker. The subtraction $(x - X_2)$ in $\mathbb{F}_p$ is computed by first computing $S = x - X_2$ and then the result is reduced (if required) by adding p with S. Let us assume that all operations are performed on 2's complement numbers. Therefore, the subtraction $S = x - X_2$ could be performed as: $S = \sum_{i=0}^{k} 2^i s_i = \sum_{i=0}^{k-1} 2^i x_i + \sum_{i=0}^{k-1} 2^i \bar{X}_{2_i} + 1$, where k represents the bit length of operands (x, X_2) and $\bar{X}_{2_i}$ corresponds to the 1's complement of X_{2_i}. The subtraction is started from the least significant bit (or LSB) by computing *sum* and *carry* bits iteratively. The formula for i-th carry bit is: $c_i = x_i \bar{X}_{2_i} \oplus x_i c_{i-1} \oplus \bar{X}_{2_i} c_{i-1}$. Similarly, the i-th sum bit is computed as: $s_i = x_i \oplus \bar{X}_{2_i} \oplus c_{i-1}$ for $k - 1 \leq i \leq 0$ with $c_{-1} = 1$.

The proposed DPA attack works by following way. The attacker first collects the power consumption traces of n number of randomly chosen public point U. We consider the simplified Hamming weight model for power leakage [20]. In this model, power consumption depends on the Hamming weight of the data being processed. Thus, we can express the power consumption W as:

$$W = \varepsilon H + \eta \tag{1}$$

where H, ε, and η represent the Hamming weight of the intermediate data, the incremental amount of power for each extra 1 in the Hamming weight, and the noise, respectively. We assume that the average of noise η is zero.

Let W be the power consumption associated with the subtraction operation $(x - X_2)$. We start from the LSB and iteratively find all bits of the x-coordinate of the secret point $S_{ID} = (x, y)$. To recover the i-th bit of x, we guess that $x_i = 0$ and divide power consumptions into two sets by $\bar{X}_{2_i} \oplus c_{i-1}$.

$$P_k = \{ W \mid \bar{X}_{2_i} \oplus c_{i-1} = k \} \quad \text{with } k = \{0, 1\}$$

Thus, the differential power consumption is:

$$\varDelta = < P_1 - P_0 > .$$

If the guess is correct, then the averages of P_1 and P_0 are, $\varepsilon(M + 1)/2$ and $\varepsilon(M - 1)/2$, where M corresponds to the bit length of S. Thus, if $\varDelta > 0$, we know that $x_i = 0$; otherwise, the averages of P_1 and P_0 is $\varepsilon(M - 1)/2$ and $\varepsilon(M + 1)/2$. Thus, if $\varDelta < 0$ then $x_i = 1$. There should be a positive peak when $x_i = 0$ and a negative peak when $x_i = 1$.

In summary, since the subtraction operation $(x - X_2)$ of line function in pairing computation is vulnerable to the proposed attack, we can recover x. Next, we can obtain the value of y-coordinate of the secret point S_{ID} by solving the curve equation.

5.1   Mounting the DPA on FPGA Platform

We perform the actual DPA attack on aforementioned pairing cryptoprocessor (or PCP). The PCP is implemented on a customized FPGA board for power analysis. We put an one ohm resistor between the VCCint pin of the FPGA chip and the on board voltage regulator. We measure the current drawn through that resistor during pairing computation by a current probe. The specification of the probe is Tektronix current probe (serial number B014316). We use the probe with a TCPA300 power amplifier in standby mode. The measured power is displayed and stored in a Tektronix TDS5032B Digital Phosphor Oscilloscope. We develop software tools to automate the whole process for varying inputs. The power consumptions are measured in terms of mV which is varying around $\pm 5mV$. The power signal is sampled at $12.5MS/s$.

We choose an x with $x_0 = 0$ and perform $(x - X_2)$ for 2000 times with 2000 different randomly chosen X_2. The respective power consumptions are stored in 2000 one dimensional vectors. Now we differentiate the the power vectors in two sets namely P_1 and P_0. A vector will be in set P_1 if $\bar{X}_{2_0} \oplus c_{-1} = 1$; $i.e.$, $X_{2_0} = 1$. Otherwise, the vector will be in set P_0. For computing the differential power consumption we subtract the average of P_0 vectors (means) from the average of

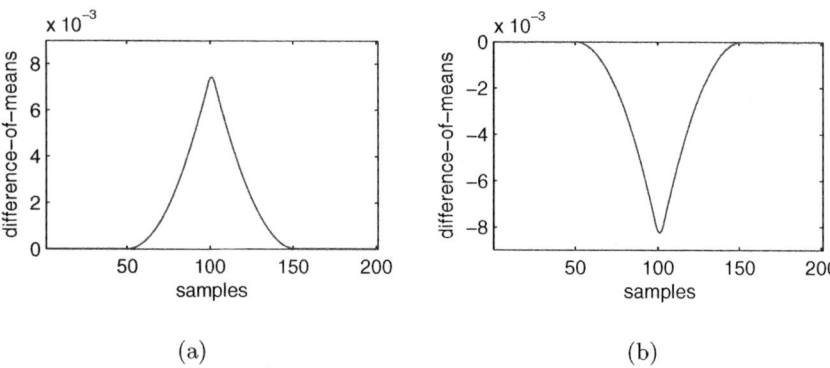

Fig. 1. The correlation between LSB and corresponding average power differences of an addition in $\mathbb{F}_p$. (a) for $x_0 = 0$ and (b) for $x_0 = 1$.

P_1 vectors. We say this differential power consumption vector as difference-of-means which is represented by Δ. Then we accumulate the samples of Δ and plot it. The respective difference-of-means is depicted in Fig. 1(a), which shows a positive peak as expected for $x_0 = 0$.

The same experiment has been repeated for another x with $x_0 = 1$. The difference-of-means in this case is plotted in Fig. 1(b). In this case the expectation of $< P_1 - P_0 >$ is negative and we got the result as expected with 2000 random X_2.

Above experimental result ensures that an attacker can easily mount the DPA attack on pairing computation over $\mathbb{F}_p$. After finding out the LSB, DPA can be performed for second LSB, and so on. The same power traces could be utilized for finding out all secret bits. The differentiation of power vectors into two sets depending on the current value of $(\bar{X}_{2_i} \oplus c_{i-1})$ upto the generation of the difference-of-means will be repeated for finding out each of the secret bits. Thus, above DPA attack iteratively finds out all bits of the x-coordinate of secret S_{ID}. After obtaining the x-coordinate, the value of y-coordinate could be obtained easily by solving the underlying elliptic curve equation.

5.2   Proposed Counteracting Technique

In the pairing computation, the secret point is only used for computing the line functions. The formula of the line function during doubling step of the Miller algorithm over $\mathbb{F}_p$ is as follows:

$$l_{T,T}(x,y) = Z_3 Z^2 y - 2Y^2 - 3X^2(Z^2 x - X),$$

where $T = (X, Y, Z)$ be the intermediate resultant point of Miller algorithm while $2T = (X_3, Y_3, Z_3)$ [14].

The formula of $l_{T,T}(x,y)$ is using the secret point $S_{ID} = (x,y)$ of identity based encryption (IBE) [19]. But, it does not use the public point $U = (X_2, Y_2)$. Therefore, this function could not be exploited by any side-channel attacks.

The second line function $l_{T,P}(x,y)$ is computed during the addition step of the Miller algorithm. In IBE scheme P is replaced by U. The formula of $l_{T,P}(x,y)$ is:

$$l_{T,U}(x,y) = (y - Y_2)Z_3 - (x - X_2)(Y_2 Z_1^3 - Y_1),$$

where $T(X_1, Y_1, Z_1)$ is the intermediate result of doubling step and (X_3, Y_3, Z_3) represents the addition result of $T + U$. In this line computation formula both public point $U = (X_2, Y_2)$ and private point $S_{ID} = (x, y)$ are used. The computation of $l_{T,U}(x,y)$ is the main weakness of pairing computation over $\mathbb{F}_p$ against side-channel attacks. The DPA attack described above can easily find out the x and y-coordinates of private point S_{ID} by exploiting the above formula.

The main drawback of the above formula is that the public and private parameters are directly involved to perform an $\mathbb{F}_p$ operation. The side-channel attack thus exploit the respective $\mathbb{F}_p$ operation for finding out the secret bits by manipulating public parameter U. To counter act on such computation against side-channel attacks it could be computed by following way.

$$l_{T,P}(x,y) = (X_2(Y_2 Z_1^3 - Y_1) - Y_2 Z_3) - (Y_2 Z_1^3 - Y_1)x + Z_3 \cdot y.$$

The above computation technique does not have any $\mathbb{F}_p$ primitive which is performed on one public parameter and one private parameter. The attacker may try to exploit the power consumption of the cryptoprocessor during the computation of $l_{T,P}(x,y)$. The private parameter x in the above formula is multiplied with an unknown parameter $(Y_2 Z_1^3 - Y_1)$. Therefore, no difference-of-mean can be computed for identifying the secret bits of x.

The second secret parameter y is multiplied with Z_3 in the modified computation of $l_{T,P}(x,y)$. The parameter Z_3 is computed by executing the formula $Z_3 = Z_1(X_2 Z_1^2 - X_1)$ which ensures Z_3 is unknown due to the unknown temporary point $T(X_1, Y_1, Z_1)$. Therefore, no difference-of-mean value can be computed based on the specific bits of Z_3 for identifying the secret bits of y. Thus, the proposed counteracting technique protects both x and y coordinates of secret point S_{ID}, which ensures the security of pairing computation against DPA attack.

5.3 Overhead of DPA Countermeasure

The respective costs of existing DPA-vulnerable formula of $l_{T,U}(x,y)$ are $6m + s$ and $14m$ in Tate and ate/optimal-ate pairings. The same in case of our proposed DPA-resistance formula are $8m+s$ and $18m$ in Tate and ate/optimal-ate pairings, respectively. For BN curves the number of iterations of Miller's loop are $r = 256$, $t = 128$, and $a = 66$ having respective Hamming weights 91, 28, and 9. The overhead of proposed DPA resistance scheme in terms of the cost for computing one $\mathbb{F}_p$-multiplication (m) is shown in Table 2.

Table 2. DPA resistance overhead for pairing computations

Pairings	Overhead in one $l_{T,U}(x,y)$	Total overhead
Tate	2m	182m
ate	4m	108m
optimal-ate	4m	32m

6   Conclusion

This paper has demonstrated an optimized scheduling of Tate pairing computation over BN curve on a dualcore pairing cryptoprocessor. The computation cost for One Tate pairing achieving 128-bit security on FPGA platform is $35.3ms$. The paper further analyzes the effect of covert power channel of the pairing cryptoprocessor against physical security. The paper has pinpointed the vulnerability of such pairing computation against DPA attack. The actual DPA has been performed on FPGA platform and respective vulnerability has been demonstrated. Finally, the paper has proposed a suitable counteract to protect secret point of pairing computation against DPA attack.

References

1. Miller, V.S.: Short Programs for Functions on Curves (1986) (unpublished manuscript)
2. Miller, V.S.: The Weil pairing, and its efficient calculation. Journal of Cryptology 17, 235–261 (2004)
3. Mrabet, N.E., Natale, G.D., Flottes, M.L., Rouzeyre, B., Bajard, J.C.: Differential Power Analysis against the Miller Algorithm. HAL: lirmm-00323684, Version 1, http://hal-lirmm.ccsd.cnrs.fr/lirmm-00323684/en/
4. Mrabet, N.E., Flottes, M.L., Natale, G.D.: A practical Differential Power Analysis against the Miller Algorithm. Research in Microelectronics and Electronics, PRIME, Ph.D (2009)
5. Kocher, P.C.: Timing Attacks on Implementations of Diffie-Hellman, RSA, DSS, and Other Systems. In: Koblitz, N. (ed.) CRYPTO 1996. LNCS, vol. 1109, pp. 104–113. Springer, Heidelberg (1996)
6. Kocher, P.C., Jaffe, J., Jun, B.: Differential power analysis. In: Wiener, M. (ed.) CRYPTO 1999. LNCS, vol. 1666, pp. 388–397. Springer, Heidelberg (1999)
7. Page, D., Vercauteren, F.: Fault and side-channel attacks on pairing based cryptography. Cryptology ePrint Archive, Report 2004/283, http://eprint.iacr.org/
8. Duursma, I., Lee, H.: Tate pairing implementation for hyperelliptic curves $y^2 = x^p - x + d$. In: Laih, C.-S. (ed.) ASIACRYPT 2003. LNCS, vol. 2894, pp. 111–123. Springer, Heidelberg (2003)
9. Hoffstein, J., Pipher, J., Silverman, J.H.: An introduction to mathmatical cryptography. Springer, Heidelberg (2008)
10. Barreto, P.S.L.M., Kim, H., Lynn, B., Scott, M.: Efficient algorithms for pairing-based cryptosystems. In: Yung, M. (ed.) CRYPTO 2002. LNCS, vol. 2442, pp. 354–368. Springer, Heidelberg (2002)

11. Kim, T.H., Takagi, T., Han, D.G., Kim, H., Lim, J.: Power analysis attacks and countermeasures on ηT pairing over binary fields. ETRI Journal 30(1), 68–80 (2008)
12. Naehrig, M., Barreto, P.S.L.M., Schwabe, P.: On compressible pairings and their computation. In: Vaudenay, S. (ed.) AFRICACRYPT 2008. LNCS, vol. 5023, pp. 371–388. Springer, Heidelberg (2008)
13. Barreto, P.S.L.M., Naehrig, M.: Pairing-friendly elliptic curves of prime order. In: Preneel, B., Tavares, S. (eds.) SAC 2005. LNCS, vol. 3897, pp. 319–331. Springer, Heidelberg (2006)
14. Chatterjee, S., Sarkar, P., Barua, R.: Efficient Computation of Tate Pairing in Projective Coordinate over General Characteristic Fields. In: Park, C.-s., Chee, S. (eds.) ICISC 2004. LNCS, vol. 3506, pp. 168–181. Springer, Heidelberg (2005)
15. Hankerson, D., Menezes, A., Scott, M.: Software implementation of pairings. In: Joye, M., Neven, G. (eds.) Identity-Based Cryptography (2008)
16. Devegili, A.J., Scott, M., Dahab, R.: Implementing Cryptographic Pairings over Barreto-Naehrig Curves. In: Takagi, T., Okamoto, T., Okamoto, E., Okamoto, T. (eds.) Pairing 2007. LNCS, vol. 4575, pp. 197–207. Springer, Heidelberg (2007)
17. Scott, M., Benger, N., Charlemagne, M., Perez, L.J.D., Kachisa, E.J.: On the final exponentiation for calculating pairings on ordinary elliptic curves. In: Shacham, H., Waters, B. (eds.) Pairing 2009. LNCS, vol. 5671, pp. 78–88. Springer, Heidelberg (2009)
18. Ghosh, S., Mukhopadhyay, D., Roychowdhury, D.: High speed flexible pairing cryptoprocessor on FPGA platform. In: Joye, M., Miyaji, A., Otsuka, A. (eds.) Pairing 2010. LNCS, vol. 6487, pp. 450–466. Springer, Heidelberg (2010)
19. Boneh, D., Franklin, M.K.: Identity-Based Encryption from the Weil Pairing. In: Kilian, J. (ed.) CRYPTO 2001. LNCS, vol. 2139, pp. 213–229. Springer, Heidelberg (2001)
20. Messerges, T.S.: Using second-order power analysis to attack DPA resistant software. In: Paar, C., Koç, Ç.K. (eds.) CHES 2000. LNCS, vol. 1965, pp. 238–251. Springer, Heidelberg (2000)

Embedded Software Security through Key-Based Control Flow Obfuscation

Rajat Subhra Chakraborty[1], Seetharam Narasimhan[2], and Swarup Bhunia[2]

[1] Department of Computer Science and Engineering
Indian Institute of Technology, Kharagpur, West Bengal, India–721302
rschakraborty@cse.iitkgp.ernet.in
[2] Department of Electrical Engineering and Computer Science
Case Western Reserve University, Cleveland, OH–44106, USA
{sxn124,skb21}@case.edu

Abstract. Protection against software piracy and malicious modification of software is proving to be a great challenge for resource-constrained embedded systems. In this paper, we develop a non-cryptographic, key-based, control flow obfuscation technique, which can be implemented by computationally efficient means, and is capable of operating with minimal hardware support. The scheme is based on matching a series of expected keys in sequence, similar to the unlocking process in a combination lock, and provides high levels of resistance to static and dynamic analyses. It is capable of protecting embedded software against both piracy as well as non-self-replicating malicious modifications. Simulation results on a set of MIPS assembly language programs show that the technique is capable of providing high levels of security at nominal computational overhead and about 10% code-size increase.

1 Introduction

The market share of embedded processors is ever-increasing, with more than 98% of the total microprocessor market share (in terms of unit sold) already occupied by them [1]. They can be found in a wide variety of electronic applications - from low-end household items such as microwave ovens to high-end 3G/4G cell phones and PDAs. Combined with this trend is the increase in computing capabilities of embedded processors (with maximum operating frequencies of up to 2 GHz in 2010) rivalling that of mainstream microprocessors [2], as they are expected to run more computation-intensive software. An example is that cutting-edge cellular devices are being increasingly used to surf the internet, play graphics intensive games and perform "mobile commerce", functionalities that were traditionally associated with personal computers. Software development for the mobile platform has also advanced immensely, with users routinely downloading, installing and using both free and commercial software for their devices.

However, this trend has increased the security concerns encompassing data confidentiality and integrity, authentication, privacy, denial of service, nonrepudiation, and digital content protection [4], which were again relevant earlier only

M. Joye et al. (Eds.): InfoSecHiComNet 2011, LNCS 7011, pp. 30–44, 2011.
© Springer-Verlag Berlin Heidelberg 2011

in the domain of commercial and personal computing. The threat is a two-edged sword - on one hand, malicious software installed in an embedded system can harm the user; on the other hand, reverse-engineering of software causes loss of millions of dollars of intellectual property (IP) revenue to the software vendors. Unfortunately, the traditional hardware or software security measures targeting personal computers are not directly applicable to embedded systems. The computational demands of secure processing often overwhelm the computing capabilities of embedded processors, and physically the portable embedded systems are often severely constrained by form factor, resulting in limited battery capacities and memory [4].

In this work, we propose a novel technique of protecting embedded software against piracy, reverse engineering and infection by obfuscating its control-flow. The obfuscation is based on a key validation mechanism that internally generates and compares a sequence of keys with their expected values loaded from memory. The keys are execution trace dependent, meaning thereby that for different input parameters to the program, the sequence and values of keys involved in the validation process are different. The normal functionality of the program is enabled only after a successful validation process, otherwise, the program produces incorrect output. In addition, it provides additional authentication features by which even if an adversary breaks the security scheme, the ownership of the software can be proven by an *authentication* mechanism based on a *digital watermark*. The proposed technique is *not based* on the weak "security through obscurity" paradigm, where the algorithm used to obfuscate the functionality is itself hidden from the adversary [5]. In our work we assume a threat scenario where the adversary only has access to the program and tries to reverse-engineer it to unveil the security scheme, and does not have access to the hardware system which is successfully running such an obfuscated software.

The rest of the paper is organized as follows: In Section 2, we describe the proposed key-based control flow obfuscation methodology with a complete illustrative example. In Section 3, we analyze the security of the scheme against a possible attack model, and estimate the computational overhead of implementing the proposed scheme. We describe the automated flow to implement the methodology for a given MIPS assembly language program [36] in Section 4. We present the simulation results for a suite of MIPS programs in Section 5. Finally, we draw conclusions and indicate future research directions in Section 6.

2 Methodology

2.1 Obfuscation Technique

The fundamental idea of the technique proposed in this work is to validate the code during execution using a "challenge-response validation" protocol. The correct execution of the program is achieved only after the correct application of a set of input values, which constitute the *validation key sequence*. The steps of the validation process are distributed throughout the program and operates concurrently with the rest of the program, thus making it difficult to bypass

---

Algorithm 1. Procedure *Enumerate_Paths_Depth_First*

Enumerate all possible control-flow paths of given assembly language program segment.

Inputs: Directed Acyclic Graph G corresponding to given assembly language program segment, *instr_stack, current_node, last_node*
Outputs: Set of edges ($\mathbb{E}$) with corresponding number of paths on which each edge lies

---
```
 1: if curr_node ≠ Φ then
 2:     push_on_stack(instr_stack, curr_node)
 3:     if curr_node == last_node then
 4:         e.pathcount ← (e.pathcount + 1) ∀ edge e on current path
 5:     end if
 6:     Enumerate_Paths_Depth_First(G, instr_stack, curr_node → left_child, last_instruction)
 7:     Enumerate_Paths_Depth_First(G, instr_stack, curr_node → right_child, last_instruction)
 8:     pop_from_stack(instr_stack)
 9: else
10:     return
11: end if
```

---

the defense mechanism [6]. The security is also increased by the fact that the required validation key sequence depends on the input argument to the program.

The keys of the *validation key sequence* are fetched from pre-determined memory locations and compared with the expected "golden" values. If all the values match, the program execution follows the normal control flow. However, if even a single comparison fails, the program executes incorrect instructions which produces an incorrect result. The main challenge in implementing this technique is the hiding of the instructions dedicated to the validation procedure in the program. Although pre-determined values are fetched from pre-determined memory locations, the key and memory location values are not hard-coded in the program. Rather, they are derived during program execution, and different sets of values are derived depending on the input argument. This makes static analysis of the code and "program profiling" to discover the validation mechanism extremely challenging, because *each and every* validation step in the obfuscated program must be identified and neutralized to ensure that the program operates properly in *every situation*. The requirement of the predicates and variables involved in obfuscation to be *opaque*, i.e. difficult to be deduced by static analysis was pointed out in [9].

The obfuscation algorithm proceeds by finding the feasible control-flow paths in the program (or a part of it) and their dependence on the input values, and then making modifications at optimal locations in the program, such that for a given code-size and run-time overhead, the modifications would have maximum overall effect. Algorithm-1 shows the pseudo-code for the algorithm to enumerate the paths of the program using a *Depth-first Search* (DFS). The procedure assumes that the given MIPS program has been modeled as a "Directed Acyclic Graph" (DAG), with the edges forming loops removed. Each instruction of the program forms a node of the graph, and each node has one child (the non-branch instructions) or two children (the non-loop branch instructions). For each node, one among the children is always the next instruction. Note that a return from a procedure call is not treated as being part of a loop, because the "directed

---

Algorithm 2. Procedure *Find_Optimal_Modifications*

Find the optimal modification locations for a set of given control-flow paths and given number of modifications.

Inputs: Set of edges $\mathbb{E}$, modification pool $\mathbb{M}$, required number of modifications (M), minimum modification radius (r_{mod})

Outputs: List of modification locations in the program

```
 1: Sort 𝔼 based on number of paths on which each edge e ∈ 𝔼 lies (i.e. e.pathcount)
 2: num_mods ← 0
 3: for all edge e ∈ 𝔼 do
 4:     e.modified ← FALSE
 5: end for
 6: /*Iterate over the ordered edges and make modifications based on r_mod constraint*/
 7: for i = 1 to |𝔼| and num_mods < M do
 8:     Set 𝔼_r = {e_j ∈ 𝔼 : |e_i − e_j| ≤ r_mod} /* |e_i − e_j| stands for the physical separation of the two
        edges */
 9:     if e.modified == FALSE ∀e ∈ 𝔼_r then
10:         Choose previously unchosen m ∈ 𝕄
11:         Insert m on e_i
12:         e_j.modified ← TRUE ∀e_j ∈ 𝔼_r
13:         num_mods ← num_mods + 1 /*Update number of modifications*/
14:     end if
15: end for
```

---

acyclic" nature of the graph can be still maintained. In addition to the regular DFS, the number of paths on which an edge lies is tracked. This information is utilized in determining optimal locations to perform modifications in the program, as described next.

Algorithm-2 shows the procedure to find the optimal locations to make M modifications for a given program (or a part of it). At first, the edges of the graph are ranked in descending order in terms of the number of paths on which the edges lie. Then, M modifications chosen greedily from a pool of modifications are inserted on the top-ranked edges, with the constraint that the modified edges are situated at least a pre-defined "modification radius" r_{mod} distance away from each other. If any edge connects two vertices which do not represent consecutive instructions in the program, jump instructions are used to connect the modification code block to the two vertices on the edge. The following points should be noted about this algorithm:

- Choosing the top-ranked edges ensures maximum effect of a single modification on multiple paths, while the r_{mod} constraint ensures that the modifications are not inserted too close to each other.
- The constraint r_{mod} determines the *average number of modifications per path*:

$$M_{av} = \frac{\sum_{i=1}^{|\mathbb{P}|} M_i}{|\mathbb{P}|} \tag{1}$$

where $|\mathbb{P}|$ denotes the total number of paths in the part of the program segment being processed, M_i denotes the number of modifications lying on the i-th path, and $1 < M_{av} \leq M$. An increase in the value of M_{av} can be thought of to signify an increase in the security of the system, because more successful validations are required on average per path to make the program run successfully. Another metric that is determined by r_{mod} is the *average distance between modifications*. Let $\mathbb{E}_{mod}$ be the list of modified edges, ordered by their positions in the program, and M be the total number of modifications inserted. Then the *average distance between modifications* is given (for $M > 1$) by:

$$D_{av} = \frac{\sum_{i=1}^{M-1} |e_{i+1} - e_i|}{M - 1} \tag{2}$$

for $e_i \in \mathbb{E}_{mod}$, with $r_{mod} \leq D_{av} < \frac{N}{M-1}$, where N is the number of in-structions in the program. If r_{mod} is small, say $r_{mod} = 1$, the minimum value possible, the top M ranked edges would be chosen which would in-crease the value of M_{av}. However, on the flip-side, the value of D_{av} might decrease, meaning that the modifications would be placed too close to each other which puts them at the risk of being more identifiable to an adversary. Also, a higher value of M_{av} also implies an increase in the average execution time of the obfuscated program with respect to the original program. Hence, the parameter r_{mod} provides a degree of freedom to balance between the quantitative metrics M_{av} and D_{av}, and the performance of the program.

– This algorithm inserts the modifications at "preferred pseudo-random" lo-cations, with preference being given to locations that would affect the max-imum possible number of paths, while being "pseudo-random" in the sense that the modification locations are distributed throughout the program, through the effect of r_{mod}.

– If a modification is inserted between two instructions which are part of a loop, then the key-validation step would be repeated as many times as the loop repeated, even if the validation is successful. To avoid this, the modification should be such that any successful validation is "remembered", so that the next time the loop is executed, the validation mechanism is not exercised. This can be implemented easily by having a "flag" register and local jumps in the modification. We have elucidated this point with an example in the next sub-section.

– To increase the level of security, the operations dedicated to deriving and comparing the keys of a sequence do not appear in the order in which the keys are compared.

Next we give a complete example program to elucidate the two algorithms de-scribed above.

2.2   Obfuscation Example

Fig. 1(a) shows an example MIPS assembly language program to calculate and display the value of the n-th Fibonacci number for a given non-negative integer

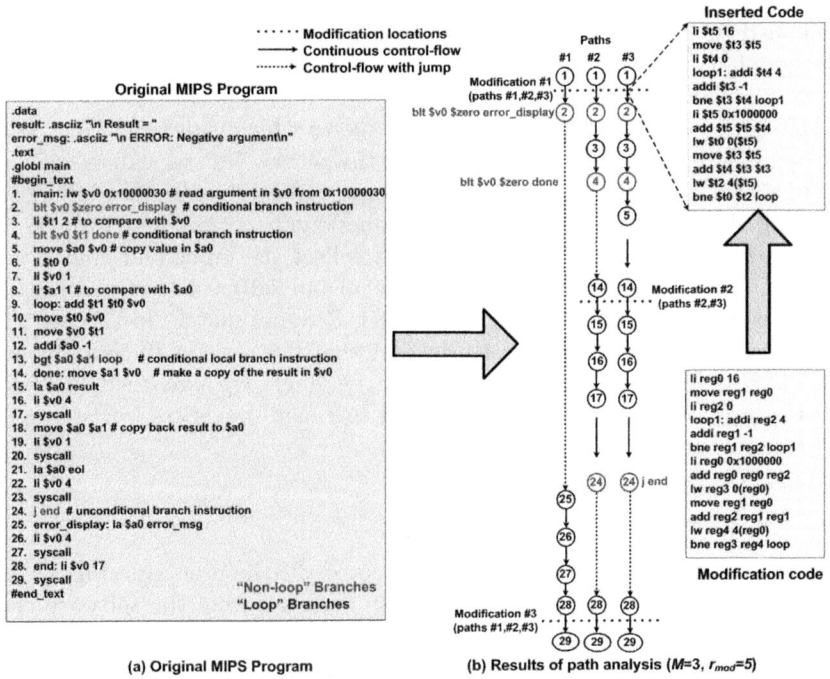

Fig. 1. Example of application of the proposed algorithm on a MIPS program to calculate the value of the n-th Fibonacci number for a given non-negative integer n

n. The main part of the program to be modified occurs between the markers *#begin_text* and *#end_text*, and the instructions between these two markers have been numbered for ease of understanding. The DAG representation of the program has been shown in Fig. 1(b). The feasible control paths of the program are then enumerated by analyzing the DAG using Algorithm-1. The feasible paths for this program (paths #1, #2 and #3) are shown in Fig. 1(b), where each instruction has been represented by its serial number. Note that the different paths are followed depending on the value of the input argument n to the program - path-1 if $n < 0$, path-2 if $0 \leq n < 2$ and path-3 if $n \geq 2$. When Algorithm-2 is applied to find the optimal modification locations for $M = 3$ modifications and $r_{mod} = 5$, the modifications are placed between instructions 1 and 2 (modification #1), between 14 and 15 (modification #2) and between 28 and 29 (modification #3). Modification #1 and #3 affect all three paths, while modification #2 affects only paths 2 and 3. The average number of modifications is per path is thus $M_{av} = (3 + 3 + 2)/3 = 2.67$, which is less than the ideal value of $M_{av} = M = 3.00$. The average distance between modifications $D_{av} = 9.00$, while the ideal value is $\frac{N}{2} = \frac{29}{2} = 14.50$.

Note that Algorithm 2 implies that the first modification would always be inserted on one of the edges connecting the "root node" to the node corresponding to the first branch instruction in the program. This feature might make the first modification identifiable to an adversary performing static analysis. This issue is handled by modifying the algorithm so that an exception is made about the position of the first modification, so that no modification appears between the "root" node and the first branch node.

An example modification has also been shown which is derived from the corresponding *modification pool* after binding the generic register names $reg0$, $reg1$ etc. to actual resisters $t5$, $t3$, etc. As mentioned before, the register binding keeps the original functionality of the program functionally correct by a *liveness analysis*. In the given case, registers $t0$ and $t2$ collect the input and golden values of the key from memory locations 0x10000040 and 0x10000044 respectively, and normal operation is allowed only if the fetched values match. In this particular case, incorrect operation is due to the fact that the register $t0$ contains an incorrect value (it should contain zero when the label *loop* is reached). In case no registers are found free to be used bound to generic registers, register spilling and restoration has to be applied.

2.3   Implementation

To make the obfuscated software operate correctly, the user must buy the software license in the form of a small support software from the software vendor to manage the key installation in memory. The user has to run this support software to install the keys in the correct memory location, and then install the main software. The security of the scheme can be increased by changing the key sequence for each instance of the licensed software, so that the support software would be bound with the particular copy of the original software which it was designed to activate.

2.4   Integration with Hardware-Assisted Approaches

The proposed software obfuscation technique can co-exist with hardware-assisted security solutions, such as *Trusted Platform Module* (TPM) [17,18], thus adding an extra level of protection. The security features provided in such platforms can be useful in situations where the adversary has physical access to the hardware successfully running the program. In addition to the proposed software obfuscation technique, if the memory contents are encrypted (e.g. in [15]) or memory addresses are re-mapped to hide the control flow (e.g. in [27]), the adversary would face an additional challenge of first breaking the hardware-assisted security scheme, and then de-obfuscating every obfuscated software individually.

3   Obfuscation Efficiency and Overheads

In this section we present theoretical analyses to obtain a quantitative estimate of the achievable security and overhead incurred by the proposed scheme.

3.1 Obfuscation Efficiency

We borrow the following metrics which have been previously proposed to estimate the success of a software obfuscation scheme [9]:

- *Potency*: the complexity in comprehending the obfuscated program compared to the unobfuscated one.
- *Resilience*: difficulty faced by an automatic de-obfuscator in breaking the obfuscation.
- *Stealth*: how well the obfuscated code blends in with the rest of the program, and
- *Cost*: how much computational overhead it adds to the obfuscated program.

A potent software obfuscation technique should provide high levels of *potency*, *resilience* and *stealth*, while incurring minimal *cost*. In particular, it should provide sufficient protection against both *dynamic* (i.e. run-time) and *static* program analyses. The technique automatically provides high levels of protection against dynamic analysis because of the fact that the particulars of the basic "challenge-response" mechanism of fetching the key from memory, comparing it with the golden key, and modifying the control-flow based on the result of the comparison, vary depending on the input arguments of the program. Because the input argument-space of most practical programs is larger beyond complete enumeration, hence, breaking the obfuscation scheme simply by observing the execution of the obfuscated program is practically infeasible. Hence, we concentrate on the protection provided by the proposed key-based obfuscation methodology against static code analysis efforts of an adversary.

Consider an assembly language program containing N instructions, to which n instructions are added to modify the control flow by the technique described above, as a result of which the code size increases to $(N + n)$. Let there be L "load" instructions in the original program, to which l "key load" instructions are added during modifications to increase the number of load instructions to $(L + l)$. Note that as pointed out earlier, these load instructions need not occur in the same order as the key comparison sequence. Similarly, let there be C "comparison-based branch" instructions in the original program to which c are added to bring the total number of branch instructions to $(C + c)$. To identify the modifications that have been made to the original program based on random choice, an adversary must perform the following steps:

- Identify the n instructions dedicated in modifying the original program, out of a total $(N + n)$ instructions in the obfuscated program. This is one out of $\binom{N + n}{n}$ possibilities.
- Identify the l "load" instructions dedicated to the obfuscation scheme out of the total $(L + l)$ "load" instructions, and from them determine the correct order in which the keys are collected from memory and compared to modify the control flow. Note that the adversary does not know a-priori the number of key comparisons for a given feasible control-flow path of a given program.

Let M_{av} be the average number of modifications performed among all the feasible control-flow paths of the given program. Then, to break the scheme, the adversary has to make exactly one out of $\left[\sum_{i=1}^{\lceil M_{av} \rceil} \binom{L+l}{i} \times i! \right]$ choices to determine the correct number and sequence of keys to be applied.

- Identify the c "comparison-based branch instructions" dedicated in control-flow modification, from a total of $(C+c)$ such instructions in the obfuscated program.
- Identify the $(n-l-c)$ dataflow operations dedicated to obfuscate the code, from among the total $(N+n-L-C-l-c)$ in the obfuscated code.

Combining the three above factors, we propose the following quantitative metric to estimate the effectiveness of the proposed key-based obfuscation scheme:

$$M_{obf,random} = \cfrac{1}{\left[\sum_{i=1}^{\lceil M_{av} \rceil} \binom{L+l}{i} \times i! \right] \times \binom{C+c}{c} \times \binom{N+n-L-C-l-c}{n-l-c}}$$

(3)

Lower values of this metric implies higher levels of *potency*, *resilience* and *stealth*. To get an idea of the numerical order of this metric, consider the example shown in Fig. 1 and the portion of the code between the two markers **#begin_text** and **#end_text**. Assuming the length of all modifications to be similar to the one shown, we have the values $\lceil M_{av} \rceil = 3$, $r_{mod} = 5$, $N = 29$, $n = 3 \times 13 = 39$, $C = 3$, $c = 3 \times 2 = 6$, $L = 1$ and $l = 3 \times 2$. This gives the value $M_{obf} \approx 9.63 \times 10^{-20}$. In real-life applications, the value of this metric would be much smaller because of larger values of N and L, which in turn would allow larger values of n and l.

3.2   Computational Overhead of the Obfuscation Technique

Time Complexity. The time complexity of the path enumeration step is essentially the time complexity of the dept-first traversal, which is $O(|\mathbb{V}| + |\mathbb{E}|)$, where $|\mathbb{V}|$ and $|\mathbb{E}|$ are the number of vertices and edges respectively in the graph [32]. However, note that in our particular case, $N - 1 \leq |\mathbb{E}| \leq 2N$, where $N = |\mathbb{V}|$ is the number of instructions in the block of the program to be obfuscated. The lower limit occurs when there is no non-loop branch instructions in the program, while the upper limit is because of the fact that no node in the graph has more than two children. However, note that an upper limit of $2N$ is overly pessimistic for real programs, because (approximately) only one in every seven instructions in real-life programs are branch instructions. Hence, the time complexity of the depth-first traversal step is $O(N)$. For the program modification step, the time complexity is $O(|\mathbb{E}|)$, which because of the argument presented just now is $O(N)$. The time complexity of ranking the instructions based on the number of paths on which they lie is $O(N \log N)$, assuming an efficient sorting algorithms such as "Heapsort". Hence, the overall time-complexity of the obfuscation procedure is $O(N \log N)$.

To estimate the value of the average number of modifications made per path (M_{av}), it is essential to find the number of modifications made on every path individually, as well as the total number of paths. The total number of paths can be found during the first depth-first search. However, finding the number of modifications made individually on each path will require $O\left(\sum_{i=1}^{|\mathbb{P}|} |p_i|\right)$ steps, where $|\mathbb{P}|$ stands for the total number of paths, and $|p_i|$ is the length of the i-th path in the set of paths $\mathbb{P}$.

Space Complexity. The space complexity of the entire procedure is $O(N)$, the space required to store the information about the instructions constituting the program. If the program to be processed is of considerable size, it should be partitioned into segments of manageable sizes; each segment can be obfuscated independently and then the obfuscated segments are to be integrated to get the obfuscated program in its entirety.

4 Automation of the Obfuscation Technique

The program obfuscation methodology described in Section 2 was implemented through an automated flow, as shown in Fig. 2. The top-level tcsh script *sobfus* accepts as input arguments the un-obfuscated MIPS program segment in a single file (let it be "file.mips"), the number of modifications (M) to be made and the *modification radius* (r_{mod}). M is estimated a-priori from the size of the modification code blocks in the modification pool, the size of the program, and the maximum code size overhead acceptable. *sobfus* invokes the TCL script *format_code* which formats the input code by removing all comments and blank lines and replacing all labels for branch instructions in the program by

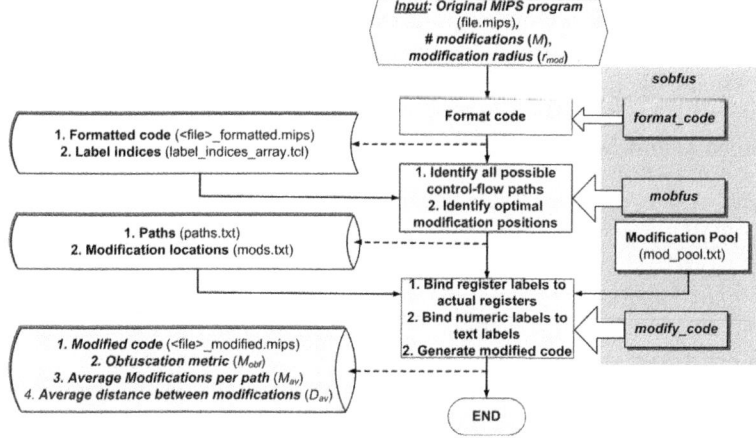

Fig. 2. Automation of the proposed obfuscation technique

Table 1. Functionality of the MIPS assembly programs used to evaluate the proposed
obfuscation technique. The test programs cover a variety of representative applications
from embedded domain.

Program	Functionality
TokenQuest.mips	One player adventure game
hanoi.mips	Recursive solution of the "Tower of Hanoi" problem
MD5.mips	MD5 hashing of a given ASCII text file
connect4.mips	Two player "Four in a Line" game
DES.mips	Digital Encryption Standard (DES) encrypter/decypter (for ASCII text files)
sudoku.mips	*Sudoku* puzzle
ID3Ediror.mips	Reading and editing of ID3 tag information in MP3 music files
string.mips	MIPS implementation of the functions of the C standard header "string.h"
cipher.txt	Various cipher techniques for ASCII text
decoder.mips	MP3 music format decoder

the corresponding destination line numbers. It produces a formatted version of
the program in the file "file_formatted.mips", and a hash of the program labels
and the corresponding line numbers in the file "label_indices_array.tcl". ***sobfus***
then calls the C program ***mobfus*** which enumerates all the possible control-flow
paths in the program segment using Algorithm-1, and finds the optimal modification locations using Algorithm-2. It reports the enumerated paths in the
file "paths.txt" and the modification locations in the file "mods.txt". ***sobfus***
then invokes the TCL script ***modify_code*** which finally produces the obfuscated program in the file "file_obfuscated.mips" by using the modification code
blocks provided in the file "mod_pool.txt", and binds the register mnemonics to
registers available at a given point in the program (as described in Section 2.1
and elucidated in Section 2.2). It also produces an estimate of the obfuscation
metric M_{obf} according to eqn. 3, and values for the metrics M_{av} and D_{av}.

To extend the proposed obfuscation technique to binary executables, one
would need to disassemble the equivalent assembly language program from a
given binary, substitute all absolute addresses by symbolic addresses, apply the
proposed obfuscation technique, and then again convert it back to the binary
form. Note that the address substitution is essential because the insertion of
modification code fragments shifts the relative positions of the instructions. Disassembly and de-compilation of binary code to assembly language code is not
very difficult, and free tools are available online [33] to serve the purpose.

5   Results

The proposed technique was applied on a suite of MIPS programs varying in
size from 109 to 21024 instructions. The test programs represent components of
various embedded applications. The functionality of the programs are listed in
Table 1. The functionality of the original and the obfuscated versions of all the
programs were verified using the *SPIM* simulator [34]. The program obfuscation

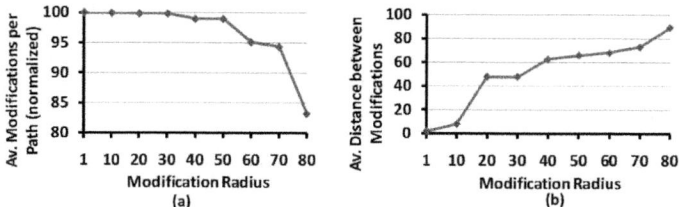

Fig. 3. Variation of (a) average modification per path (M_{av}) and (b) the average distance between modifications (D_{av}) vs. the modification radius (r_{mod}), in the program *connect4.mips*, for $M = 3$ modifications

methodology described in Section 4 was implemented and the programs were simulated on a Linux workstation with 2GB of main memory and a 2GHz quad-core processor.

We investigated the effect of variation of the *modification radius* (r_{mod}) on the average modifications per path (M_{av}) and the average distance between modifications (D_{av}) for the $N = 270$ instruction program *connect4.mips*. The number of modifications (M) was set at 3, and r_{mod} was varied between 1 and 80. Fig. 3 shows the plots of M_{av} and D_{av} vs. r_{mod}. The values for M_{av} were normalized with respect to its value at $r_{mod} = 1$ (the minimum possible value of r_{mod}). The trends are as expected, with M_{av} decreasing with r_{mod} and D_{av} increasing with r_{mod}. Note that the metrics M_{av} and D_{av} satisfy the constraints $1 < M_{av} \leq M$ and $r_{mod} \leq D_{av} < \frac{N}{M-1}$, as stated in Section 2.1.

Table 2 shows the effects of applying the proposed application technique on the MIPS program suite, at a *modification radius* ($r_{mod} = 50$), with a 10% target code-size overhead. For the largest program *decoder.mips*, only 1000 paths were considered to keep the memory requirement manageable, and r_{mod} was set to 500. As is evident from the obtained M_{obf} values, the proposed technique can provide high levels of protection at a nominal code-size overhead of 10%. Note that in larger programs and in programs with higher number of "load" and "branch" instructions, the effectiveness of the technique increases.

Table 3 shows the code-size overhead of the obfuscated program (with respect to the original program), the CPU time and average increase in execution cycles to implement algorithms 1 and 2. The run-time overheads were not calculated by direct functional simulations by SPIM, but by indirect analysis of the original and modified programs. The average increase in execution time was estimated by calculating the average increase in execution cycles per modification, and then multiplying the quantity with the average number of modifications per path. The CPU time has a strong correlation to the number of paths in the program, and a weaker correlation to the program size. These trends are consistent with the analysis of Section 3.2.

Table 2. Program obfuscation efficiency for a targeted 10% code-size overhead at a modification radius $r_{mod} = 50$

Program	Program Parameters[†]								Obfuscation Efficiency		
	N	C	L	$\|\mathbb{P}\|$	M	n	c	l	M_{obf}	M_{av}	D_{av}
TokenQuest.mips	109	19	14	11	2	18	3	3	1.09e-20	1.55	95.0
hanoi.mips	132	20	40	169	2	16	3	3	1.43e-19	1.91	67.0
MD5.mips	250	41	35	114	4	26	5	5	6.33e-33	3.67	65.33
connect4.mips	270	72	37	4146	4	26	5	5	1.30e-33	3.47	89.33
DES.mips	372	43	64	5241	6	34	7	9	1.54e-40	5.31	68.00
sudoku.mips	436	110	43	111113	8	41	9	11	2.66e-49	6.76	58.29
ID3Editor.mips	878	160	134	98724	12	89	16	19	1.71e-106	5.66	79.45
string.mips	876	156	224	111075	12	89	16	19	4.42e-103	10.90	60.55
cipher.mips	1956	231	218	150129	27	188	35	43	1.65e-222	26.23	75.12
decoder.mips[‡]	21024	174	231	1000[‡]	27	188	35	43	$<10^{-400}$	13.50	502.00[‡]

[†]The meaning and significance of these parameters are as described in Section 3.
[‡]Only 1000 paths were enumerated, and r_{mod} was set to 500.

Table 3. Overheads for the obfuscation technique (with parameters of Table 2)

Program	Overheads		
	Code-size (%)	CPU time (s)	Average Increase in Execution Cycles
TokenQuest.mips	18.85	0.10	17.83
hanoi.mips	12.12	0.40	20.06
MD5.mips	10.40	0.90	31.20
connect4.mips	9.63	1.00	29.50
DES.mips	9.14	2.00	41.60
sudoku.mips	9.40	66.00	48.17
ID3Editor.mips	10.14	112.00	54.71
string.mips	10.16	217.00	105.37
cipher.txt	10.61	1474.00	241.90
decoder.mips	0.89%	1840.00	124.50

6   Conclusions

Security of embedded software has emerged as a major challenge because of their increasing vulnerability to piracy and malicious modifications. Severe constraints on hardware and energy resources of embedded devices often limit the applicability of complex hardware and software protection approaches. We have presented a low-overhead "execution trace dependent control-flow obfuscation" technique, which requires the application of an input-dependent set of validation keys to enable a software module to function properly. The key verification mechanism is implemented by distributing the verification code throughout the program to balance the code overhead and proximity of the modifications. We have theoretically analyzed the level of security and the associated computational overhead. Application of the algorithm on a suite of MIPS programs resulted in high levels of security at nominal code size and modest computational overhead. The technique can be easily automated and applied to arbitrarily large programs by appropriate program partitioning. Future work would involve implementation of a working prototype (including proper hardware support) of the proposed obfuscation scheme.

References

1. Turley, J.: The two percent solution,
   http://www.embedded.com/story/OEG20021217S0039
2. Gwennap, L., Byrne, J.: A Guide to High-Speed Embedded Processors. The Linley Group (2008)
3. Dube, R.: Hardware-based Computer Security Techniques to Defeat Hackers. ch. 5. John Wiley and Sons, Chichester (2008)
4. Ravi, S., Raghunathan, A., Kocher, P., Hattangady, S.: Security in embedded systems: design challenges. ACM Transactions on Embedded Computing Systems 3(3), 461–491 (2004)
5. Kerckhoff, A.: La cryptographie militaire. Journal des Sciences Militaires IX, 5–38 (1883)
6. Chang, H., Atallah, M.J.: Protecting software code by guards. In: Sander, T. (ed.) DRM 2001. LNCS, vol. 2320, pp. 160–175. Springer, Heidelberg (2002)
7. Barak, B.: Can we obfuscate programs?,
   http://www.math.ias.edu/~boaz/Papers/obf_informal.html
8. Barak, B., Goldreich, O., Impagliazzo, R., Rudich, S., Sahai, A., Vadhan, S.P., Yang, K.: On the (im)possibility of obfuscating programs. In: Conference on Advances in Cryptology (2001)
9. Collberg, C., Thomborson, C., Low, D.: Manufacturing Cheap, Resilient, and Stealthy Opaque Constructs. In: ACM Symposium on Principles of Programming Languages (1998)
10. Collberg, C., Thomborson, C.: Watermarking, Tamper-Proofing, and Obfuscation – Tools for Software Protection. IEEE Transactions on Software Engineering 28(8), 735–746 (2002)
11. Collberg, C., Thomborson, C., Low, D.: Breaking abstractions and unstructuring data structures. In: International Conference on Computer Languages (1998)
12. Linn, C., Debray, S.: Obfuscation of executable code to improve resistance to static disassembly. In: ACM Conference on Computer and Communications Security (2003)
13. Hou, T.W., Chen, H.Y., Tsai, M.H.: Three control flow obfuscation methods for Java software. IEE Proceedings 153(2), 80–86 (2006)
14. Barak, B., et al.: On the (Im)possibility of obfuscating programs. In: Kilian, J. (ed.) CRYPTO 2001. LNCS, vol. 2139, pp. 1–18. Springer, Heidelberg (2001)
15. White, S.R., Comerford, L.: ABYSS: An architecture for software protection. IEEE Transactions on Software Engineering 16(6), 619–629 (1990)
16. Dallas Semiconductor, Dallas DS5240 Secure Microcontroller,
   http://datasheets.maxim-ic.com/en/ds/DS5240.pdf
17. Trusted Computing Group, Trusted Platform Module: Design Principles,
   http://www.trustedcomputinggroup.org/resources/tpm_main_specification
18. Trusted Computing Group, TCG Mobile Trusted Module Specification,
   http://www.trustedcomputinggroup.org/files/resource_files/87852F33-1D093519ADOC0F141CC6B10D/Revision_6-tcg-mobile-trusted-module-1_0.pdf

19. Leavitt Communications, Will proposed standard make mobile phones more secure?, http://www.leavcom.com/ieee_dec05.htm
20. Joepgen, H.G., Krauss, S.: Software by means of the protprog method. Elektronik 42(17), 52–56 (1993)
21. Schulman, A.: Examining the Windows AARD detection code. Dr. Dobbs Journal 18(9), 42, 448, 89 (1993)
22. Jakubowski, M.H., Saw, C.W., Venkatesan, R.: Tamper-tolerant software: Modeling and implementation. In: Takagi, T., Mambo, M. (eds.) IWSEC 2009. LNCS, vol. 5824, pp. 125–139. Springer, Heidelberg (2009)
23. Aucsmith, D.: Tamper resistant software: an implementation. In: Anderson, R. (ed.) IH 1996. LNCS, vol. 1174, pp. 317–333. Springer, Heidelberg (1996)
24. Lie, D., et al.: Architectural support for copy and tamper resistant software. ACM SIGPLAN Notices 35(11), 168–177 (2000)
25. Arora, D., Ravi, S., Raghunathan, A., Jha, N.K.: Hardware-assisted run-time monitoring for secure program execution on embedded processors. IEEE Transactions on VLSI 14(12), 1295–1308 (2006)
26. Fiskiran, A.M., Lee, R.B.: Runtime execution monitoring (REM) to detect and prevent malicious code execution. In: IEEE International Conference on Computer Design (2004)
27. Zhuang, X., Zhang, T., Lee, H.S., Pande, S.: Hardware assisted control flow obfuscation for embedded processors. In: ACM International Conference on Compilers, Architecture, and Synthesis for Embedded Systems (2004)
28. Chakraborty, R.S., Bhunia, S.: HARPOON: An obfuscation-based SoC design methodology for hardware protection. IEEE Transactions on CAD 28(10), 1493–1502 (2009)
29. Chakraborty, R.S., Bhunia, S.: RTL hardware IP protection using key-based control and data flow obfuscation. In: VLSI Design (2010)
30. Copeland, B.J. (ed.): The Essential Turing: Seminal Writings in Computing, Logic, Philosophy, Artificial Intelligence, and Artificial Life Plus the Secrets of Enigma. Oxford University Press, Oxford (2004)
31. Dube, R.B.: Hardware-based Computer Security Techniques to Defeat Hackers. ch. 5. John Wiley and Sons, Chichester (2008)
32. Cormen, T.H., Leiserson, C.E., Rivest, R.L., Stein, C.: Introduction to Algorithms, 2nd edn. ch. 22. MIT Press, Cambridge (2001)
33. The Boomerang Decompiler Project, Boomerang: A general, open source, retargetable decompiler of machine code programs, http://boomerang.sourceforge.net
34. Larus, J.: SPIM: A MIPS32 simulator, http://pages.cs.wisc.edu/~larus/spim.html
35. Balakrishnan, A., Schulze, C.: Code obfuscation literature survey, http://pages.cs.wisc.edu/~arinib/writeup.pdf
36. Patterson, D.A., Hennessy, J.L.: Computer Organization and Design: The Hardware/Software Interface (Appendix A), 4th edn. Morgan Kaufmann Publishers, San Francisco (2009)

Reversible Watermarking Using *Priority Embedding* through Repeated Application of *Integer Wavelet Transform**

Sambaran Bandyopadhyay[1], Ruchira Naskar[2], and Rajat Subhra Chakraborty[2]

[1] Department of Computer Science and Engineering
Institute of Engineering and Management, Kolkata, India–700091
sam krish89@rediffmail.com
[2] Department of Computer Science and Engineering
Indian Institute of Technology, Kharagpur, India–721302
{ruchira,rschakraborty}@cse.iitkgp.ernet.in

Abstract. *Digital Watermarking* is a well-known technique for digital content protection. *Reversible Watermarking* techniques are a special class of watermarking techniques whereby after the watermark has been extracted, the original content can be retrieved without any distortion. In this paper we present a novel high capacity reversible watermarking technique for grayscale images, based on repeated application of *integer wavelet transform*. The process is performed after determining a *priority* of the different image pixels to be used for watermark embedding. Our experimental results fare favourably when compared to other state–of–the–art reversible watermarking techniques of similar principle.

Keywords: Digital watermarking, embedding capacity, integer wavelet transform, PSNR, reversible watermarking.

1 Introduction

Digital watermarking is a class of popular techniques whereby hard–to–detect information (called the "signature" or "payload") is embedded in digital content (audio, image or video) for purposes of content authentication and intellectual property (IP) protection. Since only the creator or distributor of the digital content has knowledge about the hidden information and how to retrieve it, she can prove her ownership in case of litigation. In many application domains such as medical and military imaging, the original information is extremely sensitive and recovery of the original information in an unaltered form is of utmost importance. In such cases, *reversible watermarking* techniques have been found useful where by the very nature of the watermarking scheme, the original content can be retrieved exactly with zero distortion [3,11,12].

In this paper we present a high quality, high capacity reversible watermarking scheme for images. We use *integer wavelet transform* [3] to convert the original

---

* The work is based on our earlier work published in the *IEMCON 2011* conference.

M. Joye et al. (Eds.): InfoSecHiComNet 2011, LNCS 7011, pp. 45–56, 2011.
© Springer-Verlag Berlin Heidelberg 2011

image into a set of average and difference numbers, and then repeat the same procedure for the reduced matrix. In our scheme each row of the original image matrix [13] is replaced by a single average number and multiple difference numbers. Since usually the difference numbers can be encoded in relatively fewer number of bits, through our technique we create space to embed larger number of payload bits in the difference numbers. To embed the bits into these difference numbers, we make a *priority list* depending on the value of the hiding ability of difference numbers. The visual quality of the watermarked image compared to the original image is also found to be satisfactory, and is reflected in the calculated *peak signal-to-noise ratio* (PSNR).

The rest of the paper is organized as follows: in Section 2 we provide the mathematical formulation of integer wavelet transform based reversible watermarking. In Section 3, we describe the methodology proposed in this paper. In Section 4, we present experimental results of applying the proposed algorithm to an example image. We conclude in Section 5.

2   Background

2.1   Reversible Integer Wavelet Transform

The *integer wavelet transform* maps integers to integers, and allows for perfect invertibility with finite precision arithmetic. Also, the integer wavelet transform can be implemented with only three operations – addition, subtraction and shift, on a digital computer. This feature makes it attractive compared to other discrete wavelet transforms. For example, for the *Haar wavelet filter*, the integer wavelet transforms are:

$$l_i = \left\lfloor \frac{x_{2i} + x_{2i+1}}{2} \right\rfloor, \quad h_i = x_{2i} - x_{2i+1} \tag{1}$$

where $\lfloor \rfloor$ implies the "floor function" which means the "greatest integer less than or equal to". The corresponding inverse transforms are:

$$x_{2i} = l_i + \left\lfloor \frac{h_i + 1}{2} \right\rfloor, \quad x_{2i+1} = l_i - \left\lfloor \frac{h_i}{2} \right\rfloor \tag{2}$$

2.2   Watermarking Based on Integer Wavelet Transform

Reversible watermarking is based on applying the above integer wavelet transform on the pixel encoded values, and utilizing the high spatial redundancy in pixel values in natural images. Let (x, y) be two pixel values in a grayscale image utilizing 8–bit binary encoding, where $x, y \in [0, 255]$. Then, the following values are computed:

$$l = \left\lfloor \frac{x + y}{2} \right\rfloor, \quad h = x - y \tag{3}$$

Due to the high redundancy in natural images, the difference values h are usually comparatively smaller, and can be encoded using less than eight bits.

The space saved can be thus utilized to embed the bits of the signature to be embedded. As an example, consider $x = 205$, $y = 200$, $l = 202$, $h = 5 = 101_2$. Suppose a bit $b = 0$ of information is to be embedded at the location right after the most significant bit (MSB) in the binary representation of h. Then, the modified value of h becomes $h' = 1001_2 = 9$. Thus, the new grayscale values are:

$$x' = l + \left\lfloor \frac{h' + 1}{2} \right\rfloor = 207, \quad y' = x' - h' = 198$$

From the embedded pair (x', y'), the watermark detector can extract the embedded bit b and get back the original pair (x, y) by:

$$l' = \left\lfloor \frac{x' + y'}{2} \right\rfloor = 202, \quad h' = x' - y' = 9 = 1001_2$$

Note that the values of l and l' are the same. With the knowledge of the location of the inserted watermark bit, the original difference value $h = 5 = 101_2$ can be extracted from h', and with the average number l' and the difference number h, the original values (x, y) can be re-calculated using the inverse integer transform. The above procedure of embedding the digital watermark by expanding the difference values is generally termed as *difference expansion*.

Difficulty arises when the value of h is large, which can lead to underflow or overflow conditions with the values to be embedded. For example, let $x = 105, y = 22$, then $l = 63, h = x - y = 83 = 1010011_2$. If we embed a bit "0" in h, the new value is $h' = 10010011_2 = 147$. This leads to the embedded values $x' = 137$ and $y' = -10$. This will cause an underflow problem as grayscale values are restricted in the range $[0, 255]$. To restrict the overflow or underflow conditions, the following conditions must be satisfied:

$$0 \leq l + \left\lfloor \frac{h + 1}{2} \right\rfloor \leq 255, \quad 0 \leq l - \left\lfloor \frac{h}{2} \right\rfloor \leq 255$$

which is equivalent to

$$|h| \leq \min(2(255 - l), 2l + 1) \tag{4}$$

The least significant bit (LSB) of the difference h is usually selected as the embedding area. Since

$$h = \left\lfloor \frac{h}{2} \right\rfloor \cdot 2 + LSB(h)$$

for $LSB(h) = 0$ or 1, the difference number h is *changeable* if

$$\left| \left\lfloor \frac{h}{2} \right\rfloor \cdot 2 + b \right| \leq \min(2(255 - l), 2l + 1) \tag{5}$$

for both $b = 0$ and 1.

Note that modifying changeable h (without compression) does not provide additional storage space. The extra storage space is gained from *expandable* difference numbers. For a grayscale pixel pair (x, y), its difference number h is expandable if

$$|2 \cdot h + b| \leq \min(2(255 - l), 2l + 1) \qquad (6)$$

for both $b = 0$ and 1. For each expandable difference number, we get at least one bit of space to embed the watermark.

The information about the pixel locations and bit positions in the binary values of the pixels where the bits of the watermark are to be inserted is stored in a *location map*. The location map of the expanded difference numbers is usually in the form of a "bi-level image", where the pixel value is "1" at each location where it is expanded, and "0" otherwise. It is usually losslessly compressed using a compression technique such as JBIG2 or *run–length coding*. Similarly, the concatenation of the LSBs of the changeable difference numbers can be further compressed using *arithmetic coding* or *Huffman coding*. Optionally, a secure hash of the original digital image can be created by an algorithm such as SHA–256. All of the above bitstreams are then combined into a final bitstream and transmitted. In this work, for simplicity, we have not embedded the location map or hash information in the image, and have not applied any lossless compression algorithm to further compress these information.

3 Proposed Method

3.1 Multi–Bit Hiding

Till now we have been concerned about embedding one extra bit of the watermark per difference number. But, we can go further by checking whether more than one bit can be embedded into a single difference number. We do so by examining the *hiding ability* of the difference number h. For a given difference number h, let k be the largest integer such that:

$$|k * h + b| \leq \min(2(255 - l), 2l + 1) \qquad (7)$$

for all $0 \leq b \leq k - 1$, where the number b no longer represents the value of a single bit. In such a case, we say that the *hiding ability* of h is $\log_2 k$. Hiding ability gives us the information of how many bits we can embed into the difference number without causing an underflow or overflow. It is to be noted that higher the value of hiding ability, better the embedding capacity. In most practical images, the hiding capacity of a difference term (calculated for two adjacent pixel values) is greater than one. For a difference number to be expandable, the value of hiding ability must be at least one (since $\log_2 2 = 1$). Hiding ability can also indirectly help us to select the expandable difference numbers for data embedding. For each row of the reduced image matrix (which is in the form of a collection of average–difference value pairs), we first calculate the hiding ability of the difference terms and then examine the pairs of average values and replace them by another average–difference value pair. We repeat this procedure for the reduced average–difference matrix to have multiple difference values (not necessarily expandable) and a *single* average value for each row. Since a large fraction of the set of difference values are expandable, a large number of bits of the payload can be embedded in them. We make a list (called the *mask*) of hiding abilities of difference terms and save the mask for extraction process. Then we select the difference terms according to non–increasing order of hiding abilities to embed watermark bits. As we embed a bit, we modify the hiding ability of that difference term. As the total sum of hiding abilities is very large, the total embedding capacity of the image is also very high. Also as we are not embedding bits randomly, but assign priorities to difference terms, the quality of the process also increases. This observation and its implementation are the main contributions of this paper.

In the next section we describe the proposed watermark embedding and extraction for multi–bit hiding.

3.2   Watermark Embedding

Algorithm 1 shows the steps of the proposed watermark embedding algorithm. The algorithm embeds a given watermark in a given cover image, by giving priority to the difference terms with higher hiding ability, and repeatedly applying integer wavelet transform to the expandable difference terms. If the size of the input watermark exceeds that of the total hiding ability of the input image, the algorithm returns an error message.

As a simple example, consider a 8×8 block of an "image matrix" (with the pixel values in decimal):

$$
X = \begin{bmatrix}
129 & 128 & 129 & 134 & 149 & 171 & 196 & 220 \\
127 & 127 & 128 & 136 & 148 & 166 & 189 & 215 \\
124 & 124 & 126 & 136 & 147 & 163 & 183 & 211 \\
124 & 125 & 131 & 131 & 136 & 157 & 182 & 204 \\
122 & 122 & 126 & 133 & 138 & 158 & 181 & 203 \\
122 & 120 & 123 & 133 & 137 & 154 & 176 & 198 \\
124 & 122 & 122 & 129 & 133 & 149 & 169 & 190 \\
126 & 123 & 120 & 127 & 131 & 147 & 165 & 185
\end{bmatrix}
\tag{8}
$$

Suppose, we want to embed the payload bitstream $msg = 110110011101101 \cdots$ 00111101111101010. When X and msg are input to the watermark embedding algorithm, let w_m_image be the final image matrix. Let $mask$ be the "image mask matrix" to represent the hiding ability of each pixel; $mask1$ be the matrix showing the number of watermark bits embedded in different pixel positions, and $avgdiff$ be the matrix of average and difference terms obtained from the rows of the original cover image matrix. The evolution of the $avgdiff$ matrix over successive iterations is as follows:

Algorithm 1. *EMBED_WATERMARK*

/* Embed watermark bits into the cover image */

Input: The $m \times n$ original image matrix: *image*; the bitstream to be embedded: *msg*.

Output: The $m \times n$ watermarked image: *w_m_image*; a matrix representing hiding abilities of original average-difference matrix:*mask_image*; size of watermark embedded in bits: *len*.

1: Initialize $avgdiff$, $mask$ and w_m_image to be $m \times n$ null matrices.
2: $t \leftarrow log_2 n$
3: **for** $t1 = 0 \rightarrow t - 1$ **do**
4:    **for** $i = 1 \rightarrow m$ **do**
5:      $j \leftarrow 1$
6:      $k \leftarrow 2^{t1} + 1$
7:      **while** $(j \le n)\&\&(k \le n)$ **do**
8:        **if** $(image(i,j) + image(i,k))\%2 == 0$ **then**
9:          $avgdiff(i,j) \leftarrow \frac{image(i,j)+image(i,k)}{2}$
10:       **else**
11:          $avgdiff(i,j) \leftarrow \frac{image(i,j)+image(i,k)-1}{2}$
12:       **end if**
13:       $avgdiff(i,k) \leftarrow image(i,j) - image(i,k)$
14:       $mask(i,k) \leftarrow$ hiding ability of $(avgdiff(i,j), avgdiff(i,k))$
15:       /*Calculate the hiding ability of (i,j)th term of the reduced matrix and store it to $mask(i,j)$*/
16:       $j \leftarrow j + 2^{t1+1}$
17:       $k \leftarrow k + 2^{t1+1}$
18:     **end while**
19:   **end for**
20:   $image \leftarrow avgdiff$
21: **end for**
22: $mask\_image \leftarrow mask$
23: /*To embed the watermark msg into $avgdiff$*/
24: $l \leftarrow$ length of msg in bits
25: $p \leftarrow 1$
26: **while** $p \le l$ **do**
27:   $[ij] \leftarrow$row and column number of the largest element in $mask$
28:   **if** $mask(i,j) == 0$ **then**
29:     $error('msg$ size exceeded embedding capacity.')
30:   **end if**
31:   $avgdiff(i,j) \leftarrow avgdiff(i,j) * 2 + msg(p)$
32:   $p \leftarrow p + 1$
33:   $mask(i,j) \leftarrow mask(i,j) - 1$
34: **end while**
35: /*Apply repeated reverse integer wavelet transform to the $avgdiff$ matrix*/
36: $w\_m\_image \leftarrow avgdiff$
37: $t \leftarrow log_2 n$
38: **for** $t1 = (t-1) \rightarrow 0$ step -1 **do**
39:   **for** $i = 1 \rightarrow m$ **do**
40:     $j \leftarrow 1$
41:     $k \leftarrow 2^{t1} + 1$
42:     **while** $(j \le n)\&\&(k \le n)$ **do**
43:       $w\_m\_image(i,j) \leftarrow avgdiff(i,j) + \left\lfloor \frac{avgdiff(i,k)+1}{2} \right\rfloor$
44:       $w\_m\_image(i,k) \leftarrow avgdiff(i,j) - \left\lfloor \frac{avgdiff(i,k)}{2} \right\rfloor$
45:       $j \leftarrow j + 2^{t1+1}$
46:       $k \leftarrow k + 2^{t1+1}$
47:     **end while**
48:   **end for**
49:   $avgdiff \leftarrow w\_m\_image$
50: **end for**
51: $len \leftarrow$ size of msg in bits

1st iteration:

$$avgdifff^{(1)} = \begin{bmatrix} 128 & 1 & 131 & -5 & 160 & -22 & 208 & -24 \\ 127 & 0 & 132 & -8 & 157 & -18 & 202 & -26 \\ 124 & 0 & 131 & -10 & 155 & -16 & 197 & -28 \\ 124 & -1 & 131 & 0 & 146 & -21 & 193 & -22 \\ 122 & 0 & 129 & -7 & 148 & -20 & 192 & -22 \\ 121 & 2 & 128 & -10 & 145 & -17 & 187 & -22 \\ 123 & 2 & 125 & -7 & 141 & -16 & 179 & -21 \\ 124 & 3 & 123 & -7 & 139 & -16 & 175 & -20 \end{bmatrix}$$

2nd iteration:

$$avgdifff^{(2)} = \begin{bmatrix} 129 & 1 & -3 & -5 & 184 & -22 & -48 & -24 \\ 129 & 0 & -5 & -8 & 179 & -18 & -45 & -26 \\ 127 & 0 & -7 & -10 & 176 & -16 & -42 & -28 \\ 127 & -1 & -7 & 0 & 169 & -21 & -47 & -22 \\ 125 & 0 & -7 & -7 & 170 & -20 & -44 & -22 \\ 124 & 2 & -7 & -10 & 166 & -17 & -42 & -22 \\ 124 & 2 & -2 & -7 & 160 & -16 & -38 & -21 \\ 123 & 3 & 1 & -7 & 157 & -16 & -36 & -20 \end{bmatrix}$$

3rd iteration:

$$avgdifff^{(3)} = \begin{bmatrix} 156 & 1 & -3 & -5 & -55 & -22 & -48 & -24 \\ 154 & 0 & -5 & -8 & -50 & -18 & -45 & -26 \\ 151 & 0 & -7 & -10 & -49 & -16 & -42 & -28 \\ 148 & -1 & -7 & 0 & -42 & -21 & -47 & -22 \\ 147 & 0 & -7 & -7 & -45 & -20 & -44 & -22 \\ 145 & 2 & -7 & -10 & -42 & -17 & -42 & -22 \\ 142 & 2 & -2 & -7 & -36 & -16 & -38 & -21 \\ 140 & 3 & 1 & -7 & -34 & -16 & -36 & -20 \end{bmatrix}$$

The final watermarked image matrix output by the algorithm is:

$$w\_m\_image = \begin{bmatrix} 126 & 122 & 131 & 140 & 149 & 171 & 196 & 220 \\ 129 & 122 & 130 & 138 & 148 & 166 & 189 & 215 \\ 124 & 118 & 129 & 139 & 147 & 163 & 183 & 211 \\ 119 & 124 & 137 & 132 & 136 & 157 & 182 & 204 \\ 122 & 115 & 126 & 139 & 138 & 158 & 181 & 203 \\ 123 & 113 & 126 & 136 & 137 & 154 & 176 & 198 \\ 127 & 119 & 123 & 130 & 133 & 149 & 169 & 190 \\ 126 & 123 & 119 & 126 & 131 & 147 & 165 & 185 \end{bmatrix}$$

The values of *mask* and *mask*1 are as follows:

$$
mask = \begin{bmatrix}
0 & 6 & 6 & 5 & 1 & 3 & 1 & 1 \\
0 & 7 & 5 & 4 & 2 & 3 & 1 & 2 \\
0 & 7 & 5 & 4 & 2 & 3 & 1 & 2 \\
0 & 7 & 5 & 7 & 2 & 3 & 1 & 2 \\
0 & 7 & 5 & 5 & 2 & 3 & 1 & 2 \\
0 & 6 & 5 & 4 & 2 & 3 & 2 & 2 \\
0 & 6 & 6 & 5 & 2 & 3 & 2 & 2 \\
0 & 5 & 6 & 5 & 2 & 3 & 2 & 3
\end{bmatrix}
$$

and

$$
mask1 = \begin{bmatrix}
0 & 2 & 2 & 1 & 0 & 0 & 0 & 0 \\
0 & 3 & 1 & 0 & 0 & 0 & 0 & 0 \\
0 & 3 & 1 & 0 & 0 & 0 & 0 & 0 \\
0 & 3 & 1 & 3 & 0 & 0 & 0 & 0 \\
0 & 3 & 1 & 1 & 0 & 0 & 0 & 0 \\
0 & 2 & 1 & 0 & 0 & 0 & 0 & 0 \\
0 & 2 & 1 & 0 & 0 & 0 & 0 & 0 \\
0 & 0 & 1 & 0 & 0 & 0 & 0 & 0
\end{bmatrix}
$$

3.3   Watermark Extraction

The watermark extraction algorithm shown in Algorithm 2 works in exactly the reverse way compared to the embedding algorithm.

4   Results

The proposed technique was implemented in MATLAB and applied to a 256×256, 8 bits per pixel (bpp) grayscale version of the "Lena" and "Mandrill" images. Fig. 1 shows the original and watermarked versions of the images with 0.5 bpp embedded into both. From these two images, it is evident that the proposed approach has minimal adverse effect on the visual quality of the image. To calculate the PSNR, first the *mean square error* (MSE) was calculated as:

$$
MSE = \sum_{i=1}^{m} \sum_{j=1}^{n} \frac{(X_{org}(i,j) - X_{wm}(i,j))^2}{m \cdot n} \tag{9}
$$

where $X_{org}(i,j)$ is the (i,j)–th pixel of the original image, and $X_{wm}(i,j)$ is the (i,j)–th pixel of the watermarked image, and m and n are the dimensions of the image (here each is 256). Then, PSNR is calculated as:

$$
PSNR = 10 \log_{10} \left(\frac{MAX_I^2}{MSE} \right) = 10 \log_{10} \left(\frac{255^2}{MSE} \right) \tag{10}
$$

where MAX_I is the maximum possible pixel value of the image, which is 255 in this case because of the 8–bit grayscale nature of the image.

Algorithm 2. *EXTRACT_WATERMARK*

/* Extract watermark bits from the watermarked image */

Input: The $m \times n$ watermarked image: w_m_img; matrix representing hiding abilities of original average-difference matrix: $mask_i mage$; size of embedded watermark in bits: len.

Output: The retrieved $m \times n$ cover image: $image$; extracted watermark: msg.

1: Initialize $avgdiff$, $mask1$ and $image$ to be $m \times n$ null matrices.
2: $t \leftarrow log_2 n$
3: **for** $t1 = 0 \rightarrow t - 1$ **do**
4:    **for** $i = 1 \rightarrow m$ **do**
5:       $j \leftarrow 1$
6:       $k \leftarrow 2^{t1} + 1$
7:       **while** $(j \le n)\&\&(k \le n)$ **do**
8:          **if** $(w\_m\_img(i,j) + w\_m\_img(i,k))\%2 == 0$ **then**
9:             $avgdiff(i,j) \leftarrow \frac{w\_m\_img(i,j) + w\_m\_img(i,k)}{2}$
10:          **else**
11:             $avgdiff(i,j) \leftarrow \frac{w\_m\_img(i,j) + w\_m﬩_i mg(i,k) - 1}{2}$
12:          **end if**
13:          $avgdiff(i,k) \leftarrow w\_m\_img(i,j) - w\_m\_img(i,k)$
14:          $mask1(i,k) \leftarrow$ mask of hiding abilities of watermarked $avgdiff(i,j), avgdiff(i,k)$
15:          $j \leftarrow j + 2^{t1+1}$
16:          $k \leftarrow k + 2^{t1+1}$
17:       **end while**
18:    **end for**
19:    $w\_m\_img \leftarrow avgdiff$
20: **end for**
21: $s \leftarrow len$
22: Initialize msg and $index$ to be zero vectors of sizes $1 \times s$ and $1 \times 2s$ respectively.
23: $p \leftarrow 1$
24: **while** $p \le s$ **do**
25:    $[ij] \leftarrow$ row and column number of the largest element in $mask$
26:    $index(2 * p - 1) \leftarrow i$
27:    $index(2 * p) \leftarrow j$
28:    $mask(i,j) \leftarrow mask(i,j) - 1$
29:    $p \leftarrow p + 1$
30: **end while**
31: $p \leftarrow s$
32: **while** $p \ge 1$ **do**
33:    $t1 \leftarrow index(2 * p - 1)$
34:    $t2 \leftarrow index(2 * p)$
35:    $msg(p) \leftarrow avgdiff(t1,t2)\%2$ /*Extract the watermark bit*/
36:    $avgdiff(t1,t2) \leftarrow \left\lfloor \frac{avgdiff(t1,t2)}{2} \right\rfloor$
37:    $p \leftarrow p - 1$
38: **end while**
39: /*Apply repeated reverse integer wavelet transform to the $avgdiff$ matrix*/
40: $image \leftarrow avgdiff$
41: $t \leftarrow log_2 n$
42: **for** $t1 = t - 1 \rightarrow 0$ step -1 **do**
43:    **for** $i = 1 \rightarrow m$ **do**
44:       $j \leftarrow 1$
45:       $k \leftarrow 2^{t1} + 1$
46:       **while** $(j \le n)\&\&(k \le n)$ **do**
47:          $image(i,j) \leftarrow avgdiff(i,j) + \left\lfloor \frac{avgdiff(i,k) + 1}{2} \right\rfloor$
48:          $image(i,k) \leftarrow avgdiff(i,j) - \left\lfloor \frac{avgdiff(i,k)}{2} \right\rfloor$
49:          $j \leftarrow j + 2^{t1+1}$
50:          $k \leftarrow k + 2^{t1+1}$
51:       **end while**
52:    **end for**
53:    $avgdiff \leftarrow image$
54: **end for**

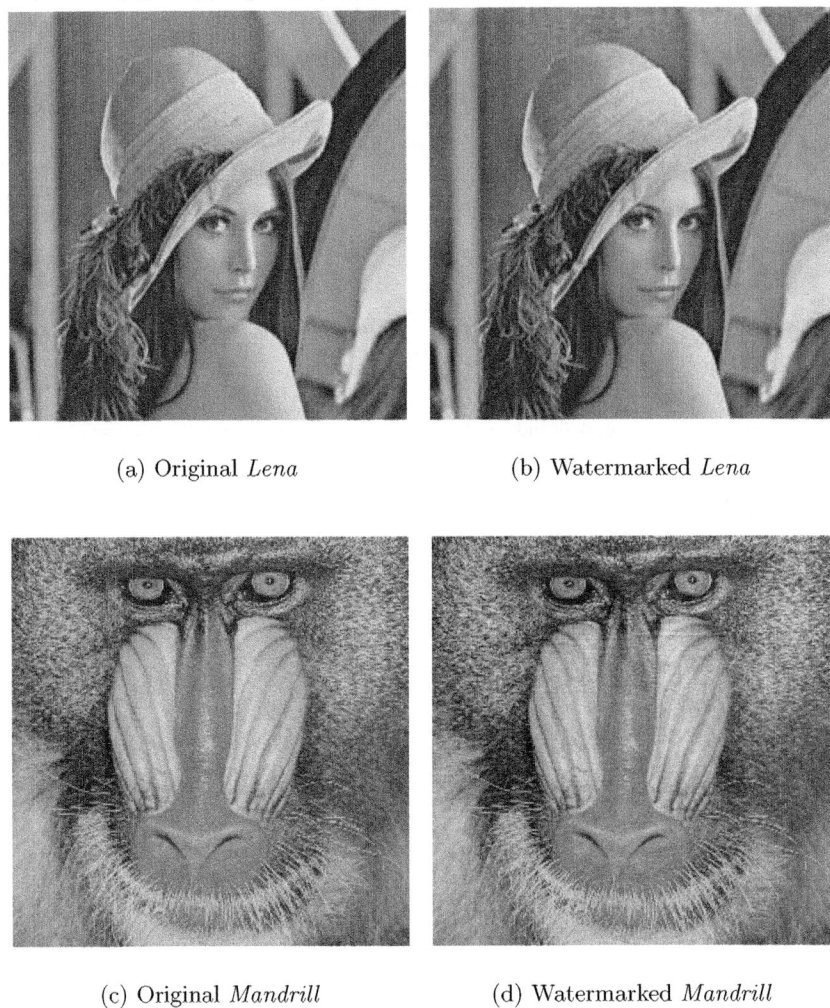

(a) Original *Lena*   (b) Watermarked *Lena*

(c) Original *Mandrill*   (d) Watermarked *Mandrill*

Fig. 1. Proposed scheme: (*Left*) Original images; (*Right*) Watermarked images with 0.5 watermark bits embedded per pixel

Fig. 2 shows a plot of the *peak signal–to–noise ratio* (PSNR, in dB) of the watermarked images against the embedded payload size (in bits per pixel). These results are compared with state–of–the–art techniques, [3,6,9], in Fig. 3, which clearly shows the superiority of the proposed technique. Note that the set of payload size values for the four techniques are not the same, as we have tabulated only those values which were available in the original publications where the techniques were described.

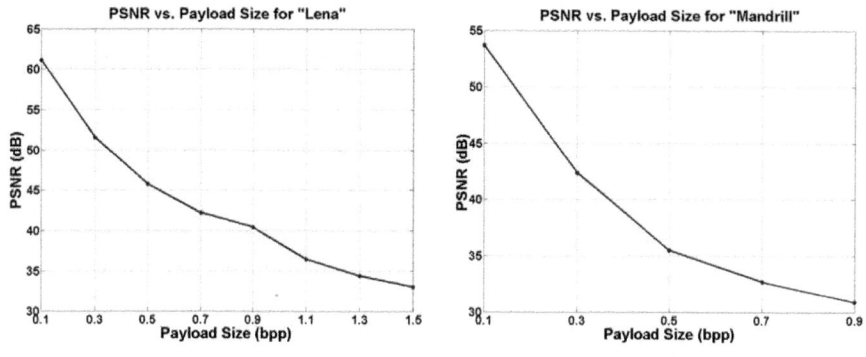

Fig. 2. Plot of PSNR vs. embedded payload size

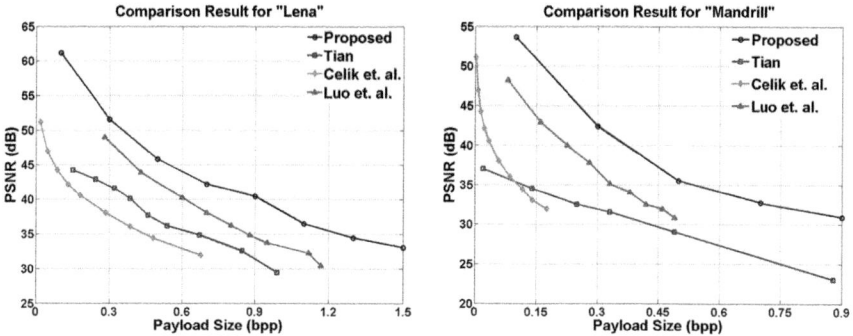

Fig. 3. Comparison with other state–of–the–art techniques

5   Conclusions

Reversible watermarking is an important class of techniques for digital content protection and authentication where it is possible to retrieve the original content with zero distortion. In this paper, we have proposed a high capacity reversible digital watermarking technique for images, where the spatial redundancy of images are utilized in embedding the watermark. The novelty of the proposed technique lies in the repeated application of the principle of *difference expansion* to decrease the number of average terms to a single average term and increase the number of difference terms, so that more bits of the payload can be embedded in the difference terms. This effectively increases the embedding capacity of the watermarked image. Experimental results on the common benchmark image "Lena" shows that the technique is capable of achieving good PSNR values even at relatively large payload sizes.

References

1. Cox, I.J., Miller, M.L., Bloom, J.A., Fridrich, J., Kalker, T.: Digital Watermarking and Steganography. Morgan Kaufmann Publishers, San Francisco (2008)
2. Feng, J.B., Lin, I.C., Tsai, C.S., Chu, Y.P.: Reversible watermarking: current status and key issues. International Journal of Network Security 2(3), 161–171 (2006)
3. Tian, J.: Wavelet–based reversible watermarking for authentication. In: Security and Watermarking of Multimedia Contents IV, vol. 4675, pp. 679–690 (2002)
4. Tian, J.: Reversible data embedding using a difference expansion. IEEE Transactions on Circuits Systems and Video Technology 13(8), 890–896 (2003)
5. Tian, J.: Reversible watermarking by difference expansion. In: Proceedings of Workshop on Multimedia and Security, pp. 19–22 (December 2002)
6. Celik, M.U., Sharma, G., Tekalp, A.M., Saber, E.: Lossless generalized-LSB data embedding. IEEE Transactions on Image Processing 14(2), 253–266 (2005)
7. Celik, M.U., Sharma, G., Tekalp, A.M., Saber, E.: Localized lossless authentication watermark (LAW). In: International Society for Optical Engineering, California, USA, vol. 5020, pp. 689–698 (January 2003)
8. Celik, M.U., Sharma, G., Tekalp, A.M., Saber, E.: Reversible data hiding. In: Proceedings of International Conference on Image Processing, pp. III-157–III-160 (Sepetmber 2002)
9. Luo, L., Chen, Z., Chen, M., Zeng, X., Xiong, Z.: Reversible image watermarking using interpolation technique. IEEE Transactions on Information Forensics and Security 5(1), 187–193 (2010)
10. Ni, Z., Shi, Y.Q., Ansari, N., Su, W.: Reversible data hiding. IEEE Transactions on Circuits and Systems for Video Technology 16(3), 354–362 (2006)
11. Ni, Z., Shi, Y.Q., Ansari, N., Su, W.: Reversible data hiding. In: Proceedings of the IEEE International Symposium of Circuits and Systems (2003)
12. Calderbank, A.R., Daubechis, I., Sweldens, W., Yeo, B.L.: Wavelet Transforms that map integers to integers. Applied and Computational Harmonic Analysis 5, 332–369 (1998)
13. Gonzalez, R.C., Woods, R.E.: Digital Image Processing, 3rd edn. Pearson education, London (2009)
14. Gonzalez, R.C., Woods, R.E., Eddins, S.L.: Digital Image Processing using MATLAB. Pearson Education, London (2004)

Access Policy Based Key Management in Multi-level Multi-distributor DRM Architecture

Ratna Dutta, Dheerendra Mishra, and Sourav Mukhopadhyay

Department of Mathematics
Indian Institute of Technology
Kharagpur–721302, India
{ratna,dheerendra,sourav}@maths.iitkgp.ernet.in

Abstract. We present a multi-level multi-distributor based DRM architecture that facilitates client mobility and propose key management mechanism for this system using Identity-Based Encryption (IBE) and Attribute-Based Encryption (ABE). The encrypted digital content sent by a package server can only be decrypted by the DRM client and is protected from attacks by other parties/servers in the system. Our key management protects the key used to encrypt a digital content during its delivery from the package server to the DRM client, not only from purchasers but also from the distribution servers and the license server. The IBE and ABE enables efficiency gains in computation time and storage over the existing certificate-based Public Key Infrastructure (PKI) based approaches as no certificate management and verification is needed by the entities in the system.

Keywords: DRM, key management, content protection, security, access structure, access policy, IBE, ABE.

1   Introduction

The core concept in DRM is the use of digital licenses. The consumer purchases a digital license granting certain rights to him instead of buying the digital content. The content access is regulated with the help of a license that contains permissions, constraints and a content decryption key. Permissions are privileges or actions that a principal can be granted to exercise against some object under some constraints. Examples of permissions include printing, playing, copying, and embedding the content into other content items. Constraints are restrictions and conditions under which permissions are executed. Constraints may include expiration date, available regional zone, software security requirements, hardware security requirements, and watermarking requirements. A set of constraints can also include another set of constraints recursively, which means that the included set of constraints must also be satisfied.

Current Digital Rights Management (DRM) systems support only two-party systems, involving the package server and purchaser [3], [4], [6], [8], [11]. However, DRM systems need to be sufficiently flexible to support existing business models

M. Joye et al. (Eds.): InfoSecHiComNet 2011, LNCS 7011, pp. 57–71, 2011.
© Springer-Verlag Berlin Heidelberg 2011

and extensible to adapt to future models. The DRM architecture in multi-party multi-level setups has been used [7], [9], [12], [13], [16] as an alternative to the traditional two-party DRM architecture.

Our Contribution: In this paper, we design a DRM system considering a network with multi-level multi-distributors. A local distributor can better explore potentially unknown markets for the owner (package server) and make strategies according to the market. In addition, the distributors can also help in handling different pricing structures of media in different countries, and share with the owner any information on price or demand fluctuation cost. We consider a hierarchy of distributors and the package server is at the top (say, level 0) of this hierarchy who appoints the level 1 distribution servers based on their access policies or attributes. In general, level i distributors appoint level $i + 1$ distributors based on their access policies or attributes for $i > 0$. In our DRM system, the DRM client has the flexibility of choosing a distributor based on his own preference. The DRM client may be mobile and roam from one region to another. The DRM client may contact the distributor who is nearest to him by location or who offers promotions/discounts on the price or offers more commissions.

We provide a secure and efficient key management scheme in our proposed DRM system using IBE and ABE instead of certificate-based Public Key Infrastructure (PKI). The ABE has the property that a user's public key is an easily calculated function of his access policy, such as $\Gamma = \langle$IIT $\cap$ CSDepartment $\cup$ ElectronicsDepartment $\cap$ DSCMember$\rangle$ or set of attributes, such as $\gamma = \{$IISc, MathematicsDepartment, M.Tech$\}$, while a user's private key can be calculated for him by a trusted authority, called Private Key Generator (PKG). The attribute-based public key cryptosystem needs verification of user's access policy or attributes only at the private key extraction phase. Consequently, the identity-based public key cryptography simplifies certificate management and verification and is an alternative for certificate-based PKI, especially when efficient key management and security are required. We obtain efficiency gains in computation time and storage over the existing certificate-based PKI approaches as no certificate management and verification are needed by the entities in our DRM system. The ABE is a generalization of IBE. In IBE system, only one attribute is used which is the identity of the receiver.

In our key management mechanism, the package server does not trust distribution servers or license server. The symmetric decryption key used to encrypt a digital content is delivered from the package server to the DRM client in a secure manner and is protected from its generation to consumption. Unlike current DRM systems which have focused on content protection from purchasers, our scheme protects the key not only from purchasers, but also from other principals such as the distribution servers and the license server. Consequently, the encrypted digital content sent by a package server can only be decrypted by the DRM client who has a valid license and no one else.

2 Preliminaries

2.1 Definitions and Notations

Definition 2.1: (**Access Structure**). *Let* $\mathcal{P} = \{P_1, \ldots, P_n\}$ *be a set of parties. A collection* $\Gamma \subseteq 2^{\mathcal{P}}$ *is monotone if for* $\forall B, C$: *if* $B \in \Gamma$ *and* $B \subseteq C$ *then* $C \in \Gamma$. *An access structure (respectively, monotone access structure) is a collection (respectively, monotone collection)* Γ *of non-empty subsets of* $\mathcal{P}$. *i.e.,* $\Gamma \subseteq 2^{\mathcal{P}} \backslash \{\emptyset\}$. *The sets in* Γ *are called the authorized sets, and the sets not in* Γ *are called the unauthorized sets.*

In our context, the role of the parties is taken by the attributes. Thus the access structure Γ will contain the authorized sets of attributes.

We describe below a tree-access structure.

Access Tree: We now describe access tree. Let $\mathcal{T}$ be a tree representing an access structure. Each non-leaf node of the tree represents a threshold gate, described by its children and a threshold value. If num_x is the number of children of a node x and k_x is its threshold value, then $0 < k_x \leq \text{num}_x$. When $k_x = 1$, the threshold gate is an OR gate and when $k_x = \text{num}_x$, it is an AND gate. Each leaf node x of the tree is described by an attribute and a threshold value $k_x = 1$.

To facilitate working with the access trees, we define a few functions. We denote the parent of the node x in the tree by $\text{parent}(x)$. The function $\text{att}(x)$ is defined only if x is a leaf node and denotes the attribute associated with the leaf node x in the tree. The access tree $\mathcal{T}$ also defines an ordering between the children of every node, that is, the children of a node are numbered from 1 to num. The function $\text{index}(x)$ returns such a number associated with the node x where the index values are uniquely assigned to nodes in the access structure for a given key in an arbitrary manner.

Satisfying an access tree: Let $\mathcal{T}$ be an access tree with root r. Denote by $\mathcal{T}_x$ the subtree of $\mathcal{T}$ rooted at the node x. Hence $\mathcal{T}$ is the same as $\mathcal{T}_r$. If the set of attributes γ satisfies the access tree $\mathcal{T}_x$, we denote it as $\mathcal{T}_x(\gamma) = 1$. We compute $\mathcal{T}_x(\gamma)$ recursively as follows. If x is a non-leaf node, evaluate $\mathcal{T}_{x'}(\gamma)$ for all children x' of node x. $\mathcal{T}_x(\gamma)$ returns 1 if and only if at least k_x children return 1. If x is a leaf node, then $\mathcal{T}_x(\gamma)$ returns 1 if and only if $\text{att}(x) \in \gamma$.

Definition 2.2: (**Linear Secret Sharing Scheme**). *A secret sharing scheme* Π *over a set of parties* $\mathcal{P}$ *is called linear (over* Z_p*) if*

1. *The shares from each party form a vector over* Z_p.
2. *There exists a matrix* $\mathcal{M}$ *called the share generation matrix for* Π. *The matrix* $\mathcal{M}$ *has* l *rows and* $n + 1$ *columns. For all* $i = 1, \ldots, l$, *the* i-th *row of* $\mathcal{M}$ *is labeled with a party named* $\overline{x}_i \in \mathcal{P}$. *When we consider the column vector* $v = (s, r_1, r_2, \ldots, r_n)$, *where* $s \in Z_p$ *is the secret to be shared, and* $r_1, \ldots, r_n \in Z_p$ *are randomly chosen, then* $\mathcal{M}v$ *is the vector of* l *shares of the secret* s *according to* Π. *The share* $(\mathcal{M}v)_i$ *belongs to party* $\overline{x}_i$.

Every linear secret sharing scheme according to the above definitions also enjoys the linear reconstruction property, defined as follows: Suppose that Π is a linear secret sharing scheme for the access structure Γ. Let $S \in \Gamma$ be any authorized set, and let $I \subset \{1, 2, \dots, l\}$ be defined as $I = \{i : \overline{x}_i \in S\}$. Then, there exists constants $\{w \in Z_p\}_{i \in I}$ such that, if $\{\lambda_i\}$ are valid shares of any secret s according to Π, then $\sum_{i \in I} w_i \lambda_i = s$. Furthermore, these constants $\{w_i\}$ can be found in time polynomial in the size of the share generation matrix $\mathcal{M}$.

Table 1 explains the meaning of symbols used throughout the paper.

Table 1. Notations

Name	Description
P	package server
$D_{i,j}$	j-th distribution server in the i-th level
L	license server
C	DRM client
ID_U	public identity of user U
S_U	private key of user U associated with ID_U
$\Gamma_{i,j}$	access policy ascribed to $D_{i,j}$
$\mathsf{SK}_{i,j}$	private key of user $D_{i,j}$ associated with $\Gamma_{i,j}$
PKG	private key generator
IBE.Enc	encryption algorithm for IBE
IBE.Dec	decryption algorithm for IBE
ABE.Enc	encryption algorithm for KP-ABE
ABE.Dec	decryption algorithm for KP-ABE
Sig	signature generation algorithm
Ver	signature verification algorithm
$\mathsf{MK}_{\mathsf{IBE}}$	master key of PKG for IBE
$\mathsf{PK}_{\mathsf{IBE}}$	public parameters of PKG for IBE
$\mathsf{MK}_{\mathsf{ABE}}$	master key of PKG for KP-ABE
$\mathsf{PK}_{\mathsf{ABE}}$	public parameters of PKG for KP-ABE
$A|B$	concatenation of A and B

2.2   Identity Based Encryption (IBE)

The concept of identity-based cryptosystem is due to Shamir [15]. Such a scheme has the property that a user's public key is an easily calculated function of his identity, such as his email address, while a user's private key can be calculated for him by a trusted authority, called Private Key Generator (PKG). The identity-based public key cryptosystem can be an alternative for certificate-based PKI, especially when efficient key management and moderate security are required.

In identity-based public key encryption, the public key distribution problem is eliminated by making each user's public key derivable from some known aspect of his identity, such as his email address. When Alice wants to send a message to Bob, she simply encrypts her message using Bob's public key which she derives from Bob's identifying information. Bob, after receiving the encrypted message, obtains his private key from a third party called a Private Key Generator (PKG), after authenticating himself to PKG and can then decrypt the message. The private key that PKG generates on Bob's query is a function of its master key and Bob's identity.

Shamir [15] introduced this concept of identity-based cryptosystem to simplify key management procedures in certificate-based public key infrastructure. The first identity-based Encryption (IBE) was proposed by Boneh and Franklin [2] in 2001 that uses bilinear pairing. Shortly after this, many identity-based cryptographic protocols were developed based on pairings and is currently a very active area of research.The identity-based public key cryptosystem can be an alternative for certificate-based PKI, especially when efficient key management and moderate security are required.

The advantage of identity-based encryption are compelling. It makes maintaining authenticated public key directories unnecessary. Instead, a directory for authenticated public parameters of PKGs is required which is less burdensome than maintaining a public key directory since there are substantially fewer PKGs than total users. In particular, if everyone uses a single PKG, then everyone in the system can communicate securely and users need not to perform on-line lookup of public keys or public parameters.

An IBE scheme consists of the following four algorithms.

Setup: This is a randomized algorithm that takes no input other than the implicit security parameter. It outputs the public parameters PK_{IBE} and a master key MK_{IBE}. PK_{IBE} is made public and used for encryption. MK_{IBE} is used to generate user private keys and is kept secret to the PKG.

Encryption: This is a randomized algorithm that takes as input a message M, a set of attributes γ, and the public parameters PK_{IBE}. It outputs the ciphertext CT.

Key Generation: This is a randomized algorithm that takes as input - a public identity ID, the master key MK_{IBE} and the public parameters PK_{IBE}. It outputs a decryption key S_{ID}

Decryption: This algorithm takes as input - the ciphertext CT that was encrypted under the public identity ID, the decryption key S_{ID} corresponding ID and the public parameters PK_{IBE}. It outputs the message M.

2.3 Attribute Based Encryption (ABE)

Current Attribute Based Encryption (ABE) schemes are built by cleverly combining the basic techniques of IBE with a linear secret sharing scheme. The ABE can be viewed as a generalization of IBE [2]. In IBE systems, only one attribute is used which is the identity of the receiver, whereas ABE systems enable the use of multiple attributes simultaneously. The ABE systems are designed to enable fine grained access control of the encrypted data. In ABE, an encryptor will associate encrypted data with a set of attributes or an access policy. An access policy is an access structure over attributes. An authority will issue users different private keys, where user's private key is associated with an access policy or a set of attributes ascribed to the user. Only the receivers who are assigned compatible access policies or sets of attributes can decrypt the encrypted message. Formally, the attributes can be considered as boolean variables with arbitrary labels, and the policies are expressed as conjunction and disjunction of attribute variables. In ABE, the access policies are written in the form of a monotonic boolean formula over the attribute variables. [5]. There are two alternatives in enforcing the access policy:

- The access policy can be embedded in the private key of a user, which leads to Key-Policy ABE (KP-ABE) [5] cryptosystem.
- The access policy can be embedded in the ciphertext, which leads to the Ciphertext-Policy ABE (CP-ABE) [1] cryptosystem.

Both KP-ABE and CP-ABE systems ensure that a group of users cannot access any unauthorized data by colluding with each other. The syntax of both KP-ABE and CP-ABE are described below.

1. *Key-Policy Attribute Based Encryption (KP-ABE) [5]*

   Key policy attribute based encryption (KP-ABE) is a generalization of Fuzzy IBE (FIBE) [14] which allows the authority to specify more advanced decryption policies. In KP-ABE, as in Fuzzy IBE, each ciphertext is labeled by the sender with a set of descriptive attributes. However, each private key is associated with an access structure (say access tree) that specifies which type of ciphertexts the key can decrypt. A particular key can decrypt a particular ciphertext only if the ciphertext attributes satisfy the access structure (tree) of the key. A KP-ABE scheme consists of the following four algorithms.

   Setup: This is a randomized algorithm that takes no input other than the implicit security parameter. It outputs the public parameters PK_{ABE} and a master key MK_{ABE}. PK_{ABE} is public and used for encryption. MK_{ABE} is used to generate user private keys and is kept secret to the PKG.

   Encryption: This is a randomized algorithm that takes as input a message M, a set of attributes γ, and the public parameters PK_{ABE}. It outputs the ciphertext CT. The set of attributes γ is sent as part of the ciphertext CT.

   Key Generation: This is a randomized algorithm that takes as input - an access structure Γ, the master key MK_{ABE} and the public parameters PK_{ABE}. It outputs a decryption key SK.

   Decryption: This algorithm takes as input - the ciphertext CT that was encrypted under the set γ of attributes, the decryption key SK for access structure Γ and the public parameters PK_{ABE}. It outputs the message M if $\gamma \in \Gamma$.

Besides, individual users can generate new private keys using their own private keys, which can then be delegated to other users using the following algorithm.

Delegate: A user with a private key SK corresponding to access structure Γ can compute a new private key $\overline{SK}$ corresponding to any access structure $\overline{\Gamma}$ which is more restrictive than Γ, *i.e.* $\overline{\Gamma} \subseteq \Gamma$. Thus the users are capable of acting as a local key authority which generate and distribute private keys to other users.

2. *Ciphertext-Policy Attribute Based Encryption (CP-ABE) [1]*

In the CP-ABE scheme, each user is associated with a set of attributes and her private key is generated based on these attributes. When encrypting a message M, the encryptor specifies an access structure which is expressed in terms of a set of selected attributes for M. The message is then encrypted based on the access structure such that only those whose attributes satisfy this access structure can decrypt the message. Unauthorized users are not able to decrypt the ciphertext even if they collude. A CP-ABE scheme consists of the following four algorithms.

Setup: This is a randomized algorithm that takes no input other than the implicit security parameter. It outputs the public parameters PK_{ABE} and a master key MK_{ABE}. PK_{ABE} is made public and used for encryption. MK_{ABE} is used to generate user private keys and is kept secret to the PKG.

Encryption: This is a randomized algorithm that takes as input a message M, an access structure Γ, and the public parameters PK_{ABE}. It outputs the ciphertext CT.

Key Generation: This is a randomized algorithm that takes as input - the set of a uses's attributes γ, the master key MK_{ABE} and the public parameters PK_{ABE}. It outputs a decryption key SK that identifies with γ.

Decryption: This algorithm takes as input - the ciphertext CT, the decryption key SK for an attribute set γ and the public parameters PK_{ABE}. It outputs the message M if γ satisfies the access structure Γ embedded in the ciphertext CT.

Besides, individual users can generate new private keys using their private keys, which can then be delegated to other users using the following algorithm.

Delegate: A user with a private key SK corresponding to a set of attributes γ can compute a new private key $\overline{SK}$ corresponding to any set of attributes

$\overline{\gamma}$ which is more restrictive than γ, *i.e.* $\overline{\gamma} \subseteq \gamma$. Thus the users are capable of acting as a local key authority which generate and distribute private keys to other users.

3   Protocol

3.1   Overview of the Proposed Multi-party Multi-level DRM Architecture

Our multi-party multi-level DRM architecture allows existence of more that one distributors arranged in a hierarchy based on attributes or access policy (*e.g.* wholesalers, retailers, or resellers). Entities involved in our DRM model are:

- package server P
- multiple levels of distribution servers $D_{i,j}$, $1 \leq i \leq k$, $1 \leq j \leq n_i$, where $D_{i,j}$ represents the j-th distribution server at the i-th level
- license server L
- DRM client C.

The distribution servers in level 1 are appointed by the package server P according to some attributes or access policy to facilitate the distribution process. Each distribution server in level 1 further appoints some subdistribution servers by attaching attributes or access policies to them and so forth. The total number of levels of distribution servers may depend upon the extent of the region to be explored and density of DRM clients. For instance, in a general business scenario such as live broadcasting and video on demand, the system may have distribution servers from University 1, distribution servers from University 2 *etc.*. The distribution servers from University 1 have further subdistribution servers such as subdistribution servers from the department of Computer Science, subdistribution servers from the department of Arts *etc.* and so on. The DRM client C is mobile and move from one region to another. C can download encrypted contents from its preferred distributor, say $D_{i,j}$, which might be location wise nearest to C or offering some promotions/discounts on the price. The owner of the package server P has raw content and wants to protect it. None of the principals except P should know how to decrypt the content.

3.2   Secure Delivery of Content Key

Our key distribution scheme makes use of the setups for IBE and KP-ABE as shown in Figure 2 and Figure 3 respectively. A similar construction can be designed using CP-ABE instead of using KP-ABE. Use of the setup of IBE instead of certificate-based setup simplifies certificate management and certificate verification.

We now describe in detail our proposed key distribution scheme.

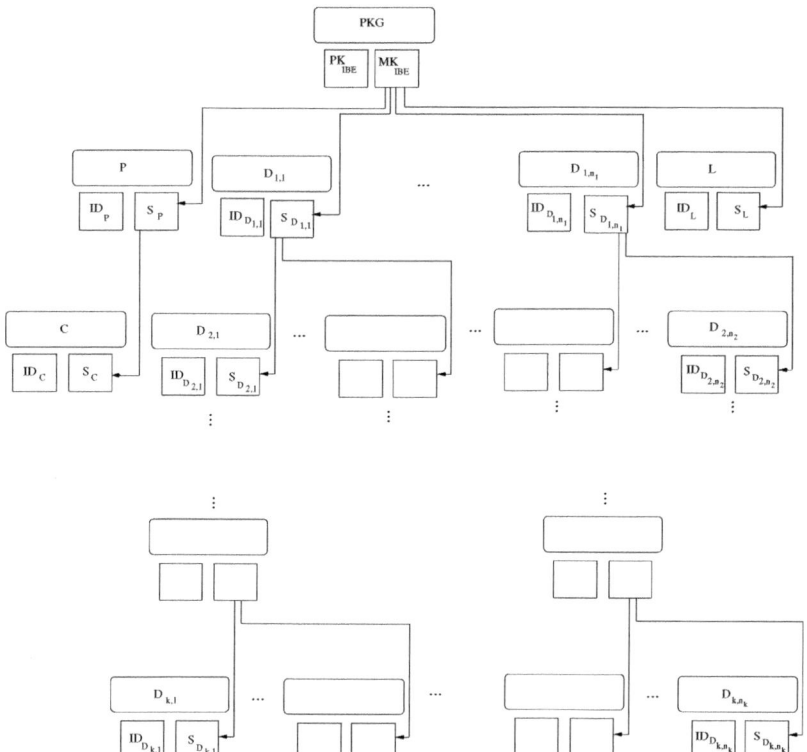

Fig. 1. IBE key setup (ID_U is the identity of user U and S_U is U's private key issued by its parent in the hierarchy)

1. *Key setup*

1.1) The principals of the package server P, and the license server L submit their public identities to PKG and obtain the corresponding private keys S_P, and S_L respectively through a secure communication channel. PKG uses its master key $\mathsf{MK}_{\mathsf{IBE}}$ to generate the principals private key after verifying the validity of the principals public identity submitted to PKG.

1.2) The principal of the DRM client C submits its public identity ID_C to the principal of the package server P and obtains the corresponding private key S_C through a secure communication channel. P uses its own private key S_P issued by PKG to generate the private key of C after verifying the validity of C's public identity ID_C submitted to P.

1.3) The principal of the distribution server $D_{1,j}$, $1 \le j \le n_1$, submits its public identities $\mathsf{ID}_{D_{1,j}}$ and access policy $\Gamma_{1,j}$ to PKG and obtains the private keys $S_{D_{1,j}}$ and $\mathsf{SK}_{1,j}$ respectively through a secure communication channel. PKG uses its master keys $\mathsf{MK}_{\mathsf{IBE}}$ and $\mathsf{MK}_{\mathsf{ABE}}$ to generate $D_{1,j}$'s private keys

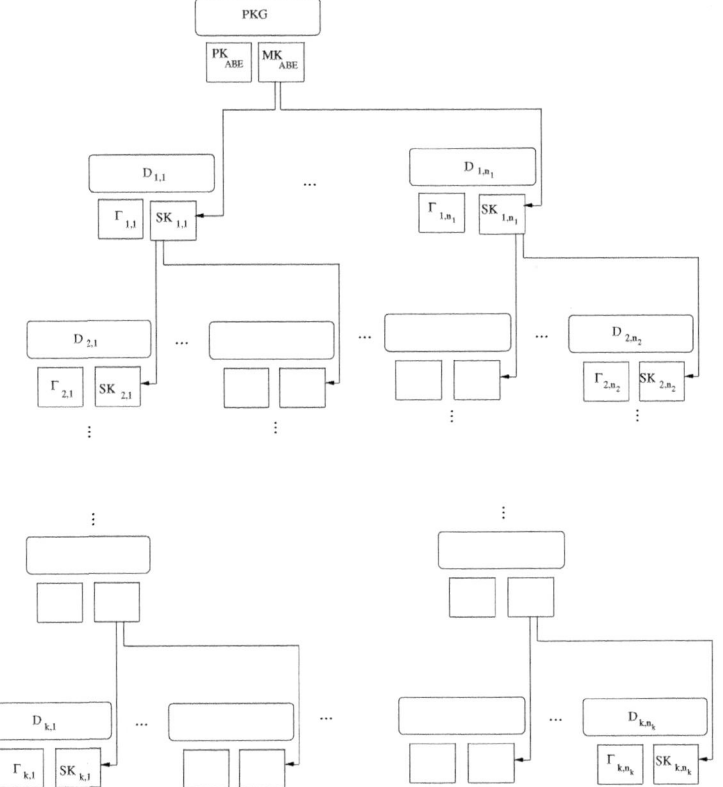

Fig. 2. KP-ABE key setup ($\Gamma_{i,j}$ is the access policy for distributor $D_{i,j}$ and $\mathsf{SK}_{i,j}$ is $D_{i,j}$'s secret key issued by its parent in the hierarchy)

$S_{D_{1,j}}$ and $\mathsf{SK}_{1,j}$ respectively after verifying the validity of $\mathsf{ID}_{D_{1,j}}$ and $\Gamma_{1,j}$ submitted to PKG.

1.4) The principal of the distribution server $D_{i,j}$, $2 \leq i \leq k$, $1 \leq j \leq n_i$ submits its public identities $\mathsf{ID}_{D_{i,j}}$ and access policy $\Gamma_{i,j}$ to the principal of its parent distribution server in the $(i-1)$-th level, say D_{i-1,j_1} in the hierarchy of the distribution servers. D_{i-1,j_1} in turn generates the corresponding private keys $S_{D_{i,j}}$ and $\mathsf{SK}_{i,j}$ respectively for $D_{i,j}$ using its own private keys $S_{D_{i-1,j_1}}$ and SK_{i-1,j_1} respectively after verifying the validity of $D_{i,j}$'s public identities $\mathsf{ID}_{D_{i,j}}$ and $\Gamma_{i,j}$. D_{i-1,j_1} then sends $S_{D_{i,j}}$ and $\mathsf{SK}_{i,j}$ to $D_{i,j}$ through a secure communication channel.

2. *Key Delivery when Packaging the Content*

The package server P creates the content key K to encrypt a raw digital content M using symmetric encryption while packaging M. P splits the content key K and distributes a different part of K to each of the license server L

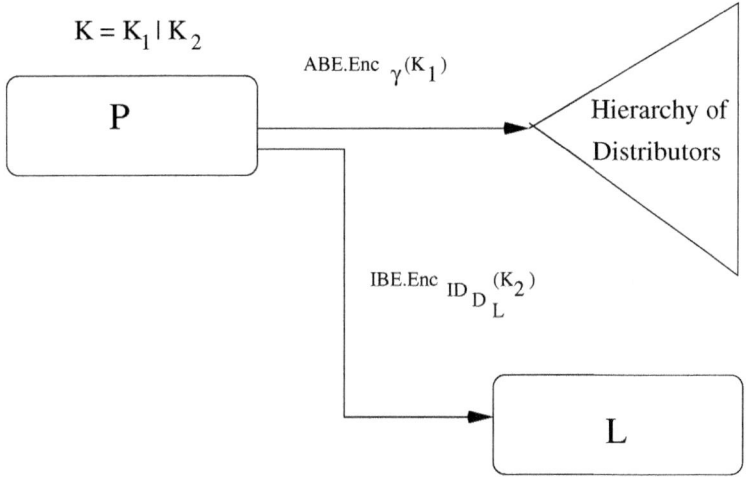

Fig. 3. Service flow during content packaging (signature and verification are not shown), γ being a set of attributes

and the distribution servers $D_{i,j}$, $1 \leq i \leq k$, $1 \leq j \leq n_i$. These servers in turn keep their respective partial content keys secret. We describe below details. The service flow is shown in Figure 4.

2.1) P splits the content key K as $K = K_1|K_2$.

2.2) P chooses a set of attributes γ, computes $Y_\gamma = \mathsf{ABE.Enc}_\gamma(K_1)$, generates signature $\sigma_{Y_\gamma} = \mathsf{sig}_{S_P}(Y_\gamma)$ using P's own private key S_P and broadcast $Y_\gamma|\sigma_{Y_\gamma}$. The set of attributed γ is sent as part of Y_γ resulting from ABE.Enc for KP-ABE system.

2.3) P computes $Y_L = \mathsf{IBE.Enc}_{\mathsf{ID}_L}(K_2)$ using L's public identity ID_L, generates signature $\sigma_{Y_L} = \mathsf{sig}_{S_P}(Y_L)$ using P's own private key S_P and sends $Y_L|\sigma_{Y_L}$ to L.

2.4) Since the ciphertext Y_γ is encrypted under a set γ of attributes, only the distribution servers who has assigned compatible access policies can decrypt it and recover K_1. For instance, the j-th distribution server in level i, $D_{i,j}$, can extract K_1 using its private key $\mathsf{SK}_{i,j}$ from Y_γ if $\gamma \in \Gamma_{i,j}$. On receiving $Y_\gamma|\sigma_{Y_\gamma}$, $D_{i,j}$ first verifies the signature σ_γ on Y_γ using P's public identity ID_P. If verification succeeds, i.e. $\mathsf{Ver}_{\mathsf{ID}_P}(Y_\gamma, \sigma_{Y_\gamma}) = \text{true}$, then $D_{i,j}$ decrypts Y_γ using its decryption key $\mathsf{SK}_{i,j}$ for access policy $\Gamma_{i,j}$, recovers $K_1 = \mathsf{ABE.Dec}_{\mathsf{SK}_{i,j}}(Y_\gamma)$ and stores K_1 to its secure database.

2.5) L upon receiving $Y_L|\sigma_{Y_L}$, verifies the signature σ_{Y_L} on Y_L using P's public identity ID_P. If verification succeeds, i.e. $\mathsf{Ver}_{\mathsf{ID}_P}(Y_L, \sigma_{Y_L}) = \text{true}$, then L

decrypts Y_L using its private key S_L, recovers $K_2 = \mathsf{IBE.Dec}_{S_L}(Y_L)$. L stores K_2 to its secure database.

3. *Key Delivery when Content Service is Provided*

Suppose a DRM client C requests the content service for encrypted content M from a distribution server, say $D_{i,j}$, which is within nearest reach to C. The following steps are executed. Figure 5 displays the service flow.

3.1) $D_{i,j}$ computes $Y_C = \mathsf{IBE.Enc}_{\mathsf{ID}_C}(K_1)$ using C's public identity ID_C, signature $\sigma_{Y_C} = \mathsf{Sig}_{S_{D_{i,j}}}(Y_C)$ using $D_{i,j}$'s own private key $S_{D_{i,j}}$, and sends $Y_C|\sigma_{Y_C}$ to L.

3.2) L on receiving $Y_C|\sigma_{Y_C}$, verifies the signature σ_{Y_C} on Y_C using $D_{i,j}$'s public identity $\mathsf{ID}_{D_{i,j}}$. If verification succeeds, *i.e.* $\mathsf{Ver}_{\mathsf{ID}_{D_{i,j}}}(Y_C, \sigma_{Y_C}) = \mathsf{true}$, L computes $Y_L = \mathsf{IBE.Enc}_{\mathsf{ID}_C}(K_2)$ using C's public identity ID_C, signature $\sigma_{Y_C|Y_L} = \mathsf{Sig}_{S_L}(Y_C|Y_L)$ using L's own private key S_L, and issues the license that contains $Y_C|Y_L|\sigma_{Y_C|Y_L}$ together with rights, content URL, and so forth.

3.3) The DRM client C analyzes the licence issued by L, verifies $\sigma_{Y_C|Y_L}$ on $Y_C|Y_L$ using L's public key ID_L. If verification succeeds, C decrypts Y_C and Y_L using its own private key S_C, extracts the partial content keys K_1 and K_2, reassembles these partial content keys to obtain the original content key $K = K_1|K_2$. Finally, C decrypts the encrypted content using the recovered content key K and can view (playback) M.

4   Analysis

We design our key management scheme keeping in mind the following specific security objectives.

- *Preventing insider attacks:* Raw content should not be exposed to unintended parties with the help of an insider.
- *Minimizing attacks by outsiders:* Unauthorized outsiders should not illegally obtain the content keys.
- *Protecting distribution channels for content key/license:* The security of the following two distribution channels should be ensured.
  - the distribution channel between the distribution servers and the license server to transport the content key
  - the distribution channel between the DRM client, the distribution servers and the license server to transport the license.

By splitting the content key, each of the distribution servers has a distinct partial content key. Thus if an insider attack on a server is successful, the partial content key obtained in the attack is insufficient to decrypt the DRM-enabled content.

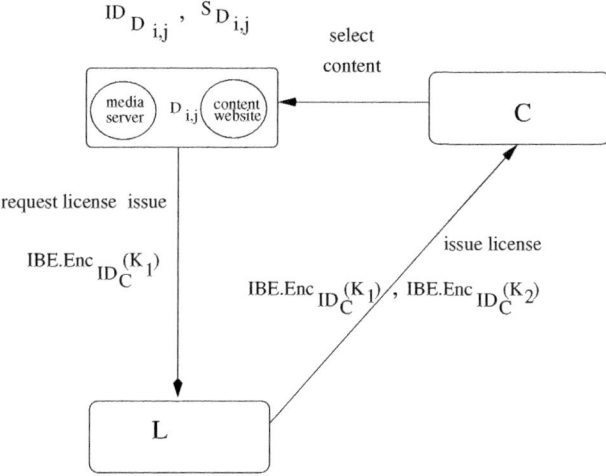

Fig. 4. Service flow when content service is provided (signature and verification are not shown)

For an outside attack to succeed, the attacker must break into the license server and any distribution server to obtain sufficient partial content keys. Thus the proposed scheme achieves multi-party security.

We use IBE and ABE and digital signature schemes to protect the content key/license distribution channel from impersonation attacks, replay attacks, man-in-the-middle attacks *etc.* Therefore, the security of the content key/license distribution channel depends on the security of the mechanisms IBE and ABE, digital signatures used for the key management.

Note that the content keys in the license file are transmitted to the client module under encryption with the client module's public key. Consequently, entities other than the client module cannot retrieve the content key even when they have obtained the license file.

The process of authentication or verification of the identities of the parties is necessary in a DRM system to ensure that the packaged digital content is from the genuine authorized content distributor. In our design, digital certificates are not used to authenticate or verify the identity of the parties involved in the system unlike certificate-based public key infrastructure, thus saving large amount of computing time and storage. Instead, we use IBE and ABE that simplifies our key management mechanism.

Our key management scheme enables the symmetric content key to be protected from the principals who manages the distribution servers and the license server. The digital content can thus be protected from attacks during the content distribution since the encrypted digital content is sent by the package server and only the DRM client can decrypt the digital content. Besides, we use IBE and ABE and digital signature instead of digital certificates. This simplifies the process of authentication or verification of the identities in the system.

The license server performs a range of tasks such as service monitoring, payment processing, license management and much information passes through it. License issuance and content key management involve time-consuming operations such as digital signature and public key encryption. Thus the license server could potentially become a bottleneck. However, the license server may consists of many subsystems arranged in a modular design that allows them to run independently to overcome this bottleneck. We have not addressed all these issues in this article and refer to Hwang *et al.*[7]. In our design, we mainly focus on ensuring security in content key management.

5 Conclusion

We propose a key management scheme for a multi-level multi-distributor DRM system where distributors and their sub-distributors are arranged in a hierarchy based on principals' access policies or attributes. Our scheme enables DRM clients to choose a distributor/subdistributor according to his own preference. The package server sits at the top of the hierarchy. In our scheme, the package server does not trust the distribution servers or the license server. The encrypted digital content sent by a package server can only be decrypted by the DRM client who has a valid license and is protected from attacks by other parties/servers in the system. We use the IBE and ABE that incurs less computation cost and storage as certificate managements are not necessary and certificate verifications are no longer needed.

References

1. Bethencourt, J., et al.: Ciphertext-Policy Attribute-Based Encryption. In: Proceedings of IEEE SP (2007)
2. Boneh, D., Franklin, M.: Identity-Based Encryption from the Weil Pairing. In: Kilian, J. (ed.) CRYPTO 2001. LNCS, vol. 2139, pp. 213–229. Springer, Heidelberg (2001)
3. Camp, L.J.: First Principles of Copyright for DRM Design. IEEE Internet Computing 7, 59–65 (2000)
4. Cohen, J.E.: DRM and Privacy. Communications of the ACM 46(4) (April 2003)
5. Goyal, V., et al.: Attribute-Based Encryption for Fine Grained Access Control of Encrypted Data. In: Proceedings of ACM CCS (2006)
6. Hartung, F., Ramme, F.: Digital Rights Management and Watermarking of Multimedia Content for M-Commerce Applications. IEEE Comm. 38, 78–84 (2000)
7. Hwang, S.O., Yoon, K.S., Jun, K.P., Lee, K.H.: Modeling and implementation of digital rights. Journal of Systems and Software 73(3), 533–549 (2004)
8. Lee, J., Hwang, S., Jeong, S., Yoon, K., Park, C., Ryou, J.: A DRM Framework for Distribution Digital Contents through the Internet. ETRI Journal 25, 423–436 (2003)
9. Liu, X., Huang, T., Huo, L.: A DRM Architecture for Manageable P2P Based IPTV System. In: IEEE Conference on Multimedia and Expo., pp. 899–902 (July 2007)

10. Liu, Q., Safavi-Naini, R., Sheppard, N.P.: Digital Rights Management for Content Distribution. In: Proceedings of Australasian Information Security Workshop Conference on ACSW Frontiers 2003, vol. 21 (January 2003)
11. Mulligan, D.K., Han, J., Burstein, A.J.: How DRM- Based Content Delivery Systems Disrupt Expectations of Personal Use. In: Proc. 2003 ACM Works. Digital Rights Management, pp. 77–88 (October 2003)
12. Rosset, V., Filippin, C.V., Westphall, C.M.: A DRM Architecture to Distribute and Protect Digital Content Using Digital Licenses. Telecommunication, 422–427 (July 2005)
13. Sachan, A., Emmanuel, S., Das, A., Kankanhalli, M.S.: Privacy Preserving Multiparty Multilevel DRM Architecture. In: IEEE Consumer Communications and Networking Conference, CCNC (January 2009)
14. Sahai, A., Waters, B.: Fuzzy identity-based encryption. In: Cramer, R. (ed.) EUROCRYPT 2005. LNCS, vol. 3494, pp. 457–473. Springer, Heidelberg (2005)
15. Shamir, A.: Identity-Based Cryptosystems and Signature Schemes. In: Blakely, G.R., Chaum, D. (eds.) CRYPTO 1984. LNCS, vol. 196, pp. 47–53. Springer, Heidelberg (1985)
16. Zhang, J., Wu, N., Luo, J., Yang, S.: A scalable Digital Rights Management Framework for Large Scale Content Distribution. In: ISPACS, pp. 761–764 (2005)

Access Polynomial Based Self-healing Key Distribution with Improved Security and Performance

Ratna Dutta

Indian Institute of Technology, Kharagpur, India
`ratna@maths.iitkgp.ernet.in`

Abstract. In this paper, we develop and analyze a computationally secure self-healing key distribution scheme with revocation capability, adopting the idea of access polynomial and a one-way hash chain. The main emphasis of our proposed scheme is that it achieves a stronger security goal, namely it can resist collusion against any number of users, while having a significant improvement in the communication overhead as compared to the existing schemes. Our design uses constant storage and hence is especially suitable for unreliable environments in which devices have limited resources. The security analysis is in an existing security model.

Keywords: self-healing key distribution, computational security, forward and backward secrecy, collusion resistance.

1 Introduction

The key distribution in wireless networks is not trivial due to unreliable lossy nature of wireless medium. The nodes/devices are powered by batteries and have the unique feature of moving in and out of range frequently. The session key has to be updated frequently due to this frequent membership change in the communication group. Self-healing is a solution for key distribution in wireless networks for efficiency and security reasons. Self-healing key distribution schemes have wide applications in military operations, rescue missions and scientific explorations. Also these scheme have found applicable in broadcast communication over low-cost channels, pay-per-view TV, information service delivering sensitive content/information to authorized recipients and several other Internet-related settings.

The concept of self-healing key distribution is that users, in a large and dynamic group communication over an unreliable network, can recover lost session keys on their own, even if they have lost some previous key distribution messages, without requesting additional transmissions from the group manager. This reduces network traffic and the risk of user exposure through traffic analysis and also decreases the work load on the group manager. The basic idea of the self-healing key distribution scheme is to broadcast information that is useful only

M. Joye et al. (Eds.): InfoSecHiComNet 2011, LNCS 7011, pp. 72–82, 2011.

Table 1. Comparison among computationally secure access polynomial based self-healing key distribution schemes in the j-th session

Schemes	Storage Overhead	Communication Overhead
Construction of [21]	$3 \log q$	$\max\{(3t+1)j, [\sum_{i=1}^{j} |G_i| + (2t+1)j]\} \log q$
Construction of [19]	$3 \log q$	$\max\{(t+1)j, [\sum_{i=1}^{j} |G_i| + 2j]\} \log q$
Construction of [14]	$4 \log q$	$\max\{(t+j+1)j, [\sum_{i=1}^{j} |G_i| + j + 1]\} \log q$
Our Construction	$2 \log q$	$(|G_j| + 2\mu + j) \log q$

for trusted users. Combined with pre-distributed secrets, this broadcast information enables a trusted user to reconstruct a session key. On the contrary, a revoked user is unable to infer useful information from the broadcast message.

Self-healing key distribution is *first* introduced by Staddon *et al.* in [18]. Following it, a number of self-healing key distribution approaches are proposed [1],[2], [9], [12], [13], [15], [16], [21], [6]. Improvements in efficiency are obtained by relaxing the security slightly - from unconditional to computational [3], [4], [10], [11]. The schemes [4], [15], [16], [20] are based on vector space access structure instead of Shamir's [17] secret sharing. The schemes [5], [14], [19], [21] use the concept of access polynomial.

Our main contribution in this article is to design a computationally secure and efficient group key distribution scheme with self-healing property and revocation capability for large and dynamic groups over unreliable wireless networks. Our scheme uses constant storage. To avoid the redundancy in the key updating broadcast message, we bind different access polynomials according to the time of users' joining and a special one-way hash function. This reduces communication bandwidth significantly as compared to the existing access polynomial based self-healing key distribution schemes [5], [14], [19], [21]. Table 1 analyzes the efficiency of our scheme compared to the previous access polynomial based constructions. (G_i being the set of legitimate active users in the session i, μ being the maximum number of joining operations during m sessions, $1 \le \mu \le m$, and t denotes the maximum number of users that can be revoked from the wireless system.) We emphasize that, unlike the existing schemes, our design holds a stronger security performance in the sense that it can deal with any number of colluding users to achieve forward and backward secrecy, and collusion resistance capability. All these results are supported by proper security analysis in an existing security framework.

The rest of the paper is organized as follows: Section 2 presents some basic definitions and the security model. In Section 3, we propose our self-healing key distribution scheme. The security analysis is provided in Section 4. Finally, we conclude in Section 5.

2 Preliminaries

2.1 One-Way Function

Our constructions for self-healing key distribution are based on the intractability of one-way function. Informally speaking, a one-way function $f : A \to B$ satisfies the following two properties where A and B are two finite set: (a) f is easy to compute; and (b) f is hard to invert, i.e., it is difficult to get x from $f(x)$. See [7] for a formal definition of one-way function.

An important component of our system is a cryptographically secure one way Hash function. The underlying principle here is that we must have a measure of the difficulty of reversing such functions. More formally a function $\mathcal{H} : A \rightarrow B$ is a cryptographically secure hash function if it satisfies the following requirements:

- $\mathcal{H}$ can be applied to any size input and produce a fixed length output.
- $\mathcal{H}$ is easy to compute.
- $\mathcal{H}$ has the one-way property, i.e. Given $\mathcal{H}(x)$ it is computationally infeasible to find x.
- $\mathcal{H}$ is weak collision resistant, i.e. Given x it is computationally infeasible to find $y \neq x$ with $\mathcal{H}(y) = \mathcal{H}(x)$.
- $\mathcal{H}$ is strong collision resistant, i.e. It is computationally infeasible to find a distinct pair (x, y) with $\mathcal{H}(x) = \mathcal{H}(y)$.

In what follows A and B are F_q. As the hash function landscape is constantly changing we do not specify a particular algorithm to compute $\mathcal{H}$, but note that our construction is not dependent on a particular hash function.

2.2   Key Distribution and Self-healing

Consider the scenario in which is a setup for pay-per-view TV channel. Suppose $\{U_1, \ldots, U_n\}$ is a dynamically changing group of users (clients) and GM $\notin \{U_1, \ldots, U_n\}$ is the group manager (the cable operator). The problem is how the GM can securely communicate with its dynamically changing group of clients over an insecure broadcast channel, so that only authorized clients (who pay) may view the content broadcast by the GM. The GM encrypts the content using a session key. We need a mechanism of distributing this session key in such a way that only the authorized users can recover this session key and decrypt the encrypted content. This mechanism is referred to as the key distribution problem. Our goal is to minimize the overhead for this key distribution keeping the following few issues in mind: (a) group-rekeying is needed on each membership change; (b) depending on specific nature of applications, we can adopt periodic group-rekeying; (c) efficient and secure revocation as well as joining mechanisms are required for dynamic groups $etc.$

On top of this, U_i may get off-line for some time due to power failure and may need to recover lost session keys immediately after being on-line. Self-healing property enables qualified users to recover lost session keys on their own, without requesting additional transmission from the GM.

2.3   Notational Convention

The following notations are used throughout the paper.

$\mathcal{U}$: set of all users in the networks
U_i : i-th user
GM   : group manager
n : total number of users in the network
m : total number of sessions
μ : total number of joining operations occurred in m sessions
G_0 : initial group members prior to the beginning of the first session
G_j : the group established by the GM in session j
F_q : a field of order q
S_i : personal secret of user U_i
SK_j : session key generated by the GM in session j
$\mathcal{B}_j$: broadcast message by the GM during session j
$Z_{i,j}$: the information learned by U_i through $\mathcal{B}_j$ and S_i
$\mathcal{H}$: a cryptographically secure one-way function
$\mathcal{E}_{\mathsf{key}}(\cdot)$: symmetric encryption function under the key key
$\mathcal{D}_{\mathsf{key}}(\cdot)$: symmetric decryption function under the key key

2.4   Security Framework

Let $\mathcal{U} = \{U_1, \ldots, U_n\}$ be the universe of the network. We assume the availability of a broadcast unreliable channel and there is a group manager GM who sets up and performs join and revoke operations to maintain a communication group, which is a dynamic subset of users of $\mathcal{U}$. Let m be the maximum number of sessions, $i \in \{1, \ldots, n\}$, $j \in \{1, \ldots, m\}$ and $G_j \in \mathcal{U}$ be the group established by the GM in session j. In the following definitions, S_i denotes the personal secret of user U_i, SK_j is the session key generated by the GM in session j, $\mathcal{B}_j$ is the broadcast message by the GM during session j, and $Z_{i,j}$ is the information learned by U_i through $\mathcal{B}_j$ and S_i.

Definition 21. *(Session Key Distribution with privacy [18]) Let $i \in \{1, \ldots, n\}$ and $j \in \{1, \ldots, m\}$.*

1) $\mathcal{D}$ is a session key distribution with privacy if
    (a) for any user U_i, the session key SK_j is efficiently determined from $\mathcal{B}_j$ and S_i.
    (b) for any set $R \subseteq \mathcal{U}$ of revoked users and $U_i \notin R$, it is computationally infeasible for users in R to determine the personal key S_i.
    (c) If we consider separately either the set of m broadcasts $\{\mathcal{B}_1, \ldots, \mathcal{B}_m\}$ or the set of n personal keys $\{S_1, \ldots, S_n\}$, then it is computationally infeasible for users $U_1, \ldots, U_n$ to compute session key SK_j (or other useful information) from either set. Information from both the sets is required in order to compute SK_j or any useful information.

2) $\mathcal{D}$ has revocation capability if given any $R \subseteq \mathcal{U}$ of users revoked in and before session j, the group manager GM can generate a broadcast $\mathcal{B}_j$, such that for all

$U_i \notin R$, U_i can efficiently recover the session key SK_j, but the revoked users cannot. i.e. it is computationally infeasible to compute SK_j from $\mathcal{B}_j$ and $\{S_l\}_{U_l \in R}$.

3) $\mathcal{D}$ is self-healing if the following is true for any j, $1 \leq j_1 < j < j_2 \leq m$:

(a) For any user U_i who is a member in sessions j_1 and j_2, the key SK_j is efficiently determined by the set $\{Z_{i,j_1}, Z_{i,j_2}\}$.

(b) Let $1 \leq j_1 < j < j_2 \leq m$. For any disjoint subsets $R, J \subset \mathcal{U}$, where the set R is a coalition of users removed before and in session j_1 and the set J is a coalition of users joined since session j_2, the set $\{Z_{l,j}\}_{U_l \in R, 1 \leq j \leq j_1} \cup \{Z_{l,j}\}_{U_l \in J, j_2 \leq j \leq m}$ cannot determine the session key SK_j, $j_1 < j < j_2$. i.e. SK_j can not be obtained by the coalition $R \cup J$. This is collusion resistance property for self-healing.

Definition 22. *(Forward and backward secrecy [12]) Let $i \in \{1, \ldots, n\}$ and $j \in \{1, \ldots, m\}$.*

1) A key distribution scheme $\mathcal{D}$ guarantees forward secrecy if for any set $R \subseteq \mathcal{U}$ of users revoked in and before session j, it is computationally infeasible for the members in R together to get any information about SK_j, even with the knowledge of group keys $\mathsf{SK}_1, \ldots, \mathsf{SK}_{j-1}$ before session j.

2) A session key distribution $\mathcal{D}$ guarantees backward secrecy if for any set $J \subseteq \mathcal{U}$ of users joined after session j, it is computationally infeasible for the members in J together to get any information about SK_j, even with the knowledge of group keys $\mathsf{SK}_{j+1}, \ldots, \mathsf{SK}_m$ after session j.

3   Scheme Description

3.1   Protocol Requirements

For our construction, we consider a setting in which there is a group manager (GM) and n users $\mathcal{U} = \{U_1, \ldots, U_n\}$. All operations take place in a finite field, F_q, where q is a large prime number ($q > n$). Let $\mathcal{E}_{\mathsf{key}}(\cdot)$, $\mathcal{D}_{\mathsf{key}}(\cdot)$ denote respectively an encryption and corresponding decryption function, which may be viewed as keyed permutations over F_q under key $\mathsf{key} \in F_q$. Let $\mathcal{H} : F_q \longrightarrow F_q$ be a cryptographically secure one-way function. This may be viewed as a random one way permutation over F_q such that $\mathcal{H}^i(u) \neq \mathcal{H}^j(u))$ for all positive integers i, j and $u \in F_q$ ($\mathcal{H}^i$ means the permutation $\mathcal{H}$ is applied i times on $u \in F_q$

3.2   Self-healing Session Key Distribution

Our self-healing key distribution consists of five phases: *Setup, Broadcast, Session Key Recovery, Addition of Group Members, Revocation of Group Members*.

(1) *Setup*: Let G_0 denotes the initial group members prior to the beginning of the first session. For each user $U_i \in G_0$, the GM selects at random a private unique

identity $\alpha_i \in F_q$. Each user $U_i \in G_0$, receives its personal secret key $S_i = \{\alpha_i\}$ from the GM via the secure communication channel between them.

(2) *Broadcast*

(i) Let $G_j = \{G_j^{(1)}, G_j^{(2)}, \ldots, G_j^{(v)}, G_j^{(v+1)}, \ldots, G_j^{(j)}\}$ be the set of legitimate active users in the session j, where $G_j^{(v)}$ denotes the set of users who joined the group in the session v and are still active in the session j. $G_j^{(v)} = \emptyset$ if there is no users joined in the session v, and $1 \le v \le j$.

(ii) In the j-th session, the GM chooses blinding values $\theta_j^{(v)} \in F_q$, $\theta_j^{(v)} \notin \{\alpha_i \in F_q | U_i \in G_j^{(v)}\}$ for $1 \le v \le j$. Using these blinding values and the private identities of legitimate active users in the group G_j, the GM constructs access polynomials:

$$A_j^{(v)}(x) = 1 + (\theta_j^{(v)} x - 1) \prod_{\{i : U_i \in G_j^{(v)}\}} (x - \alpha_i), v = 1, 2, \ldots, j \qquad (1)$$

The factor $(\theta_j^{(v)} x - 1)$ is a blinding term and $\theta_j^{(v)} \in F_q$ is randomly selected in each session j for $1 \le v \le j$ and is different from $\{\alpha_i \in F_q | U_i \in G_j^{(v)}\}$. The purpose of $(\theta_j^{(v)} x - 1)$ is to make $A_j^{(v)}(x)$ different for different session even they contain the same α's of active (authorized) users. Note that $A_j^{(v)}(\alpha_i) = 1$ for an active user $U_i \in G_j^{(v)}$. However, for a non-active user (unauthorized user) $U_i \notin G_j^{(v)}$, $A_j^{(v)}(\alpha_i)$ is a random value.

(iii) In the j-th session, the GM randomly picks an initial seed $\beta_j^{(1)} \in F_q$. It repeatedly applies the one-way function $\mathcal{H}$ to compute the one-way key chain of length j:

$$\beta_j^{(v)} = \mathcal{H}(\beta_j^{(v-1)}) = \mathcal{H}^{v-1}(\beta_j^{(1)}) \qquad (2)$$

for $1 \le v \le j$, where $\mathcal{H}^v(\cdot)$ denotes applying v times hash operation. For security, seeds of the key chain for different sessions are also different. That is, for $j_1 \ne j_2$, $\beta_{j_1}^{(1)} \ne \beta_{j_2}^{(1)}$.

(iv) The GM randomly chooses a session key $\mathsf{SK}_j \in F_q$. The GM computes

$$\Phi_j^{(v)}(x) = \beta_j^{(v)} A_j^{(v)}(x), v = 1, 2, \ldots, j. \qquad (3)$$

Henceforth, we refer $\beta_j^{(v)}$ as the masking key.

(v) Finally, the GM broadcasts the message

$$\mathcal{B}_j = \{\Phi_j^{(v)}(x) | v = 1, 2, \ldots, j\} \cup \{\mathcal{E}_{\beta_j^{(1)}}(\mathsf{SK}_1), \mathcal{E}_{\beta_j^{(2)}}(\mathsf{SK}_2), \ldots, \mathcal{E}_{\beta_j^{(j)}}(\mathsf{SK}_j)\}, \quad (4)$$

where, $\mathcal{E}_{\mathsf{key}}(\cdot)$ is a symmetric encryption function and SK_v, $1 \le v \le j$ is the session key at the v-th session randomly selected by the GM. Note that if no users joined in session v, $(v = 1, 2, \ldots, j)$, $A_j^{(v)}(x) = \emptyset$ and $\Phi_j^{(v)}(x)$ is not included in $\mathcal{B}_j$.

(3) *Session Key Recovery:* When an active (non-revoked) user $U_i \in G_j^{(v)} \subset G_j$ receives the j-th session key distribution message $\mathcal{B}_j$, it recovers the session key as follows:

(i) U_i computes the masking key $\beta_j^{(v)} = \varPhi_j^{(v)}(\alpha_i)$ for $1 \leq v \leq j$ as $A_j^{(v)}(\alpha_i) = 1$ for any active user $U_i \in G_j^{(v)}$.

(ii) U_i computes all masking keys $\{\beta_j^{(w)}\}$ for $v < w \leq j$ in the j-th key chain using equation (2).

(iii) Finally, U_i recovers the session keys SK_w for $v \leq w \leq j$ by decrypting $\mathcal{E}_{\beta_j^{(w)}}$ with corresponding keys $\beta_j^{(w)}$.

Our scheme allows the user only to recover session keys used after the user joined the group. That is, in the session j, a new user joined the group in the session v, $1 \leq v \leq j$, can recover session keys $\mathsf{SK}_v, \mathsf{SK}_{v+1}, \ldots, \mathsf{SK}_j$, and cannot recover previous session keys $\mathsf{SK}_1, \mathsf{SK}_2, \ldots, \mathsf{SK}_{v-1}$.

(4) *Addition of Group Members:* When a new user U_r wants to join the communication group starting from session j, the user gets in touch with the GM. The GM in turn picks an unique secret identity $\alpha_r \in F_q$ and allocates the personal key $S_r = \{\alpha_r\}$ to this new group member U_r via the secure communication channel between them. To handle the dynamic scenario, the GM constructs the new access polynomial $A_j^{(v)}(x)$ including $(x - \alpha_r)$, and operates as *Broadcast* phase.

(5) *Revocation of Group Members:* If a user U_w who joined the group in the session v is revoked in the session j, the GM excludes $(x - \alpha_w)$ from $A_j^{(v)}(x)$, and launches the key updating process to exclude U_w (see *Broadcast* phase).

3.3   Complexity

- *Storage overhead:* Each user U_i needs to store two field elements, its personal secret α_i and the session key SK_j. Hence the storage complexity for user U_i is $2 \log q$ bits, and is constant.
- *Communication overhead:* Communication bandwidth for key management in the j-th session is $(|G_j| + 2\mu + j) \log q$ bits, where G_j is the set of active users in the session j and μ is the maximum number of joining operations occurred in m sessions, $1 \leq \mu \leq j \leq m$. This comes from the fact that the broadcast message (see equation (4)) in the j-th session consists of a maximum μ polynomials $\varPhi_j^{(v)}(x)$ and j encrypted value. Note that if no user joined in the session v, $1 \leq v \leq j$, $A_j^{(v)}(x) = \emptyset$ and $\varPhi_j^{(v)}(x)$ is not included in $\mathcal{B}_j$.
- *Computation overhead:* The computation cost for key management for an active user U_i in the j-th session consists of j symmetric key decryption operations, $|G_j| + 1$ multiplication operations needed to find a point on

$|G_j| + 1$-degree polynomial, and a maximum j hash operations to compute the masking keys $\beta_j^{(v)}, 1 \leq v \leq j$.

4 Analysis

Theorem 41. *Our construction is computationally secure, self-healing session key distribution scheme with privacy, revocation capability with respect to Definition 21 and achieves forward and backward secrecy with respect to Definition 22 in our security model as described in Section 2.4 under the security of the symmetric encryption function.*

Proof

1) (a) An active user $U_i \in G_j$ can recover the session key SK_j as described in *Session Key Recovery* phase of our construction.

(b) For any set $R_j \subseteq \mathcal{U}$ of users revoked in and before session j, and any non-revoked user $U_i \notin R_j$, the coalition R_j is not able to compute the personal secret $S_i = \{\alpha_i\}$ of U_i unless R_j can guess α_i correctly, as α_i is selected randomly and is independent of the personal secret $S_r = \{\alpha_r\}$ for $U_r \in R_j$.

(c) The j-th session key SK_j is independent of the personal secret $S_i = \{\alpha_i\}$. Hence, using only the personal secret keys, one cannot compute session keys. On the other hand, since the masking key and the session key are selected randomly, broadcast messages cannot give any information about session keys under the assumption that the symmetric encryption function is secure. Therefore, SK_j cannot be determined by only the personal key S_i or the broadcast message $\mathcal{B}_j$.

2) (Revocation property) Let $R_j = \{R_j^{(1)}, R_j^{(2)}, \ldots, R_j^{(v)}, R_j^{(v+1)}, \ldots, R_j^{(j)}\} \subseteq \mathcal{U}$ be a collection of revoked users in the session j, where $R_j^{(v)}$ for $v = 1, 2, \ldots, j$ is the set of users who join the group in the session v and are revoked before or in the session j. It is impossible for the coalition R_j to recover the j-th session key SK_j as R_j has no information about the masking keys $\beta_j^{(v)}$, $v = 1, 2, \ldots, j$ generated in the j-th session. This is because of the fact that seeds of the key chain to generate the masking keys are different for different sessions. Moreover, since the unique identity is kept secret, the collusion of R_j cannot construct the access polynomial $A_j^{(v)}(x)$ for $v = 1, 2, \ldots, j$. The masking key $\beta_j^{(v)}$ appears randomly to all $U_i \in R_j^{(v)}$ as the value $A_j^{(v)}(\alpha_i)$ computed by $U_i \in R_j^{(v)}$ using U_i's own private unique identity α_i is random.

3) (a) (Self-healing property) Let U_i be a group member that receives session key distribution messages $\mathcal{B}_{j_1}$ and $\mathcal{B}_{j_2}$ in sessions j_1 and j_2 respectively, where $1 \leq j_1 < j_2$, but not the session key distribution message $\mathcal{B}_j$ for session j, where $j_1 < j < j_2$. User U_i can still recover all the lost session keys SK_j for $j_1 < j < j_2$ as desired by Definition 21 3(a) using the following steps.

– In the *Session Key Recovery* phase, U_i, as a member in the session j_3, $1 \leq j_1 \leq j_3$, can recover the masking key $\beta_{j_3}^{(j_1)}$.

- U_i uses $\beta_{j_3}^{(j_1)}$ to generate part of the j_3-th one-way hash key chain, $\{\beta_{j_3}^{(j_1)},$ $\beta_{j_3}^{(j_1+1)}, \ldots, \beta_{j_3}^{(j_2)}, \beta_{j_3}^{(j_2+1)}, \ldots, \beta_{j_3}^{(j_3)}\}$.

- U_i recovers session keys $\mathsf{SK}_{j_1}, \mathsf{SK}_{j_1+1}, \ldots, \mathsf{SK}_{j_2}, \mathsf{SK}_{j_2+1}, \ldots, \mathsf{SK}_{j_3}$ by decrypting respectively $\mathcal{E}_{\beta_{j_3}^{j_1}}(\mathsf{SK}_{j_1}), \mathcal{E}_{\beta_{j_3}^{j_1+1}}(\mathsf{SK}_{j_1+1}), \ldots, \mathcal{E}_{\beta_{j_3}^{j_2}}(\mathsf{SK}_{j_2}), \mathcal{E}_{\beta_{j_3}^{j_2+1}}(\mathsf{SK}_{j_2+1}),$ $\ldots, \mathcal{E}_{\beta_{j_3}^{j_3}}(\mathsf{SK}_{j_3})$ with the respective masking keys $\beta_{j_3}^{(j_1)}, \beta_{j_3}^{(j_1+1)}, \ldots, \beta_{j_3}^{(j_2)},$ $\beta_{j_3}^{(j_2+1)}, \ldots, \beta_{j_3}^{(j_3)}$.

(b) Our construction can also resist collusion. Let $1 \leq j_1 < j < j_2 \leq m$ and let $R, J \in \mathcal{U}$ be two disjoint subsets, where R is a set of revoked users from the group before session j_1 and J is a set of users who join the group from session j_2. Consider a coalition from $R \cup J$. We show the users in $R \cup J$ together are not entitled to know the j-th session key SK_j for any $j_1 \leq j < j_2 - 1$.

A user $U_r \in R$, who joined the group in the session $j', (j' < j)$ and is revoked before the session j_1, knows $S_r = \{\alpha_r\}$ and a user $U_t \in J$, who joined the group in the session $j''(j_2 < j'' \leq m)$, only knows $S_t = \{\alpha_t\}$. Note that α_r and α_t are selected randomly and the values $A_j^{(v)}(\alpha_r), A_j^{(v)}(\alpha_t)$ for $v = 1, 2, \ldots, j$ computed respectively by users $U_r \in R$ and $U_t \in J$ using their respective private unique identities α_r and α_t. This makes the masking keys $\beta_j^{(v)}$ appear randomly to users $U_r \in R, U_t \in J$. Hence, the collusion of $U_r \in R$ and $U_t \in J$ are not able to recover the masking keys $\beta_j^{(v)}$, $v = 1, 2, \ldots, j$ unless they guess $\beta_j^{(v)}$ correctly. Consequently, the collusion of users in $R \cup J$ cannot recover the session key, SK_j, for $j_1 \leq j < j_2$, assuming the encryption function is secure. We will show that our construction satisfies all the conditions required by Definition 22.

1) (Forward secrecy) Let $R_j = \{R_j^{(1)}, R_j^{(2)}, \ldots, R_j^{(v)}, R_j^{(v+1)}, \ldots, R_j^{(j)}\} \subseteq \mathcal{U}$, where $R_j^{(v)}$ for $v = 1, 2, \ldots, j-1$ is the set of users who join the group in the session v and are revoked before the session j. The coalition R_j can not get any information about the current session key SK_j even with the knowledge of group keys before session j. In order to recover the j-th session key SK_j along with all broadcast messages $\{\mathcal{B}_1, \mathcal{B}_2, \ldots, \mathcal{B}_m\}$, any user $U_l \in R_j^{(v)}$ needs to know the j-th masking key $\beta_j^{(v)}$. For any user $U_l \in R_j^{(v)}$, $A_j^{(v)}(\alpha_l)$ is a random value which means that U_l is not able to recover the masking key $\beta_j^{(v)}$ unless U_l can guess $\beta_j^{(v)}$ correctly. Hence, even all revoked users in the set R_j collude together, the session key SK_j cannot be recovered under the assumption that the symmetric encryption function is secure. Similar argument shows that the revoked users cannot compute the subsequent session keys SK_{j_1} for $j_1 > j$, as desired. This is forward secrecy from computation point of view.

2) (Backward secrecy) Let $J \subseteq U$, and each user $U_l, U_l \in J$, joins the group after the session j. The coalition J cannot get any information about any previous session key SK_{j_1} for $j_1 \leq j$ even with the knowledge of group keys after session j. This is because of the fact that the access polynomials $A_{j_1}^{(v)}(x)$, $1 \leq v \leq j_1$,

contain no private identity of any user who joined the group after the session j_1, $j_1 \leq j$, and so, $A_{j_1}^{(v)}(\alpha_l)$ is a random value for any user $U_l \in J$. Consequently, with all broadcast messages $\{\mathcal{B}_1, \mathcal{B}_2, \ldots, \mathcal{B}_m\}$, users in J cannot compute the masking keys $\beta_{j_1}^{(v)}$, $v = 1, 2, \ldots, j_1$ for $j_1 \leq j$ to perform decryption in order to recover the session keys $\mathsf{SK}_{j_1}, j_1 \leq j$. Hence, our proposed key distribution scheme achieves backward secrecy under the assumption that the symmetric encryption function is secure.   □

5   Conclusion

We present a computationally secure constant storage self-healing key distribution scheme. The users are classified according to the time of their joining. We couple the time at which a user joins the group with its capability of recovering previous session keys. We use the concept of access polynomials and a special one-way hash chain and reduce the redundancy in the communication bandwidth. Additionally, we have shown in an existing security model that the proposed self-healing key distribution scheme is able to deal with any number of colluding users to achieve the forward secrecy, backward secrecy and collusion resistance capability. We feel that our scheme guarantees stronger security and performance as compared to the existing similar schemes.

References

1. Blundo, C., D'Arco, P., Santis, A., Listo, M.: Design of Self-healing Key Distribution Schemes. Design Codes and Cryptology 32, 15–44 (2004)
2. Blundo, C., D'Arco, P., Santis, A., Listo, M.: Definitions and Bounds for Self-Healing Key Distribution Schemes. In: Díaz, J., Karhumäki, J., Lepistö, A., Sannella, D. (eds.) ICALP 2004. LNCS, vol. 3142, pp. 234–245. Springer, Heidelberg (2004)
3. Dutta, R., Chang, E.-C., Mukhopadhyay, S.: Efficient self-healing key distribution with revocation for wireless sensor networks using one way key chains. In: Katz, J., Yung, M. (eds.) ACNS 2007. LNCS, vol. 4521, pp. 385–400. Springer, Heidelberg (2007)
4. Dutta, R., Mukhopadhyay, S., Das, A., Emmanuel, S.: Generalized Self-healing Key Distribution Using Vector Space Access Structure. In: Das, A., Pung, H.K., Lee, F.B.S., Wong, L.W.C. (eds.) NETWORKING 2008. LNCS, vol. 4982, pp. 612–623. Springer, Heidelberg (2008)
5. Dutta, R., Mukhopadhyay, S., Dowling, T.: Enhanced Access Polynomial Based Self-healing Key Distribution. In: Gu, Q., Zang, W., Yu, M. (eds.) SEWCN 2009. Lecture Notes of the Institute for Computer Sciences, Social Informatics and Telecommunications Engineering, vol. 42, pp. 13–24. Springer, Heidelberg (2010)
6. Sáez, G.: Self-healing Key Distribution Schemes with Sponsorization. In: Dittmann, J., Katzenbeisser, S., Uhl, A. (eds.) CMS 2005. LNCS, vol. 3677, pp. 22–31. Springer, Heidelberg (2005)
7. Goldreich, O.: Foundations of Cryptography: Basic Tools. Cambridge University Press, Cambridge (2001)

8. Simmons, G.J., Jackson, W., Martin, K.: The Geometry of Secret Sharing Schemes. Bulletin of the ICA 1, 71–88 (1991)
9. Hong, D., Kang, J.: An Efficient Key Distribution Scheme with Self-healing Property. IEEE Communication Letters 9, 759–761 (2005)
10. Jiang, Y., Lin, C., Shi, M., Shen, X.: Self-healing Group Key Distribution with Time-limited Node Revocation for Wireless Sensor Networks. Ad Hoc Networks 5(1), 14–23 (2007)
11. Kausar, F., Hassian, S., Park, J.H., Masood, A.: Secure Group Communication with Self-healing and Rekeying in Wireless Sensor Networks. In: Zhang, H., Olariu, S., Cao, J., Johnson, D.B. (eds.) MSN 2007. LNCS, vol. 4864, pp. 737–748. Springer, Heidelberg (2007)
12. Liu, D., Ning, P., Sun, K.: Efficient Self-healing Key Distribution with Revocation Capability. In: Proceedings of the 10th ACM CCS 2003, pp. 27–31 (2003)
13. More, S., Malkin, M., Staddon, J.: Sliding-window Self-healing Key Distribution with Revocation. In: ACM Workshop on Survivable and Self-regenerative Systems 2003, pp. 82–90 (2003)
14. Xu, Q.Y., He, M.X.: Improved Constant Storage Self-healing Key Distribution with Revocation in Wireless Sensor Network. In: Chung, K.-I., Sohn, K., Yung, M. (eds.) WISA 2008. LNCS, vol. 5379, pp. 41–55. Springer, Heidelberg (2009)
15. Saez, G.: On Threshold Self-healing Key Distribution Schemes. In: Smart, N.P. (ed.) Cryptography and Coding 2005. LNCS, vol. 3796, pp. 340–354. Springer, Heidelberg (2005)
16. Saez, G.: Self-healing Key Distribution Schemes with Sponsorization. In: Dittmann, J., Katzenbeisser, S., Uhl, A. (eds.) CMS 2005. LNCS, vol. 3677, pp. 22–31. Springer, Heidelberg (2005)
17. Shamir, A.: How to Share a Secret. Communications of the ACM 22(11), 612–613 (1979)
18. Staddon, J., Miner, S., Franklin, M., Balfanz, D., Malkin, M., Dean, D.: Self-healing key distribution with Revocation. In: Proceedings of IEEE Symposium on Security and Privacy 2002, pp. 224–240 (2002)
19. Tian, B., Han, S., Dillon, T.-S.: An Efficient Self-Healing Key Distribution Scheme. In: Proceedings of the 2nd IFIP Internal Conference on New Technologies, Mobility and Security (2008)
20. Tian, B., Han, S., Dillon, T.-S., Das, S.: A Self-Healing Key Distribution Scheme Based on Vector Space Secret Sharing and One Way Hash Chains. In: Proceedings of IEEE WoWMoM (2008)
21. Zou, X.K., Dai, Y.S.: A Robust and Stateless Self-Healing Group Key Management Scheme. In: ICCT 2006, vol. 28, pp. 455–459 (2006)

An ID-Based Proxy Multi Signature Scheme without Bilinear Pairings

Namita Tiwari and Sahadeo Padhye

Department of Mathematics
Motilal Nehru National Institute of Technology
Allahabad-211004, India
{namita.mnnit,sahadeomathrsu}@gmail.com

Abstract. As a variation of ordinary digital signature scheme, a proxy signature scheme enables a proxy signer to sign messages on behalf of the original signer. Proxy multi-signature is an extension of the basic proxy signature primitive, and permits two or more entities to delegate their signing capabilities to some other entity. Many identity-based proxy multi signature (IBPMS) schemes using bilinear pairings have been proposed. But the relative computation cost of the pairing is approximately more than ten times of the scalar multiplication over elliptic curve group. In order to save the running time and the size of the signature, in this paper, we propose an IBPMS scheme without bilinear pairings. We also prove the security of our scheme against adaptive chosen message attack under random oracle model. With the running time being saved greatly, our scheme is more applicable than the previous related schemes for practical applications.

Keywords: Digital signature, Identity-based cryptography, Proxy-multi signature, Elliptic curve discrete log problem.

1 Introduction

The central idea of identity based cryptography (Shamir [14]), is to simplify public-key and certificate management by using a users identity(e.g., its email address) as its public key. For this to be possible, the system requires a trusted third party, typically called a Private Key Generator (PKG), to generate users secret keys from its master secret and the users identity. Only the PKG has a traditional public key. In an identity based signature scheme, the verifier verifies a signature by using the signer's identity and the PKG's public key, the verification information does not include any certificate or any individual public key for the signer.

The notion of proxy signature scheme was firstly introduced by Mambo et al. [12]. A proxy signature scheme allows an entity called original signer to delegate his signing capability to another entity, called proxy signer. Since it is proposed, the proxy signature schemes have been suggested for use in many applications, particularly in distributed computing where delegation of rights is

M. Joye et al. (Eds.): InfoSecHiComNet 2011, LNCS 7011, pp. 83–92, 2011.

quite common. Since the proxy signature primitive was introduced, various extensions of the basic proxy signature primitive have been considered. These include threshold proxy signature, blind proxy signature, one-time proxy signature, multi proxy signature, proxy multi-signature, and multi-proxy multi-signature, etc.

Proxy multi-signature means a proxy signer can generate the signature for a message on behalf of several original signers. It can be used in the following scenario: A company releases a document that may involve the financial department, engineering department, and program office, etc. The document must be signed jointly by these entities, or signed by a proxy signer authorized by these entities. One solution to the latter case of this problem is to use a proxy multi-signature scheme.

Using bilinear pairings, many new ID-based signature schemes [1,2,10], ID-based proxy signature(IBPS) schemes [7,8,11,16,17] and proxy multi signature schemes [3,15] etc. were proposed. All the above IBPS schemes are very practical, but they are based on bilinear pairings and the pairing is regarded as the most expensive cryptography primitive. According to [9], the relative computation cost of a pairing is approximately more than ten times of the scalar multiplication over elliptic curve group [4]. Therefore, IBPMS schemes without bilinear pairings would be more appealing in terms of efficiency. In this paper, we present an IBPMS scheme without pairings. To achieve $1024 - bits$ RSA level security, $512 - bits$ supersingular elliptic curve and $160 - bits$ non-supersingular elliptic curves are used in applications. In general pairing is defined on the supersingular elliptic curve. But the ECC uses non supersingular elliptic curves. Because our scheme is based on the elliptic curve cryptosystem, it is efficient and have smaller key size than pairing based system. The proposed scheme is based on the elliptic curve discrete logarithm problem (ECDLP). With the pairing-free realization, proposed schemes overhead is lower than that of previous schemes [3,15] in computation.

Organization: The rest of this paper is organized as follows: In Section 2, we introduce the complexity assumption. In Section 3, we define a formal model of identity-based proxy multi-signature scheme and it's security. In Section 4, we propose a new identity-based proxy multi-signature scheme, and we prove its security using the model in Section 5. In Section 6, we compare the efficiency of our scheme with that in [3,15]. Finally, Section 7 concludes the paper.

2   Preliminaries

2.1   Background of Elliptic Curve Group

Let the symbol E/F_p denote an elliptic curve E over a prime finite field F_p, defined by an equation
$$y^2 = x^3 + ax + b, \ a, b \in F_p, \text{ and}$$
discriminant $\Delta = 4a^3 + 27b^2 \neq 0$

The points on E/F_p together with an extra point O called the point at infinity form a group $G = \{(x,y) : x,y \in F_p, E(x,y) = 0\} \cup \{O\}$.

Let the order of G be n. G is a cyclic additive group under the point addition " $+$ " defined as follows: Let $P, Q \in G$, l be the line containing P and Q (tangent line to E/F_p if $P = Q$), and R, the third point of intersection of l with E/F_p. Let l' be the line connecting R and O. Then $P + Q$ is the point such that l' intersects E/F_p at R and O and $P + Q$.

Scalar multiplication over E/F_p can be computed as follows:
$tP = P + P + \dots\dots + P(t\ times)$.

2.2   Complexity Assumption

The following problem defined over G are assumed to be intractable within polynomial time.

Elliptic curve discrete logarithm problem (ECDLP): For $x \in_R Z_n^*$ and P the generator of G , given $Q = x.P$ compute x.

3   Formal Model of Identity-Based Proxy-Multi Signature Scheme

Based on the work of [7,9], we give a formal definition and security model for identity-based proxy multi-signature schemes.

3.1   Identity-Based Proxy Multi Signature Scheme

In an identity-based proxy multi-signature scheme, there is one proxy signer and a group of original signers. Let $A_1, A_2, \dots..A_l$ be the original signers and A_0 be the proxy signer designated by original signers. A_i ($\forall i = 0,1,2...l$) has an identity ID_i.

Definition 1. An identity-based proxy multi-signature scheme is a tuple IBPMS =(Setup; Extract; Delgen; Delverif; PKGen; PMSign; PMVerif).

Setup: The parameters generation algorithm, takes as input a security parameter k, and returns a master secret key x and system parameters Ω. This algorithm is performed by KGC.

Extract: Given an identity $ID_i \in \{0,1\}^*$, the master secret key s and params Ω, KGC uses this algorithm to generate the private key D_i of ID_i. The master entity will use this algorithm to generate private keys for all entities participating in the scheme and distribute the private keys to their respective owners through a secure channel.

Delgen: The delegation algorithm, takes A_i's secret key D_i and warrant m_w as inputs and outputs the delegation $W_{A_i \rightarrow A_0}, \forall i = 1,2...l$.

DelVerif: This algorithm, takes $ID_i, W_{A_i \rightarrow A_0}$ as input and verifies whether $W_{A_i \rightarrow A_0}$ is a valid delegation came from $A_i, \forall i = 1, 2...l$.

PKgen: The proxy key generation algorithm, takes $W_i, \forall i = 1, 2...l$ and some other secret information (for example, the secret key of the executor) as input, and outputs a signing key D_p for proxy signature.

PMSign: The proxy signing algorithm, takes a proxy signing key D_p and a message $m \in \{0, 1\}^*$ as input, and outputs a proxy signature (m, δ).

PMVerif: The proxy verification algorithm, takes $ID_i, \forall i = 0, 1, 2...l$, and a proxy signature (m, δ) as input, and outputs 0 or 1. In the later case, (m, δ) is a valid proxy multi-signature for m by the proxy signer on behalf of the original signers.
    We consider an adversary T which is assumed to be a probabilistic Turing machine which takes as input the global scheme parameters and a random tape.

Definition 2. For an ID-based proxy multi signature scheme IBPMS, we define an experiment Exp_T^{IBPMS} of adversary T and security parameter k as follows [7]:

1. A challenger C runs Setup and gives the system parameters Ω to T.
2. $C_{list} \leftarrow \phi, D_{list} \leftarrow \phi, G_{list} \leftarrow \phi, S_{list} \leftarrow \phi$. ($\phi$ means null).
3. Adversary T can make the following requests or queries adaptively.

Extract(.): This oracle takes user's ID_i as input, and returns the corresponding private key D_i. If T gets $D_i \leftarrow ExtractID_i$, let $C_{list} \leftarrow C_{list} \bigcup \{ID_i, D_i\}$.

Delgen(.): This oracle takes the designator's identity ID_i and a warrant m_w as input, and outputs a delegation $W_{A_i \rightarrow A_0}$. If T gets $W_{A_i \rightarrow A_0} \leftarrow Delegate\{ID_i, m_w\}$, let $D_{list} \leftarrow D_{list} \bigcup \{ID_i, m_w, W_{A_i \rightarrow A_0}\}$.

PKgen(.): This oracle takes the proxy signer's ID_0 and a delegation W as input, and outputs a proxy signing key D_p. If T gets $D_p \leftarrow PKgen(ID, W)$, let $G_{list} \leftarrow G_{list} \bigcup (ID_0, m_w, W)$.

PSign(.): This oracle takes the delegation W and message $m \in \{0, 1\}^*$ as input, and outputs a proxy signature created by the proxy signer. If T gets $(m, \delta) \leftarrow PSign(W, m)$, let $S_{list} \leftarrow S_{list} \bigcup \{(m, \delta)\}$.

4. T outputs $(ID_i, m_w, W_{A_i \rightarrow A_0})$ or (W, m, δ).
5. If T's output satisfies one of the following terms, T's attack is successful.

    $a)$ The output is $(ID_i, m_w, W_{A_i \rightarrow A_0})$, and satisfies: DelVerif$(W_{A_i \rightarrow A_0}, ID_i) = 1$ where $(ID_i, .)$ is not in C_{list}, $(ID_i, .)$ is not in G_{list} and $(ID_i, m_w, .)$ is not in D_{list}. $Exp_T^{IBPMS}(k)$ returns 1.
    $b)$ The output is (W, m, δ), and satisfies PVerif$((m, \delta), ID_i, ID_0) = 1$, $(W, m, .)$

not in S_{list} and $(ID_0, .)$ not in C_{list}. $(ID_0, W, .)$ not in G_{list}, where ID_i and ID_0 are the identities of the designator and the proxy signer defined by W, respectively. $Exp_T^{IBPMS}(k)$ returns 2.

Otherwise $Exp_T^{IBPMS}(k)$ returns 0.

Definition 3   [7]. An ID-based proxy digital signature scheme IBPS is said to be existential delegation and signature unforgeable under adaptive chosen message and ID attacks (DS-EUF-ACMIA), if for any polynomial-time adversary T, $Pr[Exp_T^{IBPMS}(k) = 1]$ and $Pr[Exp_T^{IBPMS}(k) = 2]$ are negligible.

4   Proposed Scheme

In this section, we present an ID-based proxy multi signature scheme without pairing. Our scheme is based on the intractability of ECDLP.

Setup: Takes a security parameter k, returns system parameters and a master key. Given k, KGC does as follows.

1. Chooses a k-bit prime p and determines the tuple $F_p, E/F_p, G, P$ as defined in Section 2.

2. Chooses the master private key $x \in Z_n^*$ and computes the master public key $P_{pub} = x.P$.

3. Chooses two cryptographic secure hash functions $H_1 : \{0,1\}^* \rightarrow Z_n^*$ and $H_2 : \{0,1\}^* \times G \rightarrow Z_p^*$.

4. Publishes $\{F_p, E/F_p, G, P, P_{pub}, H_1, H_2\}$ as system parameters Ω and keep the master key x secretly.

Extract: Takes system parameters, master key, and a users identity as input, returns the users ID-based private key. With this algorithm, KGC works as follows for each user A_i with identity ID_i $(0 \leq i \leq l)$.

1. Chooses at random $r_i \in Z_n^*$, computes $R_i = r_i.P$ and $h_i = H_1(ID_i, R_i)$.

2. Computes $D_i = r_i + h_i x$.

A_i's private key is the tuple (D_i, R_i) and is transmitted to A_i via a secure channel.

A_i can validate her private key by checking whether the equation $D_i P = R_i + h_i P_{pub}$ holds. The private key is valid if the equation holds and vice versa.

Delgen: Let $A_1, A_2, ...A_l$ be the original signers and A_0 be the proxy signer designated by original signers. This algorithm takes A_i's secret key D_i $(\forall i = 1, 2...l)$ and a warrant m_w as input, and outputs the delegation $W_{A_i \rightarrow A_o}$ as follows:

For each $(1 \leq i \leq l)$

1. Generates a random $a_i \in Z_n^*$, computes $K_i = a_i.P$.

2. Computes $e_{i_1} = H_2(m_w, ID_0, K_i)$ and $\sigma_i = e_{i_1} D_i + a_i \bmod n$.

Each A_i sends individual delegation $W_{A_i \to A_o} = \{ID_i, R_i, ID_0, m_w, K_i, \sigma_i\}$ to proxy signer A_0.

DelVerif: To verify the delegation $W_{A_i \to A_o}$ for each $(1 \leq i \leq l)$ and message m_w, proxy signer A_0 first computes
$e_{i_1} = H_2(m_w, ID_0, K_i)$ and $h_i = H_1(ID_i, R_i)$,
then checks whether $\sigma_i P = e_{i_1}[R_i + h_i P_{pub}] + K_i$.
Accept if it is equal, otherwise reject.

PKgen: If A_0 accepts the each delegation $W_{A_i \to A_o}$, he computes the proxy signing key D_p for each $(1 \leq i \leq l)$ as:
$$D_{p_i} = \sigma_i + D_0 e_{i_2}, \text{ where } e_{i_2} = H_2(m_w, ID_i, K_i)$$
$$D_p = \sum_1^l D_{p_i}.$$
D_p is the proxy signing key.

PMSign: Takes system parameters, the proxy signing key D_p and a message m as inputs, returns a signature of the message m. The user A_0 does as follows:

1. Chooses at random $b \in Z_n^*$ to compute $R = bP$.
2. Computes $h = H_2(m, R)$.
3. Verifies whether the equation gcd $(b + h, n) = 1$ holds, continue if it does, otherwise return to step 1.
4. Compute $s = (b + h)^{-1} D_p \mod n$.
5. The resulting signature is $((ID_i, R_i, K_i, (\forall i = 1, 2, ...l)), ID_0, R_0, m_w, m, R, s)$.

PMVerif: To verify the signature $((ID_i, R_i, K_i, (\forall i = 1, 2, ...l)), ID_0, R_0, m_w,$ $m, R, s)$ for message m, a verifier first checks if the proxy signer and the message confirm to m_w, then he computes

$$h_i = H_1(ID_i, R_i), h_o = H_1(ID_0, R_0)$$
$$e_{i_1} = H_2(m_w, ID_0, K_i), \ e_{i_2} = H_2(m_w, ID_i, K_i)$$
$$h = H_2(m, R), \ K = \sum_1^l K_i,$$

then checks whether $s(R+hP) = \sum_1^l e_{i_1}(R_i+h_i P_{pub})+K+\sum_1^l e_{i_2}(R_0+h_0 P_{pub})$,
Accept if it is equal, otherwise reject.

Correctness: Since $R = bP$ and $s = (b + h)^{-1} D_p \mod n$, we have
$s(R + hP) = (b + h)^{-1} D_p(bP + hP)$

$$= D_p P$$
$$= (\sum_1^l \sigma_i).P + D_0 \sum_i^l e_{i_2}.P$$
$$= \sum_1^l e_{i_1}(R_i + h_i.P_{pub}) + K + \sum_1^l e_{i_2}(R_0 + h_0.P_{pub}).$$

5   Security Analysis

Assume there is an adversary T who can break our ID based proxy multi signature scheme $\sum$. We will construct a polynomial-time algorithm F that, by simulating the challenger and interacting with T, solves the ECDLP.

Theorem 1. Consider an adaptively chosen message attack in the random oracle model against $\sum$. If there is an attacker T that can break $\sum$ with at most q_{H_2} H_2-queries and q_s signature queries within time bound t and non-negligible probability ε. Then we can solve the ECDLP with non-negligible probability.

Proof. Suppose an attacker T can break $\sum$ through adaptively chosen message attack then $Pr[Exp_T^{IBPMS}(k) = 1]$ and $Pr[Exp_T^{IBPMS}(k) = 2]$ are non negligible. Our aim is to show that using the ability of T one can construct an algorithm F for solving the ECDLP.

Suppose F is challenged with a ECDLP instance (P, Q) and is tasked to compute $x \in Z_n^*$ satisfying $Q = xP$. For this purpose F sets $\{F_p, E/F_p, G, P, P_{pub}, H_1, H_2\}$ as system parameters and answers T's queries (described in Definition 2) as follows.

Extract-query: T is allowed to query the extraction oracle for an identity ID_i. There exist a simulator S that simulates the oracle as follows.
It chooses $a_i; b_i \in Z_n^*$ at random and sets
$$R_i = a_i.P_{pub} + b_i.P, \qquad D_i = b_i$$
$$h_i = H_1(ID_i, R_i) \leftarrow -a_i \bmod n.$$ Note that (D_i, R_i) generated in this way satisfies the equation $D_i.P = R_i + h_i P_{pub}$ in the extract algorithm. It is a valid secret key. F outputs (D_i, R_i, h_i) as the secret key of ID_i and stores the value of (D_i, R_i, h_i) in the C_{list} table (we modify the content of C_{list} table).

Delgen-query: T queries the delegate oracle for a warrant m_w, ID_0 and original signer's identity group $\{ID_i, \forall i = 1, 2, ..l\}$, F first checks that whether ID_0, and $\{ID_i, \forall i = 1, 2, ..l\}$ have been queried for the extraction oracle before. If yes, it just retrieves $(D_i, R_i, h_i), \forall i = 1, 2, ..l\}$ from the table and uses these values to delegate a warrant m_w, according to the delgen algorithm described in the scheme.

It outputs the delegation $W_{A_i \rightarrow A_o} = \{ID_i, R_i, ID_0, m_w, K_i, \sigma_i\}, \forall i = 1, 2, ..l$ and stores the values in the hash table D_{list} for consistency. If ID_0, and $\{ID_i, \forall i = 1, 2, ..l\}$ has not been queried to the extraction oracle, F executes the simulation of the extraction oracle and uses the corresponding secret key to sign the message.

Since F knows every users private key(described in Extract-query), he can simulate Delgen-query, DelVerif-query, PKgen-query, PMSign-query, and PMVerif-query as he simulates Delgen-query. There are two following cases:

Case 1. If T can forge a valid delegation on warrant m_w with the probability $Pr[Exp_T^{IBPMS}(k) = 1] = \varepsilon \geq 10(q_{H_2} + 1)(q_{H_2} + q_s)/2^k$ where m_w has not been queried to the signature oracle, then a replay of F with the same random tape but different choice of H_2 will output two valid delegations $(\{ID_i, R_i, ID_0, m_w, K_i, \sigma_i, e_{i_1}\}$, and $\{ID_i, R_i, ID_0, m_w, K_i, \sigma_i', e_{i_1}'\}$, $\forall i = 1, 2, ..l)$. Then we have

$$\sigma_i.P = e_{i_1}[R_i + h_i P_{pub}] + K_i, \text{ and}$$
$$\sigma'_i.P = e'_{i_1}[R_i + h_i P_{pub}] + K_i.$$

Let $K_i = a_i.P$, $R_i = a_i.P_{pub} + b_i.P$, $P_{pub} = Q = x.P$, then
$$\sigma_i.P = e_{i_1}[a_i.P_{pub} + b_i.P + h_i.x.P] + a_i.P \text{ (a)}$$
$$\sigma'_i.P = e'_{i_1}[a_i.P_{pub} + b_i.P + h_i.x.P] + a_i.P \text{ (b)}$$
Subtracting (b) to (a) we have,
$$(e_{i_1}a_i + e_{i_1}h_i - e'_{i_1}a_i - e'_{i_1}h_i).x.P = (\sigma_i - \sigma'_i - e_{i_1}.b_i + e'_{i_1}.b_i).P$$

Let $u_i = (e_{i_1}a_i + e_{i_1}h_i - e'_{i_1}a_i - e'_{i_1}h_i)^{-1} \mod n$ (inverse exist with high probability, if not then repeat the queries),

and $v_i = (\sigma_i - \sigma'_i - e_{i_1}.b_i + e'_{i_1}.b_i) \mod n$,

then we get $x = u_i v_i \mod n \ \forall i = 1, 2, ...l$.
According to Lemma 4 [6] the ECDLP can be solved with probability $\varepsilon' \geq 1/9$ and time $t' \leq 23q_{H_2}t/\varepsilon$.

Case 2. From Case 1, we know the adversary T can not generate a valid delegation. In this case we prove, if T can forge a valid signature on message m under the delegation $W_{A_i \to A_o} = \{ID_i, R_i, ID_0, m_w, K_i, \sigma_i\} \ \forall i = 1, 2, ..l$, with the probability $Pr[Exp_T^{IBPMS}(k) = 2] = \varepsilon \geq 10(q_{H_2} + 1)(q_{H_2} + q_s)/2^k$ where m has not been queried to the signature oracle, then a replay of F with the same random tape but different choice of H_2 will output two valid signatures $((ID_i, R_i, K_i,), ID_0, R_0, m_w, m, R, s, e_{i_1}, e_{i_2}, h)$ and $((ID_i, R_i, K_i), ID_0, R_0, m_w, m, R, s', e_{i_1}, e_{i_2}, h'), (\forall i = 1, 2, ...l)$.
Then we have
$$s(R + h.P) = \sum_1^l e_{i_1}(R_i + h_i.P_{pub}) + K + \sum_1^l e_{i_2}(R_0 + h_0.P_{pub})$$
$$s'(R + h'.P) = \sum_1^l e'_{i_1}(R_i + h_i.P_{pub}) + K + \sum_1^l e'_{i_2}(R_0 + h_0.P_{pub})$$

Since $K = \sum_1^l K_i = \sum a_i.P$, $R = b.P$,
$R_i = a_i.P_{pub} + b_i.P$, and $P_{pub} = Q = x.P$,
then we have
$$s(b + h) = \sum_1^l e_{i_1}(a_i.x + b_i + h_i.x) + \sum_1^l a_i$$
$$+ \sum_1^l e_{i_2}(a_0.x + b_0 + h_0.x) \mod n, \text{ (c)}$$
$$s'(b + h') = (\sum_1^l e'_{i_1}(a_i.x + b_i + h_i.x) + \sum_1^l a_i$$
$$+ \sum_1^l e'_{i_2}(a_0.x + b_0 + h_0.x)). \mod n, \text{ (d)}$$

Since there are two equations $(c), (d)$ and two unknowns b and x. Thus output x is the solution of the ECDLP with probability $\varepsilon' \geq 1/9$ and time $t' \leq 23q_{H_2}t/\varepsilon$ (Lemma 4 [6]).

6   Comparative Analysis

In this section, we will compare the efficiency of our new scheme with Wang and Cao scheme [15] and Cao and Cao scheme [3]. To analyze the computational efficiency of different schemes, we use the method given in [5,13]. We compare the computational efficiency of these schemes to our scheme only for a single user. According to the running time calculations in millisecond (ms) given in [9], the running time of one pairing operation is 20.04 ms, ECC-based scalar multiplication is 2.21 ms and Map-to-point hash function is 3.04 ms. Computational cost and running time analysis of our scheme with schemes [3,15] are given in table 1 and table 2 respectively.

Table 1. Computational Cost Comparison

Scheme	Extract	Delgen	DelVerif	PKgen
scheme [15]	$2M_P + 2H_M$	$3M_P + 1H_M$	$1M_P + 3H_M + 3O_P$	0
scheme [3]	$1M_P + 1H_M$	$2M_P + 1H_M$	$2H_M + 3O_P$	$1M_P$
Our scheme	$1M_E$	$1M_E$	$2M_E$	0

Scheme	PMsign	PMverif	Total
scheme [15]	$3M_P + 1H_M$	$2M_P + 5H_M + 3O_P$	$11M_P + 12H_M + 6O_P$
scheme [3]	$2M_P + 1H_M$	$1M_P + 3H_M + 4O_P$	$7M_P + 8H_M + 7O_P$
Our scheme	$1M_E$	$4M_E$	$9M_E$

Where M_E, M_P, H_M, O_P stand for one ECC based scalar multiplication, pairing based scalar multiplication, Map-to-point hash function and pairing operation respectively.

Table 2. Running Time Comparison(in ms)

Scheme	Extract	Delgen	DelVerif	PKgen	PMsign	PMverif	Total
scheme [15]	18.84	22.18	75.62	0	22.18	88.08	226.90
scheme [3]	9.42	15.80	66.20	6.38	15.80	95.66	209.26
Our scheme	2.21	2.21	4.42	0	2.21	8.84	19.89

According to these running time computations, the running time of PMSign algorithm of our scheme is 13.98% of Cao and Cao scheme [3] and 9.96% of Wang and Cao [15] scheme. Total running time of our scheme is 8.76% of the Wang and Cao scheme [15] and 9.50% percent of the Cao and Cao scheme [3].

7   Conclusion

In this paper, we have proposed an efficient identity-based proxy multi signature scheme without using bilinear pairings. We also prove the security of the proposed scheme against adaptive chosen message attack under random oracle model. Compared with previous schemes, the new scheme reduces the running time heavily. Therefore, our scheme is more practical than the previous related schemes for practical application.

References

1. Barreto, P.S.L.M., Libert, B., McCullagh, N., Quisquater, J.-J.: Efficient and Provably-Secure Identity-Based Signatures and Signcryption from Bilinear Maps. In: Roy, B. (ed.) ASIACRYPT 2005. LNCS, vol. 3788, pp. 515–532. Springer, Heidelberg (2005)
2. Cha, J.C., Cheon, J.H.: An Identity-Based Signature from Gap Diffie-Hellman Groups. In: Desmedt, Y.G. (ed.) PKC 2003. LNCS, vol. 2567, pp. 18–30. Springer, Heidelberg (2002)
3. Cao, F., Cao, Z.: A secure identity-based proxy multi-signature scheme. Information Sciences 179, 292–302 (2009)
4. Chen, L., Cheng, Z., Smart, N.P.: Identity-based key agreement protocols from pairings. International Journal of Information Security, 213–241 (2006)
5. Cao, X., Kou, W., Du, X.: A pairing-free identity-based authenticated key agreement protocol with, minimal message exchanges. Information Sciences 180, 2895–2903 (2010)
6. David, P., Jacque, S.: Security arguments for digital signatures and blind signatures. Journal of Cryptology 13(3), 361–396 (2000)
7. Gu, C., Zhu, Y.: Provable security of ID-based proxy signature schemes. In: Lu, X., Zhao, W. (eds.) ICCNMC 2005. LNCS, vol. 3619, pp. 1277–1286. Springer, Heidelberg (2005)
8. Gu, C., Zhu, Y.: An efficient ID-based proxy signature scheme from pairings. In: Pei, D., Yung, M., Lin, D., Wu, C. (eds.) Inscrypt 2007. LNCS, vol. 4990, pp. 40–50. Springer, Heidelberg (2008)
9. He, D., Chen, J., Hu, J.: An ID-Based proxy signature schemes without bilinear pairings. Annalas of Telicommunications, doi:10.1007/s12243-011-0244-0
10. Hess, F.: Efficient identity based signature schemes based on pairings. In: Nyberg, K., Heys, H.M. (eds.) SAC 2002. LNCS, vol. 2595, pp. 310–324. Springer, Heidelberg (2003)
11. Ji, H., Han, W., Zhao, L., et al.: An identity-based proxy signature from bilinear pairings. In: 2009 WASE International Conference on Information Engineering (2009)
12. Mambo, M., Usuda, K., Okamoto, E.: Proxy signatures: Delegation of the power to sign messages. IEICE Transactions Fundamentals E79-A(9), 1338–1353 (1996)
13. The Certicom Corporation, SEC 2: Recommended Elliptic Curve Domain Parameters, www.secg.org/collateral/sec2_final.pdf
14. Shamir, A.: Identity-based cryptosystems and signature schemes. In: Blakely, G.R., Chaum, D. (eds.) CRYPTO 1984. LNCS, vol. 196, pp. 47–53. Springer, Heidelberg (1985)
15. Wang, Q., Cao, Z.: Identity based proxy multi-signature. The Journal of Systems and Software 80, 1023–1029 (2007)
16. Wu, W., Mu, Y., Susilo, W., et al.: Identity-based proxy signature from pairings. In: Xiao, B., Yang, L.T., Ma, J., Muller-Schloer, C., Hua, Y. (eds.) ATC 2007. LNCS, vol. 4610, pp. 22–31. Springer, Heidelberg (2007)
17. Zhang, J., Zou, W.: Another ID-based proxy signature scheme and its extension. Wuhan Univ. Journal of Natural Science 12, 133–136 (2007)

Distributed Signcryption Schemes with Formal Proof of Security

Indivar Gupta and P.K. Saxena

SAG, DRDO, Metcalfe House Complex, Delhi-110054, India
{indivargupta,pksaxena}@sag.drdo.in

Abstract. A distributed signcryption scheme was proposed by Mu and Varadharajan [18] in 2000 . Since then some more distributed signcryption schemes have been proposed [11,13]. But formal security models and security proofs have not been presented in any of these schemes.

In this paper, we propose formal security model for distributed signcryption for confidentiality and unforgeability. We also modify schemes proposed by Mu & Varadharajan [18] and Gupta et al [11] to achieve formally provable security. We show that these modified schemes provide confidentiality against chosen ciphertext attack and unforgeability against chosen message attack.

Keywords: Signcryption, Distributed Signcryption, Formal Security Model, Confidentiality, Unforgeability, Security Proofs, Gap Diffie Hellman Problem.

1 Introduction

In a normal secure communication on a network, confidentiality of the message is provided usually through encryption and authenticity is achieved through digital signatures. Traditionally, the message is first signed and then encrypted for securing the information. This two-step approach is called *sign-then-encryption* technique. To accomplish the two tasks, 'digital signature' and 'encryption' in a single logical step, Zheng [24] introduced the notion of *signcryption* in 1997[1]. The motivation was to achieve significantly lower computational cost and communication overheads while achieving both message confidentiality and authenticity.

There are certain applications that demand a suitable & efficient protocol and schemes for 'individual' to 'group' or 'group' to 'group' communication ensuring security as well as authentication. For example, when the communicating parties are big organizations (groups), the Head of the establishment (group manager) may not send/receive all messages herself/himself but may delegate authority to subordinate officers (group members) to communicate within and outside the group. Such authorization may be restricted to only some individuals based on subject such as 'Legal', 'Negotiations', 'Finance', 'Administrative'

---

[1] In symmetric key cryptography the equivalent notions is Authenticated Encryption [12].

M. Joye et al. (Eds.): InfoSecHiComNet 2011, LNCS 7011, pp. 93–110, 2011.
© Springer-Verlag Berlin Heidelberg 2011

etc. Similarly in case of grid/cluster computing, where the users/groups are connected through network, such restricted authorization to nodes for decryption of information is needed. In sharing of information by intelligence agencies also, there may be requirements of encryption as well as authentication of individual recipients within the agencies involved. In case of pay TV channels where the broadcast companies may restrict their programs to be viewed by only authorized subscribers by signcrypting the programs and distributing to their authorized subscribers. In all of these example, signcrypted message is to be received by a group of receivers/multiple parties but in restricted way through authorization. The concept of "signcryption" as proposed by Zheng supported multiple parties receiving signcrypted message sent by a sender, instead of just point-to-point communication application. To design such kind of protocols/schemes, mainly two approaches can be followed: (i) either the group of authorized receivers/legitimate subscribers share the common private key with the same public key, or (ii) group of receivers share common group public key but corresponding private keys are different. The first case is not recommended in 'individual/user' to 'group'/'group' to 'group' secure communication since if any member of the receiving group is dishonest and leaks the private key, it would be difficult to trace her/him and also because the group manager (server) or the controlling authority has no role to play in the protocol. *Therefore case (ii) is preferred for meeting some of specific requirements as discussed above. The concept is termed as 'Distributed Signcryption'.*

Distributed Signcryption was first introduced by Mu and Varadharajan [18] in 2000 (scheme called MVS-DSC here onwards). In this scheme, a signcrypted message can be de-signcrypted by any member of the receiving designated group. This definition can be extended for transmission of information between two or more designated groups. This means that any member of the designated group can signcrypt the message on behalf of the group and distribute it to the receiving group. Signcrypted message can be de-signcrypted by any member of the receiving group. A scheme which offers communication between two designated groups is known as *group signcryption*. In both of the schemes proposed by Mu and Varadharajan [18], the computational complexity and communication overheads depend on the number of members in the designated group and it becomes very cumbersome if the number of users in the group increases. Kwak and Moon [13] also proposed distributed signcryption scheme as group signature, which provided sender identity confidentiality but had the same weaknesses as Mu and Varadharajan scheme had. Gupta, Pillai and Saxena [11] proposed a scheme (called GPSS here onwards) where such weaknesses were overcome upto a great extent.

In all the schemes mentioned above, authors did not include formal security notions and proofs. Kwak and Moon [13], however, gave some heuristic arguments for security analysis of their scheme (Distributed Signcryption proposed by Kwak and Moon would be referred as KMS-DSC and their Group Signcryption as KMS-GSC). Bao, Cao and Quin [3] analyzed KMS-DSC and showed that the Distributed signcryption scheme with sender ID confidentiality proposed by

Kwak and Moon actually did not provide sender ID confidentiality since the verification step in Kwak and Moon scheme requires sender ID. Thus there was no significant advantage of KMS-DSC over MVS-DSC. DongJin Kwak et al proposed a secure extension of KMS-GSC [14] and gave some informal proofs for unforgeability and coalition-resistance along with heuristic arguments for other security notions.

In this paper, we propose a formal security model for distributed signcryption for the two aspects of security i.e. confidentiality of the message and unforgeability (for authenticity of message). We also propose modifications to the schemes proposed by Mu & Varadharajan and Gupta et al and give formal security proofs. We show that our modified schemes ensure message confidentiality against chosen ciphertext attack and unforgeability against chosen message attacks.

The paper is organized as follows. In section 2, we present a generic distributed signcryption and a formal security model for confidentiality and unforgeability. In section 3, we review the two distributed signcryption schemes - MVS and GPSS. In section 4, we propose modifications to both of these, calling the modified schemes as MMVS and MGPSS respectively. In section 5, we give security proofs for the confidentiality and unforgeability of MGPSS and also sketch the proof of security for MMVS. The paper ends with conclusion in section 6 followed by Acknowledgments and References.

2 Security Model for Distributed Signcryption

2.1 Generic Scheme for Distributed Signcryption

In normal signcryption between two members in a group, each member has its individual public key, kept in a public directory, whereas in case of distributed signcryption, the designated group as a whole has a common public key with the individual members having different individual private keys. The Group Manager (called $\mathcal{GM}$ here onward) of the designated group also has the secret parameters which are referred as *group secret parameters* (gsp). The public key associated with the group is referred as *group public key* (gpk). A group with a single member (who is $\mathcal{GM}$ himself) would be referred as *single user*. If $n+1$ persons are in the group (including $\mathcal{GM}$), the $\mathcal{GM}$ selects $(n+1)$ pairs of integers or a set of integers randomly from $\mathbb{Z}_q^*$ (where q is a prime) and then uses these integers for initialization of the designated group. The group public key (gpk), the group secret parameters(gsp) and individual members secret keys (member secret key is denoted by msk) are to be computed at the time of initialization of the designated group. The Keys are distributed in the following way. The gpk being common to all members of the group, is kept in public directory. The $\mathcal{GM}$ keeps gsp secret and distributes individual secret keys to group members. In case of a *single user*, the $\mathcal{GM}$ has only one public - secret key pair (pk, sk) (i.e $gpk = pk$, $gsp = sk$) and scheme works as ordinary signcryption scheme.

We now define basic algorithms for distributed signcryption required in the rest of the paper.

Setup: Based on the input of unary string $1^{\Re_{\mathfrak{p}}}$, where $\Re_{\mathfrak{p}}$ is the security parameter, it generates common system parameters referred as *'params'*.

SenKeyGen: On the input of *params*, this algorithm generates the keys for the sender returning the secret / public key pair (sk_S, pk_S).

RecKeyGen: On the input of $(params, n)$, this algorithm generates the keys of receiving designated group returning gpk, gsp and the members' secret keys for each individual members of the group. We denote member secret key of lth member by msk_l.

DisSignCrypt: DisSignCrypt is an algorithm which accepts the sender's secret key sk_S, the recipients public key (gpk) as well as the message m as input and outputs a ciphertext C.

DisDeSignCrypt: DisDeSignCrypt is an algorithm which accepts the sender's public key pk_S and the recipient's (a member of the group) secret key (msk) and ciphertext a C and outputs a message m, or the special symbol $\perp$ in the case of an invalid ciphertext.

It is noted that *Setup, SenKeyGen, RecKeyGen* and *DisSignCrypt* are randomized algorithms and *DisDeSignCrypt* is a deterministic algorithm. For consistency of the whole scheme, we must have the following:

$C \leftarrow DisSignCrypt(sk_S, gpk, m)$ & $\hat{m} \leftarrow DisDeSignCrypt(C, msk_l)$, then $\hat{m} = m \ \forall l$.

Thus our generic method of distributed signcryption and security model as described above can be viewed as generalization of signcryption.

2.2   Security Models for Distributed Signcryption

Recently, many authors proposed several public key schemes and presented security models also for their schemes [1, 5, 8, 9, 10]. Formal models for security of signcryption have also been discussed by many authors [2, 15, 16, 23]. However, a formal models of security for distributed signcryption has not yet been proposed. In this section, we present a formal security model for confidentiality and unforgeability of distributed signcryption. We call the confidentiality security notion as *IND-DSC-CCA* (indistinguishability of distributed signcryption against chosen ciphertext attacks).

Definition 2.1. *We say that a distributed signcryption scheme ensures message confidentiality against chosen-ciphertext attacks i.e. IND-DSC-CCA if no probabilistic polynomial time adversary has a non-negligible advantage in the following game:*

1. *Challenger $\mathcal{CH}$ generates two pairs (sk_U, pk_U) and (msk_G, gpk_G) where sk_U and pk_U denote the secret key and the public key of a user U, msk_G denotes the secret key of any member of the group G and gpk_G denotes the public key of the group G. sk_U and msk_G are kept secret, while gpk_G and pk_U are sent to the adversary $\mathcal{A}$.*

2. $\mathcal{A}$ *performs a series of queries of the following kinds:*
DisSignCrypt queries: $\mathcal{A}$ submits a message $m \in M$ (message space) and an arbitrary group public key gpk_{G_R} of the receiving group R (which may differ from gpk_G) to $\mathcal{CH}$ for the result of $DisSignCrypt(m, sk_U, gpkG_R)$.
DisDeSignCrypt queries: $\mathcal{A}$ submits a pair (pk_S, C) to $\mathcal{CH}$ and requires the result of $DisDeSignCrypt(C, msk_G, pk_S)$. It is noted that pk_S may be different from pk_U. $\mathcal{CH}$ returns a plaintext or rejects symbol $\perp$ after running DisDeSignCrypt.

These queries can be asked adaptively i.e. each query may depend on the answer of previous ones. After a number of queries, $\mathcal{A}$ outputs two plaintexts m_0, $m_1 \in M$ and an arbitrary private key of the form sk_S. $\mathcal{CH}$ flips a coins $b \in_R \{0, 1\}$ to compute a distributed signcrypted message $C^* = DisSignCrypt$ (m_b, sk_S, gpk_G) of m_b with the sender's private key sk_S under the attacked group public key gpk_G. Ciphertext C^* is sent to $\mathcal{A}$ as challenge.
3. $\mathcal{A}$ *performs number of new queries as in the first stage with a restriction that $\mathcal{A}$ may not ask the DisDeSignCrypt query of the challenged ciphertext C^*. At the end of the game, $\mathcal{A}$ outputs a bit b' and wins if $b' = b$.*

$\mathcal{A}$'s *advantage is defined to be* $Adv^{IND-DSC-CCA}(\mathcal{A}) = 2Pr[b' = b] - 1$.

Definition 2.2. *A distributed signcryption scheme ensures existentially unforgeability against chosen-message attack (EUF-DSC-CMA) if no probabilistic polynomial time forger $\mathcal{F}$ has a non-negligible advantage in the following game:*

1. *Challenger $\mathcal{CH}$ generates two key pairs (sk_U, pk_U) and (msk_G, gpk_G) as in step 1 of IND-DSC-CCA game (Definition 2.1). sk_U and msk_G are kept secret while pk_U and gpk_G are given to forger $\mathcal{F}$.*
2. $\mathcal{F}$ *makes series of $DisSignCrypt(m, sk_U, gpk_{G_R})$ and DisDeSignCrypt (C, msk_G, pk_S) adaptive queries exactly in the same way as in step 2 of IND-DSC-CCA game (Definition 2.1).*
3. $\mathcal{F}$ *produces a ciphertext C^* and a key pair $(msk_{G_{R^*}}, gpk_{G_{R^*}})$ and wins the game if (i) $DisDeSignCrypt(C^*, msk_{G_{R^*}}, pk_U)$ returns a signed message m^* (ii) the query $(m^*, gpk_{G_{R^*}}, sk_U)$ has not been submitted as input to DisSignCrypt oracle during the game.*

3 Distributed Signcryption Schemes - MVS and GPSS

3.1 Mu and Varadharajan Scheme(MVS) [13, 18]

Let p be a large prime number, $\mathbb{Z}_p^*$ the multiplicative group of order $q(= p - 1)$ and $g \in \mathbb{Z}_p^*$ a primitive element. Assume that $Hash()$ denotes a strong one-way function, $Hash_k()$ a keyed one-way hash function with key k, and $E_k(D_k)$ denotes a symmetric encryption (decryption) function.

Initialization of a Group. In order to construct a group including n members, the manager selects a set of integers $\epsilon_i \in_R \mathbb{Z}_q$ $(i = 1, 2, \cdots, n)$, and computes the coefficients $\alpha_0, \cdots, \alpha_n \in \mathbb{Z}_q$ of the polynomial:

$$f(x) = \prod_{i=1}^{n}(x - \epsilon_i) = \sum_{i=1}^{n} \alpha_i x^i \bmod q.$$

Define $g_i = g^{\alpha_i} \bmod p$ $(i = 0, 1, \cdots, n)$ which produces

$$F(\epsilon_l) = \prod_{i=0}^{n} g_i^{\epsilon_l^i} = 1 \bmod p,$$

where ϵ_l is an element of $\{\epsilon_i\}$. This is because $F(\epsilon_l) = g^{f(\epsilon_l)}$ and $f(\epsilon_l) = 0$ in $\mathbb{Z}_q$. This is an important property of the system. However, there is a weak point if $\{g_i\}_{i=1}^{n}$ is used as group public key. In that case, an adversary would add another illegal ϵ_i' to the set $\{\epsilon_i\}$ by using the g_i polynomial. Thus to avoid this weakness, the method given in [17] is adopted. For the given $(\alpha_0, \alpha_1, \cdots, \alpha_n)$, a new set is defined as $(\alpha_0', \alpha_1', \cdots, \alpha_n')$, where $\alpha_0' = \alpha_0$, $\alpha_n' = \alpha_n$, $\alpha_1' = \cdots = \alpha_{n-1}' = \sum_{i=1}^{n-1} \alpha_i$. Define $\beta_i = g^{\alpha_i'}$ and $A_l = \sum_{i=1, j=1, i \neq j}^{n-1} \alpha_j \epsilon_l^i$, then for all $\epsilon_l|_{l=1}^{n}$

$$F'(\epsilon_l) = g^{-A_l} \prod_{i=0}^{n} \beta_i^{\epsilon_l^i} = g^{-A_l} g^{\sum_{i=0}^{i=n} \alpha_i' \epsilon_l^i} = 1 \bmod p.$$

Thus function F and F' have the same properties at $\{\epsilon_l\}_{l=1}^{n}$. The $\mathcal{GM}$ picks a random number $\gamma \in_R \mathbb{Z}_q$, then computes its inverse γ^{-1} and $\rho_l = -\gamma A_l \bmod q$ for member l. The group public key is defined as $n + 2$ tuple, $\{\beta_0, \cdots, \beta_{n+1}\} = \{\beta_0, \cdots, \beta_n, g^{\gamma^{-1}}\}$. The manager keeps γ and all $\{\alpha_i\}$ secret and gives ϵ_l and ρ_l to the group member l as his/her secret key pair.

Description of MVS. Assume that A is the sender who signcrypts a message m and sends the message to a designated group. Further, let B be a member of the designated group who De-signcrypts the message.

Setup: On giving the security parameters, the algorithm generates common system parameter $(p, \mathbb{Z}_p^*, g, q, Hash, Hash_k)$.

SenKeyGen: A picks $x_a \in \mathbb{Z}_q$, and runs SenKeyGen to generate the public-private key pair $(x_a, y_a = g^{x_a})$.

RecKeyGen: This generates $gpk = (\{\beta_0, \cdots, \beta_n, g^{\gamma^{-1}}\})$, $gsp = (\alpha_i|_{i=0}^{n}, \gamma)$, and the individual members' secret keys (ϵ_l, ρ_l) for $l = 1, \cdots, n$. Assume that B is the lth member of group with the secret key (ϵ_l, ρ_l).

DisSignCrypt: To signcrypt the message m, A follows the following steps:

Step 1. Choose $z \in_R \mathbb{Z}_q$, and compute $k = g^z \bmod p$.
Step 2. Split k into k_1 and k_2.

Step 3. Compute $r = Hash_{k_2}(m)$, $s = z(kr + x_a)^{-1} \bmod q$ and $w = Hash(m)$.

Step 4. Generates the signcrypted message as follows:

$$c_1 = \{a_0, \cdots, a_n, a_{n+1}\} = \{g^{kr}\beta_0^w, \beta_1^w, \cdots, \beta_{n+1}^w\}, \ \& \ c_2 = E_{k_1}(m)$$

Step 5. A sends the ciphertext $C = (c_1, c_2, r, s)$ to B.

DisDeSignCrypt: On receiving $C = (c_1, c_2, r, s)$, B can de-signcrypt the signcrypted message as per following steps.

Step 1 B computes the secret key k as follows:

$$k = (y_a a_0 (\prod_{i=1}^{n} a_i^{\epsilon_i}) a_{n+1}^{\rho_l})^s = (y_a g^{rk} \prod_{i=0}^{n} g^{w\alpha_i \epsilon_i})^s = (y_a g^{rk} g^{wf(\epsilon_l)})^s = g^z \bmod p$$

Step 2. B splits k into k_1 and k_2 as agreed earlier.

Step 3. B computes $m? = D_{k_1}(c_2)$ and verifies that $r? = Hash_{k_2}(m)$.

3.2 Gupta, Pillai and Saxena Scheme(GPSS) [11]

Let $\mathcal{C}$ be a hyperelliptic curve (HEC) of genus g defined over the finite field F_q of characteristic p and let $J(F_q)$ be the Jacobian of $\mathcal{C}$ such that the discrete logarithm problem in $J(F_q)$ is hard. Each element of $J(F_q)$ has an unique representation as a *reduced divisor* $D(a, b)$. Let $H_\tau : F_q^g \longrightarrow \mathbb{Z}_N$ denote one way keyed hash function with key τ. Assume that π and π_1 are maps from g-tuple of F_q elements to a set of keys (of desired length). Further, let ENC_χ and DEC_χ denote the encryption and the decryption functions of the symmetric key cipher with key χ.

Initialization of a Group. For the construction of a group of $n + 1$ members with one $\mathcal{GM}$ in it, the $\mathcal{GM}$ selects a base point $D \in J(F_q)$ of prime order (say N) and a set of distinct pairs of nonzero integers $(x_0, y_0), (x_1, y_1), \ldots, (x_n, y_n) \in_R \mathbb{Z}_N$. Then the group manager computes the Lagrange's interpolation polynomial: $f(x) = \sum_{i=0}^{n} \beta_i x^i \bmod N$, passing through the points $(x_i, y_i)_{i=0}^{i=n}$. Clearly the polynomial $f(x)$ satisfies the condition: $f(x_i) = y_i \bmod N$, $0 \le i \le n$. We can rewrite the polynomial in the form:

$$f(x) = \beta_0 + \sum_{j=1}^{n} \beta_j \sum_{k=1}^{n} x^k - \sum_{j=1, k=1, j \neq k}^{n} \beta_j x^k \bmod N$$

or

$$f(x) = \beta_0 + \beta\delta_1(x) - \delta_2(x) \bmod N,$$

where $\beta = \sum_{j=1}^{n} \beta_j$, $\delta_1(x) = \sum_{j=1}^{n} x^j$ and $\delta_2(x) = \sum_{j=1, k=1, j \neq k}^{n} \beta_j x^k$.

Consider the polynomials $F_i(x) = f(x) - y_i \bmod N (i = 0, 1, \ldots, n)$. Clearly, the polynomial $F_i(x)$ vanishes at x_i for each value of i. Define a new function $F_i^*(x, D) = F_i(x) \cdot D$ on divisors of the HEC. Then $F_i^*(x_i, D) = \mathcal{O} \bmod N$ for $0 \le i \le n$ ($\mathcal{O} \in \mathcal{C}$ is a point at infinity).

For construction of *gpk*, the group manager keeps β_i secret for all i and computes $\beta_0 \cdot D$ and $\beta \cdot D$. Then he selects a random number $\gamma \in_R \mathbb{Z}_N^*$ and computes the parameters ρ_l for $l = 0, 1, \ldots, n$ such that $\rho_l = \overline{\gamma}\delta_2(x_l) \bmod N$ where $\overline{\gamma}$ is the multiplicative inverse of γ. Finally, the group manager computes $\gamma \cdot D$ and keeps it secret. Observe that *gpk* is defined by the triplet $(D_{\beta_0} = \beta_0 \cdot D, D_\beta = \beta \cdot D, D_\gamma = \gamma \cdot D)$. The group manager registers the public key in the public directory and distributes the secret keys (x_l, y_l, ρ_l) to the group members l $(0 \leq l \leq n)$.

Distributed Signcryption on HEC. Let A denote a person who wants to communicate with the designated group. Let B be the lth member of the designated group who receives the message. The algorithms work as follows.

Setup: On giving the security parameters, this algorithm generates common system parameters $(\mathcal{C}, g, \mathbb{F}_q, J(\mathbb{F}_q), D, H_\tau, \pi, \pi_1, ENC_\chi, DEC_\chi)$ as described earlier.

SenKeyGen: A runs SenKeyGen to get his / her public key-private key pair (x_a, D_{x_a}).

RecKeyGen: The group manager runs RecKeyGen and generates $gpk = (D_{\beta_0} = \beta_0 \cdot D, D_\beta = \beta \cdot D, D_\gamma = \gamma \cdot D)$ and the individual member's secret keys (x_l, y_l, ρ_l), $l = 0, 1, \cdots, n$ which are distributed to its members securely.

DisSignCrypt: To signcrypt a message m, A carries out the following steps.

Step 1. A chooses random numbers k, k_1 & $k_2 \in_R \{2, 3, \ldots, N-2\}$ and computes $D_k = k \cdot D$, $E = k_1 \cdot D$ and $k_2 \cdot D$. It may be noted that D_k is the short form of $D_k(\hat{d}, \hat{e})$ for some polynomials $\hat{d}$ (a polynomial of degree g with leading coefficient 1) and $\hat{e}$ (a polynomial of degree $g-1$) where $\hat{d} = <\hat{d}_{g-1}, \ldots, \hat{d}_1, \hat{d}_0 >$ and $\hat{e} = <\hat{e}_{g-1}, \ldots, \hat{e}_1, \hat{e}_0>$. Here $d_i|_{i=0}^{g-1}$ and $e_i|_{i=0}^{g-1}$ denote the coefficients of the polynomial $\hat{d}$ and $\hat{e}$ respectively.
Step 2. A computes $E_0 = k_2 \cdot D + k_1 \cdot D_{\beta_0}$, $E_1 = k_1 \cdot D_\beta$, $E_2 = k_1 \cdot D_\gamma$.
Step 3. A computes the encryption key $\chi = \pi(\hat{d} \oplus \hat{e})$ and the hash key $\chi_1 = \pi_1(\hat{d} \oplus \hat{e})$ (as in the step 2 of Section 2.1) and $r = H_{\chi_1}(m)$.
Step 4. A computes the signature: $s = (k - k_2 - x_a r) \bmod N$ on the message.
Step 5. A computes $c = ENC_\chi(m)$.
Step 6. A sends the ciphertext $C =< E, E_0, E_1, E_2, r, s, c >$ to B.

DisDeSignCrypt: To de-signcrypt the message, B follows the following steps.

Step 1. B computes $\rho_l \cdot E_2$, $s \cdot D$ and $r \cdot D_{x_a}$.
Step 2. B computes $w_l \cdot E_1 = (x_l + x_l^2 + \cdots + x_l^n) \cdot E_1$ and $y_l \cdot E$.
Step 3. B computes $D_k = s \cdot D + E_0 + w_l \cdot E_1 - \rho_l \cdot E_2 + r \cdot D_{x_a} - y_l E$ which is $D_k(\hat{d}, \hat{e})$ for some polynomials $\hat{d}$ & $\hat{e}$, where $\hat{d} = <\hat{d}_{g-1}, \ldots, \hat{d}_1, \hat{d}_0 >$ and $\hat{e} = <\hat{e}_{g-1}, \ldots, \hat{e}_1, \hat{e}_0>$. B then computes two keys $\chi = \pi(\hat{d} \oplus \hat{e})$ and $\chi_1 = \pi_1(\hat{d} \oplus \hat{e})$.
Step 4. B computes $m' = DEC_\chi(c)$.
Step 5. B verifies if $r = H_{\chi_1}(m')$ and accepts the signature. He thus recovers the message m and also verifies its authenticity.

This scheme had advantage over MVS in the sense of computational complexity and communication overhead. Details of the comparison can be found in [11].

4   Modifications in Distributed Signcryption Schemes MVS and GPSS

Merits of a protocol /scheme also depend on its security proof. As the original schemes MVS and GPSS did not have security proofs, both MVS and GPSS needed modifications to enable one to give security proofs for these schemes.

4.1   Modified Mu and Varadharajan Scheme [MMVS]

With all the symbols and notations as used in section 3.1, let $H : \{0,1\}^* \to \{0,1\}^\lambda$, $H_1 : \{0,1\}^* \to <g>$ and $H_2 : \{0,1\}^* \to \mathbb{Z}_q$ be three hash functions. The group manager selects $z \in_R \mathbb{Z}_q$ and computes g^z. The group public /secret keys are $gpk = \{(\beta_0, \cdots, \beta_n, \beta_{n+1} = g^{\gamma^{-1}}), \beta_{n+2} = g^z\}$, $gsp = (\alpha_0, \cdots, \alpha_n, z)$. Assume that π is a permutation function over $\mathbb{Z}_q$.

DisSignCrypt: To signcrypt a message m, A follows the following steps:

Step 1. Choose $z' \in_R \mathbb{Z}_q$, and compute $k = g^{zz'} \mod p$.

Step 2. Compute encryption key $\tau = H(g^{z'}, g^{zz'})$ of desired length λ.

Step 3. Compute $g^r = H_1(m, g^{zz'}, g^z, g^{z'}, g^{x_a})$ and $w = H_2(m, g^{z'}, g^{zz'})$. Then Compute $r' = \pi(g^{z'}.g^r \mod q)$, and $s = kg^{(x_a r - z')r'} \mod p$.

Step 4. The message is signcrypted as follows:

$$c_1 = \{a_0, \cdots, a_n, a_{n+1}, a_{n+2}\} = \{g^{x_a - x_a r}\beta_0^w, \beta_1^w, \cdots, \beta_{n+1}^w, g^{z'}\} \text{ and } c_2 = E_\tau(m)$$

Step 5. A sends the ciphertext $C = (c_1, c_2, g^r, s)$ to B.

DisDeSignCrypt: B can de-signcrypt the message in the following steps.

Step 1 First compute $r' = \pi(g^{z'}.g^r)$ and then the secret key k as follows:
$k = (y_a^{-1}g^{z'}a_0(\prod_{i=1}^{i=n} a_i^{\epsilon_i})a_{n+1}^{\rho_l})^{r'} s = (g^{-x_a}g^{z'}g^{x_a - x_a r}\prod_{i=0}^{i=n}g^{w\alpha_i \epsilon_i})^r kg^{(x_a r - z')r'} = (g^{z'-x_a r}g^{wf(\epsilon_l)})^{r'}kg^{(x_a r - z')r'} \mod p$

Step 2. Compute key $\tau = H(g^{z'}, g^{z'z})$.

Step 3. Compute $m? = D_\tau(c_2)$ and verify that $g^r? = H_1(m, g^{zz'}, g^z, g^{z'}, g^{x_a})$.

4.2   Modified Gupta, Pillai and Saxena Scheme [MGPSS]

With all symbols and notations as used in the section 3.2 being same, let $H : \{0,1\}^* \to \{0,1\}^\lambda$ and $H_1 : \{0,1\}^* \to <D>$ be two hash functions. The group manager selects $k \in \mathbb{Z}_n$ and computes $D_k = k \cdot D$. The group public key gpk is $(D_{\beta_0}, D_\beta, D_\gamma, D_k)$ and group secret parameters gsp is $(\beta_0, \beta, \gamma, k)$. Assume that π is a map from g-tuple of F_q element to a set of integers.

DisSignCrypt:

Step 1. A chooses random numbers k', k_1, $\in_R \{2, 3, \ldots, N-2\}$ and computes $\mathcal{K} \cdot D = D_{\mathcal{K}} = k' \cdot D_k = kk' \cdot D$, $E = k_1 \cdot D$.

Step 2. A computes the encryption key $\chi = H(k' \cdot D, \mathcal{K} \cdot D), rD = D(\tilde{d}, \tilde{e}) = H_1(m, D_{x_a}, D_{k'}, D_k, D_\mathcal{K})$ and $r' = \pi(\tilde{d} \oplus \tilde{e})$.

Step 3. A computes $E_0 = k_1 \cdot D_{\beta_0} + x_a r \cdot D - D_{x_a}$. E_1 and E_2 are same as in the original scheme, GPSS.

Step 4. A computes $S = k'k \cdot D + r'(k' \cdot D - x_a r \cdot D) \bmod N$.

Step 5. A computes $c = ENC_\chi(m)$.

Step 6. A sends the ciphertext $C = < E, E_0, E_1, E_2, k'D, S, r \cdot D, c >$ to B.

DisDeSignCrypt:

Step 1. B computes $w_l \cdot E_1 = \left(x_l + x_l^2 + \cdots + x_l^n \right) \cdot E_1, \rho_l \cdot E_2, y_l \cdot E$.

Step 2. B computes $D_\mathcal{K} = \mathcal{K} \cdot D = S + r'(E_0 + w_l \cdot E_1 - \rho_l \cdot E_2 - y_l \cdot E + D_{x_a} - k' \cdot D)$.

Step 3. B computes the encryption key $\chi = H(k' \cdot D, \mathcal{K} \cdot D)$ and $m' = DEC_\chi(c)$. B checks whether $r \cdot D = H_1(m', D_{x_a}, D_{k'}, D_k, D_\mathcal{K})$? If yes then B accepts the signature. Thus he recovers the message.

5   Security Analysis of MMVS and MGPSS

There are many models for proof of security for any public key scheme [19, 21, 22, 23] but we prove security for present cases in random oracle model [4]. The security of MGPSS relies on the intractability of the Hyperelliptic Curve Gap Diffie-Hellman Problem whereas the security of MMVS relies on the intractability of Gap Diffie-Hellman Problem. Before giving security proofs, we briefly recall such computationally intractable problems.

Discrete Logarithm Problem (DLP)is the base of many public key cryptosystems and has been used to derive many other intractable problems such as *Decisional Diffie-Hellman Problem (DDHP)* [6], *Gap Diffie-Hellman Problem* [20] and Gap Discrete Log Problem (GDLP). We first discuss definitions on a natural multiplicative group then we extend these definitions on an algebraic group.

For a security parameter $\mathfrak{K}'_\mathfrak{p} \in \mathbb{Z}_n$, let $(\mathbb{G}, .)$ be a finite cyclic group of order $n > 2^{\mathfrak{K}'_\mathfrak{p}}$, and let g be a random generator of $\mathbb{G}$. Let O^{DDH} denote a Decision Diffie-Hellman Oracle that solves DDHP i.e. which answers whether a given quadruple $(g, g^{a'}, g^{b'}, g^{c'})$ from $\mathbb{G}$ is a Diffie-Hellman quadruple or not where $a', b', c' \in_R \mathbb{Z}_n$. Given g, g^a, g^b in $\mathbb{G}$ for some $a, b \in_R \mathbb{Z}_n$, finding g^{ab} with the help of a O^{DDH} is called **Gap Diffie Hellman Problem (GDHP)** [20]. The "advantage" of any probabilistic, polynomial-time algorithm $\mathcal{A}$ in solving GDHP in $\mathbb{G}$ is defined as follow:

$$\mathbf{Adv}_{\mathcal{A},\mathbb{G}}^{\text{GDHP}} = \text{Prob}[\mathcal{A}(\mathbb{G}, g, n, g^a, g^b | O^{\text{DDH}}(\cdot, \cdot, \cdot, \cdot)) = g^{ab} \ : \ a, b \in_R \mathbb{Z}_n].$$

The Gap Diffie-Hellman assumption is that for every probabilistic, polynomial time algorithm $\mathcal{A}$, $\mathbf{Adv}_{\mathcal{A},\mathbb{G}}^{\text{GDHP}}$ is negligible. It is a function of the security parameter $\mathfrak{K}'_p$ and can be written as $\mathfrak{negl}(\mathfrak{K}'_p)$. In GDLP attacker, in addition to g^a whose discrete log with respect to a given base g is desired, the attacker is also given access to a restricted DDH oracle in which the first two elements g, g^a of the quadruple are fixed. Further details of these problems can be found in [2, 6, 20].

Some of these definitions can easily be extended to Hyperelliptic curves over finite fields by replacing the group $(G, .)$ by its Jacobian which forms a group under composition-divisor addition. Let $\mathcal{C}$ be a hyperelliptic curve of genus g defined over the finite field F_q of characteristic p and let $J(F_q)$ be the Jacobian of $\mathcal{C}$ of order $\mathfrak{N}'$. Let D be any element of $J(F_q)$. For a security parameter $\mathfrak{K}_p \in \mathbb{N}$, let order of D be $\mathfrak{N} > 2^{\mathfrak{K}_p}$. It is clear that $\mathfrak{N} \mid \mathfrak{N}'$. Given a reduced divisor D of order $\mathfrak{N}$ and the random reduced divisor $\mathfrak{a} \cdot D$, $\mathfrak{b} \cdot D$ and $\mathfrak{c} \cdot D$ in $< D >$ for some $\mathfrak{a}, \mathfrak{b}, \mathfrak{c} \in_R \mathbb{Z}_{\mathfrak{N}}$, the **Hyperelliptic Curve Decisional Diffie-Hellman Problem (HECDDHP)** is to determine if $\mathfrak{a}\mathfrak{b} \cdot D = \mathfrak{c} \cdot D$. If $\mathfrak{a}\mathfrak{b} \cdot D = \mathfrak{c} \cdot D$ then the quadruple $(D, \mathfrak{a} \cdot D, \mathfrak{b} \cdot D, \mathfrak{c} \cdot D)$ in $< D >$ is called an HECDDH quadruple. Let $O^{HECDDH}_{J(F_q)}$ denote a Hyperelliptic Curve Decision Diffie-Hellman Oracle that solve HECDDHP i.e. which answers whether a given quadruple is a Diffie-Hellman quadruple or not. Given a reduced divisor $\mathfrak{a} \cdot D$, $\mathfrak{b} \cdot D$ and $\mathfrak{c} \cdot D$ in $< D >$ for some $\mathfrak{a}, \mathfrak{b}, \mathfrak{c} \in_R \mathbb{Z}_{\mathfrak{N}}$, finding the reduced divisor $\overline{D} = \mathfrak{a}\mathfrak{b} \cdot D$ with the help of a HECDDHP is a Hyperelliptic Curve Diffie-Hellman quadruple or not) is called **Hyperellipic Curve Gap Diffie Hellman Problem (HECGDHP)**. The "advantage" in term of probability and HEC-GDL can also be defined similarly as done for GDHP.

In the following Theorems, we prove that MGPSS is secure under assumption of the hardness of HECGDHP. To prove confidentiality and unforgeability of the scheme, we the follow approach as given by Libert and Quisquater [15, 16]. We also assume that hash functions used in the scheme are modelled as random oracle.

Theorem 5.1. *Assume that an adversary $\mathcal{A}$ is allowed to have a limited access to O^{HECDDH}. If $\mathcal{A}$ has non-negligible advantage ϵ over the $IND-DSC-CCA$ security of the MGPSS when running in a time t and asking q_h and q_{h_1} queries to the random oracle H and H_1 respectively, q_{DSC} queries to DisSignCrypt oracle and q_{DDSC} queries to DisDeSignCrypt oracle then for any $0 \leq \nu \leq \epsilon$, there exists*

- *an algorithm $\mathcal{B}$ that can solve the HECGDHP in the groups $J(F_q)$ with the probability $\epsilon' \geq \epsilon - \nu - q_{DDSC}/2^{\mathfrak{K}_p} - q_{h_1}q_{DDSC}/2^{2\mathfrak{K}_p}$ within time $t' \leq t + O(q_h + q_{h_1} + q_{DDSC})t^{HECDDH}_O$, where t^{HECDDH}_O denotes the time required for running the oracle O^{HECDDH}.*
- *a passive adversary breaking the semantic security of the symmetric key encryption scheme (ENC, DEC) with the advantage ν within time t'.*

Proof. It is given that the adversary has non negligible advantage over the $IND-DSC-CCA$. Our aim is to build an algorithm $\mathcal{B}$ that solves HECGDHP. Algorithm $\mathcal{B}$ starts with a common parameter generation subroutine and then interacts with $\mathcal{A}$ with the public key. Thus $\mathcal{B}$ uses $\mathcal{A}$ as a subroutine to solve HECGDHP. Our aim is to compute $\mathfrak{a}\mathfrak{b} \cdot D$ given $\mathfrak{a} \cdot D$ and $\mathfrak{b} \cdot D$ with the help of O^{HECDDH} oracle. We assume that $(\mathfrak{a} \cdot D, \mathfrak{b} \cdot D)$ is any random instant of HECGDHP. Let $gpk_G = (D_{\beta_0^*}, D_{\beta^*}, D_{\gamma^*}, D_{\mathfrak{b}})$ be challenged public key of any group G and secret key-public key pair of user U be $(sk_U, pk_U) = (x_a, D_{x_a})$. Algorithm $\mathcal{B}$ runs subroutine $\mathcal{A}$ with challenged $gpk_G = (D_{\beta_0^*}, D_{\beta^*}, D_{\gamma^*}, D_{\mathfrak{b}})$. $\mathcal{A}$

adaptively performs the hash queries, DisSignCrypt queries and DisDeSignCrypt queries. As the scheme uses two hash functions H, H_1, $\mathcal{B}$ maintains the lists for handling the queries to keep track of the answers given to random oracles H and H_1. We assume that H-queries are handled using lists L and L' and H_1-queries are handled using list L_1 and L'_1. All the queries are performed as follows:

H-*queries:* When a hash query H is made on the input $(D_{k'_i}, D_{\mathcal{K}_i})$, $\mathcal{B}$ first checks if $(D, D_{k'_i}, D_\mathfrak{b}, D_{\mathcal{K}_i})$ is valid HECDDH quadruple by using O^{HECDDH} oracle. If it is then

- $\mathcal{B}$ checks if $D_{k'} = \mathfrak{a} \cdot D$, and halts outputting $D_{\mathcal{K}_i} = \mathfrak{a}\mathfrak{b} \cdot D$ which is a solution that it was looking for.
- If $D_{k'} \neq \mathfrak{a} \cdot D$ then $\mathcal{B}$ does the following:
  $\mathcal{B}$ checks if L' contains an entry of the form $(D_{k'_i}, \cdots h_i)$. If it contains, $\mathcal{B}$ returns $h_i \in \{0,1\}^\lambda$ and includes $(D_{k'_i}, D_\mathfrak{b}, D_{\mathcal{K}_i}, h_i, 1)$ in the list L. (It may be noted that 1 is indicating here a output of O^{HECDDH} oracle). If there is no entry of the form $(D_{k'_i}, \cdots h_i)$ in the list L', $\mathcal{B}$ selects the random string $h_i \in_R \{0,1\}^\lambda$ and inserts $(D_{k'_i}, D_\mathfrak{b}, D_{\mathcal{K}_i}, h_i, 1)$ in the list L.

If $(D, D_{k'_i}, D_k, D_{\mathcal{K}_i})$ is not a HECDDH quadruple then the random simulator stores the 5-tuple $(D_{k'_i}, D_k, D_{\mathcal{K}_i}, h_i, 0)$.

H_1-*queries:* When a hash query H_1 is made on the input $(m, D_{x_a}, D_{k'_i}, D_\mathfrak{b}, D_{\mathcal{K}_i})$, $\mathcal{B}$ follows the same procedure as in H-queries and maintains the list L'_1 and L_1.

DisSignCrypt queries: $\mathcal{A}$ selects the plaintext m and the group public key $gpk_{G_R} = (D_{\beta_0}, D_\beta, D_\gamma, D_k)$ of the receiver and submits it for DisSignCrypt queries. On receiving (m, gpk_R), $\mathcal{B}$ does the following:

- $\mathcal{B}$ selects k' and computes $\mathcal{K} \cdot D = k'(k \cdot D)$ and $E_3 = k' \cdot D$. It may be noted that $k \cdot D$ has been picked up from the challenged group public key.
- $\mathcal{B}$ simulates the hash functions H and H_1 to obtain $h = H(k' \cdot D, \mathcal{K} \cdot D)$ and $\mathcal{H}_1 = H_1(m, D_{x_a}, D_{k'}, D_k, D_{\mathcal{K}_i})$.
- $\mathcal{B}$ computes $S = \mathcal{K} \cdot D + r'(k' \cdot D - x_a \mathcal{H}_1) \mod N$. Then $\mathcal{B}$ computes $c = ENC_h(m)$. Finally $\mathcal{B}$ computes E, E_0, E_1, E_2, and returns the ciphertext $C =< E, E_0, E_1, E_2,$
  $E_3, S, \mathcal{H}_1, c >$.

DisDeSignCrypt queries: $\mathcal{A}$ submits the pair (C, pk_S) for DisDeSignCrypt queries where $C =< E, E_0, E_1, E_2, E_3, \mathcal{H}_1, S, c >$ denotes the ciphertext and $pk_S = \tilde{D}_{s_k}$ is the public key of the sender. On receiving (C, D_{s_k}), $\mathcal{B}$ computes $\tilde{\mathcal{K}} \cdot \tilde{D}$ using $msk_G = (\tilde{x}_l, \tilde{y}_l, \tilde{\rho}_l)$ and $\tilde{D}_{s_k}$. It may be noted that there are chances that $\mathcal{A}$ has selected the ciphertext randomly in which some of the reduced divisors / sender public key are not the elements of $< D >$. In that case, $\tilde{\mathcal{K}} \cdot \tilde{D}$ and $E_3 = \tilde{D}_{\tilde{k}'}$ will not be the elements of $< D >$ and the ciphertext will be rejected. Thus we assume that all the reduced divisors are present in the ciphertext C and $\tilde{D}_{s_k}$ is the element of $< D >$ (i.e. $\tilde{D}_{s_k} = D_{s_k}, \tilde{D}_{\tilde{k}'} = D_{\tilde{k}'}, \tilde{\mathcal{K}} \cdot \tilde{D} = \tilde{\mathcal{K}} \cdot D$). Now $\mathcal{B}$ checks if the list L contains the unique 5-tuple $(D_{\tilde{k}'}, D_\mathfrak{b}, D_{\tilde{\mathcal{K}}}, h, 1)$.

- If yes, this implies $(D, D_{\tilde{k}'}, D_{\mathfrak{b}}, D_{\tilde{K}})$ is HECDDH quadruple and $H(D_{\tilde{k}'}, D_{\tilde{K}})$ was set to h. Thus $\mathcal{B}$ obtains $\chi = h = H(D_{\tilde{k}'}, D_{\tilde{K}})$. $\mathcal{B}$ then computes $m = DEC_\chi(c)$ and simulates H_1 on the input $(m, D_{s_k}, D_{\tilde{k}'}, D_{\mathfrak{b}}, D_{\tilde{K}})$. Finally $\mathcal{B}$ checks whether $r \cdot D = \mathcal{H}_1 = H_1(m, D_{s_k}, D_{\tilde{k}'}, D_{\mathfrak{b}}, D_{\tilde{K}})$. If yes, $\mathcal{B}$ returns message signature pair (m, S) otherwise rejects the ciphertext.
- If not, $\mathcal{B}$ selects $h \in_R \{0,1\}^\lambda$ and inserts a record $(D_{\tilde{k}'}, \cdots, h)$ in the list L' for answering subsequent H queries on the input $(D_{\tilde{k}'}, D_{\mathfrak{b}}, D_{\tilde{K}}, \cdots h)$. Since $h = H(D_{\tilde{k}'}, D_{\mathfrak{b}}, D_{\tilde{K}}, h)$, $\mathcal{B}$ computes $c = DEC_\chi(m)$ using encryption key $\chi = h$. $\mathcal{B}$ now checks the list L_1' for answering the hash query $H_1(m, D_{s_k}, D_{\beta_0}, D_{\tilde{k}'}, D_{\mathfrak{b}}, D_{\tilde{K}})$, if it does not contain tuple of the form $(m, D_{s_k}, D_{\tilde{k}'}, D_{\mathfrak{b}}, D_{\tilde{K}}, \mathcal{H}_1)$, it is inserted so as to answer subsequent H_1 query. $\mathcal{B}$ now verifies whether

$$r \cdot D = \mathcal{H}_1 = H_1(m, D_{s_k}, D_{\tilde{k}'}, D_{\mathfrak{b}}, D_{\tilde{K}})?.$$

If yes, $\mathcal{B}$ returns (m, S) otherwise rejects the ciphertext.

At the end of the first stage, $\mathcal{A}$ provides $\mathcal{B}$ the two plaintexts m_0 and m_1 which have never been queried to DisSignCrypt together with an arbitrary senders private key x_{sk}(say) and requires a challenge ciphertext built under the group public key $gpk_G = (D_{\beta_0^*}, D_{\beta^*}, D_{\gamma^*}, D_{\mathfrak{b}})$. $\mathcal{B}$ randomly picks $b \in_R \{0,1\}$, binary string $h^* \in \{0,1\}^\lambda$ and $\mathcal{H}_1^* \in_R < D >$. Then $\mathcal{B}$ computes $E_0, E_1, E_2, E_3, S, r'$ as follows:

- $\mathcal{B}$ computes E_0, E_1, E_2, E_3 and r' as described in the section 4.2.
- $\mathcal{B}$ sets $\chi = h$ and $r \cdot D = \mathcal{H}_1$
- $\mathcal{B}$ selects $\mathfrak{a}'$ and sets $S = \mathfrak{a}'\mathfrak{a} \cdot D + r'(\mathfrak{a}' \cdot D - x_{sk}r \cdot D)$.
- $\mathcal{B}$ computes $c = ENC_\chi(m_b)$
- $\mathcal{B}$ sends the tuple: $< E, E_0, F_1, E_2, E_3, S, r \cdot D, c >$ to $\mathcal{A}$ as a challenged ciphertext.

Once $\mathcal{A}$ receives the challenged ciphertext, $\mathcal{A}$ performs second series of queries. These queries are handled as in the first stage. But $\mathcal{A}$ is not allowed to DisDe-SignCrypt query of the challenged ciphertext.

In the distributed signcryption, a symmetric scheme (ENC, DEC) has been used for encryption of message. If this scheme is semantically secure against passive adversary, it is clear that $\mathcal{A}$ will not be able to guess whether challenged cipher text is DisSignCrypt of m_0 or m_1. Thus $\mathcal{A}$'s observation will be independent from the hidden bit $b \in \{0,1\}$ unless $\mathcal{A}$ queries a tuple containing $\mathfrak{a}\mathfrak{b} \cdot D$ to random oracles H or H_1. If $\mathcal{A}$ makes hash queries for H and H_1, then the solution of the HECGDHP will be obtained while answering H and H_1 queries.

As we have assumed that the adversary $\mathcal{A}$ has non-negligible advantage ϵ over $IND - DSC - CCA$, we have to find the probability of success of $\mathcal{B}$ in solving HECGDHP. Let $AskHq$ denote an event that $\mathcal{A}$ asks the hash value of the tuple containing $\mathfrak{a}\mathfrak{b} \cdot D$ during the simulation of H and H_1. As we know that attacker wins the game if $b = b'$ and attacker advantage over the game is defined as $Adv^{IND-DSC-CCA}\mathcal{A}* = 2 \times Pr[b = b'] - 1 \Rightarrow Pr[b = b'] = \frac{(\epsilon+1)}{2}$, we first determine the probability for which $b = b'$. Let Evt_1 be an event in which attacker wins the game i.e. $b = b'$ and Evt_2 be an event in which $\mathcal{A}$ has not asked H and H_1 hash queries. We assume that the simulation of the attack's environment is perfect i.e an attack where $\mathcal{A}$ interacts with oracles. Then the probability for $AskHq$ to happen is the same as in a real attack. Thus we have $Pr[Evt_1] = Pr[Evt_1|Evt_2]Pr[Evt_2] + P[Evt_1|\neg Evt_2]Pr[\neg Evt_2]$, which implies that:

$$Pr[b = b'] = Pr[b = b'|\neg AskHq]Pr[\neg AskHq] + Pr[b = b'|AskHq]Pr[AskHq]$$
$$\leq Pr[b = b'|\neg AskHq](1 - Pr[AskHq]) + Pr[AskHq]$$
$$\leq \frac{(1+\nu)}{2}(1 - Pr[AskHq]) + Pr[AskHq] \leq \frac{1}{2}Pr[AskHq] + \frac{(1+\nu)}{2}$$
$$\Rightarrow \frac{(\epsilon+1)}{2} \leq \frac{1}{2}Pr[AskHq] + \frac{(1+\nu)}{2}$$

Here ν denotes the maximal advantage of any passive adversary against the semantic security of the symmetric key encryption scheme (ENC, DEC). Thus $Pr[AskHq] \geq \epsilon - \nu$.

In case the simulation fails, one needs to handle the only two possibilities. In the first case, when the random challenge ciphertext had been submitted to the DisDeSignCrypt oracle before the challenge phase and in the second case when the simulation is not perfect. The first event will occur with the probability smaller than $q_{DDSC}/2^{\aleph_p}$. In the second event, there is a chance in which DisDeSignCrypt oracle rejects the valid ciphertext. Since the hash function h_1 is used to decide the acceptance of the message. The probability to reject the valid ciphertext is not greater than $q_{h_1}q_{DDSC}/2^{2\aleph_p}$. Thus the success probability of $\mathcal{B} = \epsilon' = Pr[AskHq] - q_{DDSC}/2^{\aleph_p} - q_{h_1}q_{DDSC}/2^{2\aleph_p} \geq \epsilon - \nu - q_{DDSC}/2^{\aleph_p} - q_{h_1}q_{DDSC}/2^{2\aleph_p}$. Hence $\mathcal{B}$ would be able to solve HECGDHP with the success probability $\epsilon' \geq \epsilon - \nu - q_{DDSC}/2^{\aleph_p} - q_{h_1}q_{DDSC}/2^{2\aleph_p}$.

Finally, we compute the running time t' of the algorithm $\mathcal{B}$. On H and H_1 queries, $\mathcal{B}$ runs oracle O^{HECDDH} to check whether given tuple is on HECDH tuple. The oracle is also called by $\mathcal{B}$ on DisDeSignCrypt queries. Thus maximum number of possibilities for which $\mathcal{B}$ runs O^{HECDDH} is proportional to $O(q_h + q_{h_1} + q_{DDSC})$. Thus $\mathcal{B}$ can solve HECGDHP in time $t' \leq t + O(q_h + q_{h_1} + q_{DDSC})t_O^{HECDDH}$.   □

Theorem 5.2. *Let a forger $\mathcal{F}$ be allowed to have a limited access to O^{HECDDH}. If the forger $\mathcal{F}$ has non-negligible advantage ϵ over the $EUF - DSC - CMA$ security of the MGPSS when running in time t, and asking q_h and q_{h_1} queries to the random oracle H and H_1 respectively, q_{DSC} queries to DisSignCrypt oracle and q_{DDSC} queries to DisDeSignCrypt oracle, then there is an algorithm $\mathcal{B}$ that can solve the HECGDHP in groups $J(F_q)$ with the probability $\epsilon' \geq \epsilon - q_{DSC}/2^{\aleph_p}(q_{h_1} + q_{DSC} + q_{DDSC}) - q_{h_1}q_{DDSC}/2^{2\aleph_p} - 1/2^{\aleph_p}$ within time $t' \leq t + O(q_h + q_{h_1} + q_{DDSC})t_O^{HECDDH}$ where t_O^{HECDDH} denotes the time required for running the oracle O^{HECDDH}.*

Proof. We first assume that there exists a forger $\mathcal{F}$ who wins the game of EUF-DSC-CMA as defined in definition 2.2. It would be shown that, we can construct an algorithm $\mathcal{B}$ that solves HECGDHP.

We follow the same procedure as in theorem 5.1. We assume that $(\mathfrak{a} \cdot D, \mathfrak{b} \cdot D)$ is any random instant of HECGDHP. Let $pk_U = D_\mathfrak{b}$ be the challenged public key of any group user U. The forger $\mathcal{F}$ adaptively performs hash queries, DisSignCrypt queries and DisDeSignCrypt queries. All the queries are performed as follows:

H-queries: H queries are handled similar to as in the Theorem 5.1.

H_1-queries: H_1 queries are handled using the list L_1. When the H_1 query is received on the input $(m, D_\mathfrak{b}, D_{k_i'}, D_{k_i}, D_{\mathcal{K}_i})$, $\mathcal{B}$ first checks if the query tuple $(m, D_\mathfrak{b}, D_{k_i'}, D_{k_i},$
$D_{\mathcal{K}_i})$ is already in the list L_1. If it exists, $\mathcal{B}$ returns existing defined value. If not exist then $\mathcal{B}$ picks $r \in_R \mathbb{Z}_N$ and defines $H_1(m, D_\mathfrak{b}, D_{k_i'}, D_{k_i}, D_{\mathcal{K}_i}) = r(\mathfrak{a} \cdot D)$. In this case $\mathcal{B}$ returns $r(\mathfrak{a} \cdot D)$ to $\mathcal{A}$ and updates list L_1 accordingly.

DisSignCrypt queries: $\mathcal{A}$ the selects plaintext m and the group public key $gpk_{G_R} = (D_{\beta_0}, D_\beta, D_\gamma, D_k)$ of receiver and submits it for DisSignCrypt queries. On receiving (m, gpk_{G_R}), $\mathcal{B}$ does the following:

- $\mathcal{B}$ selects k' and computes $\mathcal{K} \cdot D = k'(k \cdot D)$ and $k' \cdot D$.
- $\mathcal{B}$ simulates the hash function H to obtain $h = H(k' \cdot D, \mathcal{K})$.
- $\mathcal{B}$ checks list L_1 if H_1 is already defined on the input $(m, D_\mathfrak{b}, D_{k'}, D_k, D_\mathcal{K})$. In this case, $\mathcal{B}$ outputs 'failure' and halts. Otherwise, $\mathcal{B}$ picks $r \in \mathbb{Z}_N$ and return $\mathcal{H}_1 = r \cdot D$ as an answer of H_1 query and updates the list L_1 accordingly.
- $\mathcal{B}$ computes r' and $S = \mathcal{K} \cdot D + r'(k' \cdot D - \mathfrak{b}r \cdot D)$. Then $\mathcal{B}$ computes $c = ENC_h(m)$. Finally $\mathcal{B}$ computes E, E_0, E_1, E_2, E_3, S and returns the ciphertext $C = <E, E_0, E_1, E_2,$
$E_3, \mathcal{H}_1, S, c>$.

DisDeSignCrypt queries: These queries on the input (C, pk_S) are answered in the similar way as in the Theorem 5.1.

At the end of the first stage, the forger $\mathcal{F}$ provides a ciphertext C^* and a key pair (msk_{G_R}, gpk_{G_R}). $\mathcal{B}$ performs DisDeSignCrypt operation as discussed above on the input of (C^*, msk_{G_R}, pk_U) where $pk_U = D_\mathfrak{b} = \mathfrak{b} \cdot D$ is the challenged public key. If the ciphertext is valid then DisDeSignCrypt(C^*, msk_{G_R}, pk_U) returns the valid message signature pair (m^*, S) for the sender public key $\mathfrak{b} \cdot D$ and $\mathcal{H}_1 = H_1(m^*, D_\mathfrak{b}, D_{k'}, D_k, D_\mathcal{K})$. If $\mathcal{F}$ had not made H_1 query on the input $(m^*, D_\mathfrak{b}, D_{k'}, D_k, D_\mathcal{K})$ during the simulation then $\mathcal{B}$ reports failure and stops. Otherwise, there must be entry in L_1 for $H_1(m^*, D_\mathfrak{b}, D_{k'}, D_k, D_\mathcal{K})$ and it must be in the form of $r^*\mathfrak{a} \cdot D$ for some $r^* \in \mathbb{Z}_N$. The value of $\mathfrak{a}\mathfrak{b} \cdot D$ can be computed using the signature, $kk' \cdot D$ and $k' \cdot D$ as follows:

$$r^{*-1}(k' \cdot D - r'^{-1}(S - k'k \cdot D))$$
$$= r^{*-1}(k' \cdot D - r'^{-1}r'(k' \cdot D - \mathfrak{b} \cdot H_1(m^*, D_\mathfrak{b}, D_{k'}, D_k, D_\mathcal{K})))$$
$$= r^{*-1}(k' \cdot D - (k' \cdot D - \mathfrak{b}r^*\mathfrak{a} \cdot D))$$
$$= r^{*-1}(\mathfrak{b}r^*\mathfrak{a} \cdot D)) = r^{*-1}(r^*\mathfrak{a}\mathfrak{b} \cdot D))$$
$$= \mathfrak{a}\mathfrak{b} \cdot D \bmod N.$$

This yields solution of Diffie-Hellman Problem. Now, we compute the probability of success of $\mathcal{B}$ in solving HECGDHP. We first consider the cases where the simulation fails. Only three situations arise: (i) H_1 is already defined on given input when DisSignCrypt query is made (ii) hash value $H_1(m^*, D_\mathfrak{b}, D_{k'}, D_k, D_\mathcal{K})$ was not asked during the simulation or (iii) simulation is not perfect. Since there is atmost $(q_{h_1} + q_{DSC} + q_{DDSC})$ elements in the list L_1 for each DisSignCrypt query, the probability of the first case can not be greater than $q_{DSC}(q_{h_1} + q_{DSC} + q_{DDSC})/2^{\aleph_\mathfrak{p}}$. The probability that the hash was not asked for during the simulation is at most $1/2^{\aleph_\mathfrak{p}}$. In the last case, the probability when simulation is not perfect can not exceed $q_{DDSC}q_{h_1}/2^{2\aleph}$. As we have assumed that the forger $\mathcal{F}$ has non-negligible advantage ϵ over the $EUF - DSC - CMA$, $\mathcal{B}$ would be able to solve HECGDHP with the success probability $\epsilon' \geq \epsilon - q_{DSC}/2^{\aleph_\mathfrak{p}}(q_{h_1} + q_{DSC} + q_{DDSC}) - q_{h_1}q_{DDSC}/2^{2\aleph_\mathfrak{p}} - 1/2^{\aleph_\mathfrak{p}}$. □

In the following theorems, we give proofs of security of MMVS. Here also we assume that the hash function used are modelled as random oracle.

Theorem 5.3. *Assume that an adversary $\mathcal{A}$ is allowed to have a limited access to O^{DDH}. If $\mathcal{A}$ has non-negligible advantage ϵ over the $IND - DSC - CCA$ security of the MMVS when running in a time T and asking q_h and q_{h_i} ($i = 1, 2$) queries to the random oracle H and H_i respectively, q_{DSC} queries to DisSign-Crypt oracle and q_{DDSC} queries to DisDeSignCrypt oracle then, for any $0 \leq \nu_1 \leq \epsilon_1$, there exist*

- *an algorithm $\mathcal{B}$ that can solve the GDHP in group $\mathbb{G} = \mathbb{Z}_p^*$ with the probability $\epsilon'_1 \geq \epsilon_1 - \nu_1 - q_{DDSC}/2^{\aleph'_\mathfrak{p}}(1 + q_{h_1}/2^{\aleph'_\mathfrak{p}} + q_{h_2}/2^{\aleph'_\mathfrak{p}})$ within time $T' \leq T + O(q_h + q_{h_1} + q_{DDSC})T_O^{DDH}$, where T_O^{DDH} denotes the time required for running the oracle O^{DDH}.*
- *a passive adversary breaking the semantic security of the symmetric key encryption scheme (E, D) with the advantage ν_1 within time T'.*

Proof. Suppose (g^a, g^b) is any random instant of $GDHP$. It is required to compute g^{ab}. The proof is similar to Theorem 5.1. The probability that the simulation is not perfect is atmost $1/2^{2\aleph'_\mathfrak{p}}q_{DDSC}(q_{h_1} + q_{h_2})$.

Theorem 5.4. *Let a forger $\mathcal{F}$ be allowed to have a limited access to O^{DDH}. Assume that $\mathcal{F}$ has non-negligible advantage ϵ over the $EUF - DSC - CMA$ security of the MMVS when running in a time T and asking q_h and q_{h_i} ($i = 1, 2$) queries to the random oracle H and H_i respectively, q_{DSC} queries to Dis-SignCrypt oracle and q_{DDSC} to DisDeSignCrypt oracle. Then there is an algorithm $\mathcal{B}$ that can solve the GDHP in groups $\mathbb{G} = \mathbb{Z}_p^*$ with the probability*

$\epsilon' \geq \epsilon - q_{DSC}/2^{\aleph'_p}(q_{h_1} + q_{DSC} + q_{DDSC}) - (q_{h_1} + q_{h_2})q_{DDSC}/2^{2\aleph_p} - 1/2^{\aleph_p}$ *within time* $T' \leq T + O(q_h + q_{h_1} + q_{DDSC})T_O^{DDH}$ *where* T_O^{DDH} *denotes the time required for running the oracle* O^{DDH}.

Proof. The proof is similar to Theorem 5.2 and is omitted.

6   Conclusion

In this paper, we gave a generic model for distributed signcryption and proposed formal security notions for two security aspects IND-DSC-CCA and EUF-DSC-CMA. We proposed a modified distributed signcryption scheme MMVS (MVS proposed by Mu & Varadharajan) and a modified scheme MGPSS (GPSS proposed by Gupta, Pillai and Saxena) and gave Security proofs of IND-DSC-CCA and EUF-DSC-CMA for both the modified schemes in the random oracle model. Such proofs of security were not there in MVS & GPSS. As far as the complexity of the MMVS and MGPSS is concerned, it is of the same order as that of MVS and GPSS respectively. The communication overheads in modified schemes are also comparable to those in the original schemes. Further work on other security models and security proofs for both schemes MGPSS and MMVS is being carried out.

Acknowledgments. The authors would like to thank Prof. Rana Barua, ISI Kolkata for technical discussions and valuable suggestions. Authors would also like to thank Prof C. E. Veni Madhavan, Prof A. Tripathi, Dr. S S Bedi, Dr. Meena Kumari and N R Pillai for continuous encouragement and support they gave.

References

1. An, J.H., Dodis, Y., Rabin, T.: On the Security of Joint Signature and Encryption. In: Knudsen, L.R. (ed.) EUROCRYPT 2002. LNCS, vol. 2332, pp. 83–107. Springer, Heidelberg (2002)
2. Baek, J., Steinfeld, R., Zheng, Y.: Formal Proofs for the Security of Signcryption. Journal of Cryptology 20, 203–235 (2007)
3. Bao, H., Cao, Z., Qian, H.: On the Security of a Group Signcryption Scheme from Distributed Signcryption Scheme. In: Desmedt, Y.G., Wang, H., Mu, Y., Li, Y. (eds.) CANS 2005. LNCS, vol. 3810, pp. 26–34. Springer, Heidelberg (2005)
4. Bellare, M., Rogaway, P.: Random Oracles Are Practical: A Paradigm for Designing Efficient Protocols. In: Proceedings of the First ACM Conference on Computer and Communications Security, pp. 62–73. ACM Press, New York (1993)
5. Bellare, M., Desai, A., Pointcheval, D., Rogaway, P.: Relations among Notions of Security for Public-Key Encryption Schemes. In: Krawczyk, Y. (ed.) CRYPTO 1998. LNCS, vol. 1462, pp. 26–45. Springer, Heidelberg (1998)
6. Boneh, D.: The Decision Diffie-Hellman Problem. In: Buhler, J.P. (ed.) ANTS 1998. LNCS, vol. 1423, pp. 48–63. Springer, Heidelberg (1998)
7. Boyen, X.: Multipurpose Identity-Based Signcryption: A Swiss Army Knife for Identity-based Cryptography. In: Boneh, D. (ed.) CRYPTO 2003. LNCS, vol. 2729, pp. 383–399. Springer, Heidelberg (2003)

8. Cramer, R., Shoup, V.: A Practical Public Key Cryptosystem Provably Secure against Adaptive Chosen Ciphertext Attack. In: Krawczyk, H. (ed.) CRYPTO 1998. LNCS, vol. 1462, pp. 13–25. Springer, Heidelberg (1998)
9. Cramer, R., Shoup, V.: Design and Analysis of Practical Public-Key Encryption Schemes Secure Against Adaptive Chosen Ciphertext Attack. Report 2001/108, International Association for Cryptographic Research (IACR), ePrint Archive (2001)
10. Goldwasser, S., Micali, S., Rivest, R.: A Digital Signature Scheme Secure against Adaptive Chosen Message Attacks. SIAM Journal of Computing 17(2), 281–308 (1988)
11. Gupta, I., Pillai, N.R., Saxena, P.K.: Distributed Signcryption Scheme on Hyperelliptic Curve. In: Proceedings of the Fourth IASTED International Conference on Communication, Network and Information Security, CNIS 2007, pp. 33–39. Acta Press, Calgary (2007)
12. Julta, C.S.: Encryption Modes with Almost Free Message Integrity. In: Pfitzmann, B. (ed.) EUROCRYPT 2001. LNCS, vol. 2045, pp. 529–544. Springer, Heidelberg (2001)
13. Kwak, D., Moon, S.: Efficient Distributed Signcryption Scheme as Group Signcryption. In: Zhou, J., Yung, M., Han, Y. (eds.) ACNS 2003. LNCS, vol. 2846, pp. 403–417. Springer, Heidelberg (2003)
14. Kwak, D., Moon, S., Wang, G., Deng, R.H.: A Secure Extension of the Kwak-Moon Group Signcryption Scheme. Computer & Security 25, 435–444 (2006)
15. Libert, B., Quisquater, J.: Efficient Signcryption with Key Privacy from Gap Diffie-Hellman Groups. In: Bao, F., Deng, R., Zhou, J. (eds.) PKC 2004. LNCS, vol. 2947, pp. 187–200. Springer, Heidelberg (2004)
16. Libert, B.: New Secure Applications of Bilinear Maps in Cryptography. PhD Thesis, Microelectronics Laboratory Laboratory, Université Catholique de Louvain (2006)
17. Mu, Y., Varadharajan, V., Nguyen, K.Q.: Delegated decryption. In: Walker, M. (ed.) Cryptography and Coding 1999. LNCS, vol. 1746, pp. 258–269. Springer, Heidelberg (1999)
18. Mu, Y., Varadharajan, V.: Distributed signcryption. In: Roy, B., Okamoto, E. (eds.) INDOCRYPT 2000. LNCS, vol. 1977, pp. 155–164. Springer, Heidelberg (2000)
19. Naor, M., Yung, M.: Public-Key Cryptosystems Secure against Chosen Ciphertext Attacks. In: 22nd ACM Symposium on Theory of Computing, pp. 427–437. ACM Press, New York (1990)
20. Okamoto, T., Pointcheval, D.: The Gap-Problems: A New Class of Problems for the Security of Cryptographic Schemes. In: Kim, K. (ed.) PKC 2001. LNCS, vol. 1992, pp. 104–118. Springer, Heidelberg (2001)
21. Schnorr, C.P., Jakobsson, M.: Security of Signed ElGamal Encryption. In: Okamoto, T. (ed.) ASIACRYPT 2000. LNCS, vol. 1976, pp. 73–89. Springer, Heidelberg (2000)
22. Shoup, V.: Sequences of Games, A Tool for Taming Complexity in Security Proofs. Report 2004/332, International Association for Cryptographic Research (IACR) ePrint Archive (2004)
23. Tsiounis, Y., Yung, M.: On the Security of ElGamal Based Encryption. In: Imai, H., Zheng, Y. (eds.) PKC 1998. LNCS, vol. 1431, pp. 117–134. Springer, Heidelberg (1998)
24. Zheng, Y.: Digital Signcryption or How to Achieve Cost (Signature & Encryption) << Cost(Signature) + Cost(Encryption). In: Kaliski, B. (ed.) CRYPTO 1997. LNCS, vol. 1294, pp. 165–179. Springer, Heidelberg (1997)

Identity Based Online/Offline Encryption and Signcryption Schemes Revisited

S. Sharmila Deva Selvi, S. Sree Vivek, and C. Pandu Rangan*

Theoretical Computer Science Laboratory,
Department of Computer Science and Engineering,
Indian Institute of Technology Madras,
Chennai, India
{sharmila,svivek}@cse.iitm.ac.in, prangan@cse.iitm.ac.in.

Abstract. Consider the situation where a low power device with limited computational power has to perform cryptographic operation in order to do secure communication to the base station where the computational power is not limited. The most obvious way is to split each and every cryptographic operations into resource consuming, heavy operations and the fast light weight operations. This concept can be efficiently implemented through online/offline cryptography. In this paper, we show the security weakness of an identity based online offline encryption scheme proposed in ACNS 09 by Liu et al. [9]. The scheme in [9] is the first identity based online offline encryption scheme in the random oracle model, in which the message and recipient are not known during the offline phase. We have shown that this scheme is not CCA secure. We have also proposed a new identity based online offline encryption scheme in which the message and receiver are not known during the offline phase and is efficient than the scheme in [9].

Online/Offline signcryption is a cryptographic primitive where the signcryption process is divided into two phases - online and offline phase. To the best of our knowledge there exists three online/offline signcryption schemes in the literature: we propose various attacks on two of the existing schemes. Then, we present an efficient and provably secure identity based online/offline signcryption scheme. We formally prove the security of the new scheme in the random oracle model.

Keywords: Identity Based Cryptography, Encryption, Signcryption, Confidentiality, Unforgeability, Online/Offline, Cryptanalysis, Random Oracle Model.

1 Introduction

Separating the process of signing or encrypting into two phases namely, online phase and offline phase is the concept of "Online/Offline" cryptography. This notion was first introduced in the context of digital signatures by Even, Goldreich and Micali [5]. Their construction is inefficient as it increases the size of

---

* Currently Head, Indian Statistical Institute, Chennai, India.

M. Joye et al. (Eds.): InfoSecHiComNet 2011, LNCS 7011, pp. 111–127, 2011.
© Springer-Verlag Berlin Heidelberg 2011

each signature by a quadratic factor. Shamir and Tauman [13] proposed an improved version which makes use of a new paradigm called "hash-sign-switch" to design more efficient online/offline signature schemes. During the offline phase, heavy computations like exponentiation and bilinear pairing are done and in the online phase, only light weight integer operations (multiplication and addition) and hashing are performed to make the computations faster. In an online/offline signature scheme the message is not known in the offline phase and in an online/offline encryption scheme both the message and receiver are not known in the offline phase. Thus, online/offline schemes find use in low power devices such as PDA's, sensor networks, hand held devices including mobile phones and smart-cards.

Adi Shamir introduced the concept of identity based cryptography and proposed the first identity based signature scheme. The idea of identity based cryptography is to enable an user to use any arbitrary string that uniquely identifies him as his public key. Identity based cryptography serves as an efficient alternative to Public Key Infrastructure (PKI) based systems. Most of the identity based encryption (IBE) schemes use the costly bilinear pairing operation and the concept of online/offline computation is an important area of research with respect to IBE. The first identity based online/offline encryption scheme was proposed by Guo et al.[7]. It should be noted that, the major difference between online/offline signature and encryption schemes is that, the message and the receiver are not known during the offline phase of encryption schemes. This makes it subtle and interesting to explore for new directions in constructing efficient and elegant online/offline encryption schemes. Few motivating examples for online/offline encryption schemes can be found in [7] and [9].

Related Works

Online/Offline Encryption: Guo et al. [7] have shown natural extension of the IBE of Boneh and Boyen [2] and Gentry [6]. They have also given constructions which efficiently divide the IBE schemes in [2] and [6]. All the schemes are in the standard model. In 2009, Joseph. K. Liu et al. [9] have proposed an identity based online/offline encryption scheme. It was proved to be chosen ciphertext (CCA) secure in the random oracle model and was claimed to be much efficient that the scheme in [7] (obviously true due to random oracle assumption). Recently, Chow et al. in [3] proposed a CPA secure identity based online/offline encryption scheme and have given a KEM (Key Encapsulation Mechanism) based CCA construction. Although they are giving a generic transformation from identity based online/offline KEM (IBOOKEM) to CCA secure identity based online/offline encryption, there is no concrete IBOOKEM scheme discussed in the paper. Hence, we do not compare our results with the results reported in [3].

Online/Offline Signcryption: Confidentiality and authenticity are two fundamental properties offered by public key cryptography which are achieved through encryption schemes and digital signatures respectively. In scenarios where both these properties are needed, a Sign-then-Encrypt approach was used earlier. In 1997, Zheng [17] introduced the concept of signcryption where both these properties are achieved in a single logical step, but in a more efficient way. The notion of online/offline signcryption was first discussed in An et al. [1]. In their paper, they did not give any concrete method, but they have given general security proof notions for signcryption schemes. Zhang et al. [16] extended the work of An et al. [1] and provided a concrete scheme making use of short signatures. However, Zhang's scheme [16] is PKI based scheme and the focus of our paper is on identity based signcryption schemes. Sun et al. [14] were the first to propose an identity based online/offline signcryption scheme. In their paper, they formally defined the identity based online/offline signcryption and its security model. They also proposed a new scheme where the offline computations can be done before the message is available and the online computations are done after the message is received. After this, Sun et al. proposed another generic scheme in [15].

Our Contribution: In this paper, we show that the scheme in [9] is not CCA secure, i.e. an adversary can distinguish the challenge ciphertext by accessing the decryption oracle. Although the authors of [9] (footnote 4) claim that a bug in [9] was identified and presented in the conference, we are unable to trace any record of its presence. In view of this we present the details of the attack here explicitly. We provide a fix for the bug in the scheme and also propose a new efficient construction for identity based online/offline encryption. We prove the new scheme in the random oracle model.

Moreover, to the best of our knowledge there are three online/offline signcryption schemes in the literature: two schemes by sun et al. [15], [14] and one scheme by Liu et al. [8]. In this paper, we point out some weaknesses in the generic scheme by Sun et al. [15] and forgeability attack on the specific scheme by Sun et al [14]. Then, we present a new online/offline identity based signcryption scheme. In our scheme the online phase includes only modular addition operations and an XOR operation. The striking feature of our scheme is that the sender does not require the knowledge of receiver identity as well as the message in the offline phase. The security of the scheme is proved under random oracle model.

2   Preliminaries

2.1   Bilinear Pairing

Let $\mathbb{G}_1$ be an additive cyclic group generated by P, with prime order q, and $\mathbb{G}_2$ be a multiplicative cyclic group of the same order q. Let $\hat{e}$ be a bilinear pairing $\hat{e} : \mathbb{G}_1 \times \mathbb{G}_1 \to \mathbb{G}_2$.

2.2   Computational Assumptions

In this section, we recall the computational assumptions related to bilinear maps[4] that are relevant to the security of our scheme.

Modified BDHI for k values (k-mBDHIP): k-mBDHIP is the bilinear variant of the k-CAA problem. Given $(P, aP, (x_1+a)^{-1}P, ..., (x_k+a)^{-1}P) \in \mathbb{G}_1^{k+2}$

for unknown $a \in Z_q^*$ and known $x_1, ..., x_k \in Z_q^*$, the k-mBDHIP problem is to compute $\hat{e}(P, P)^{(a+x^*)^{-1}}$ for some $x^* \notin \{x_1, ..., x_k\}$.

The advantage of any probabilistic polynomial time algorithm $\mathcal{A}$ in solving the k-mBDHIP problem in $\mathbb{G}_1$ is defined as

$$\begin{aligned} \text{Adv}_{\mathcal{A}}\,^{k-mBDHIP} &= \Pr[\mathcal{A}(P, aP, (x_1 + a)^{-1}P, ..., (x_k + a)^{-1}P, x_1, ..., x_k) \\ &= \hat{e}(P, P)^{(a+x^*)^{-1}} | a, x^* \in_R Z_q^*, x^* \notin \{x_1, ..., x_k\}]. \end{aligned}$$

We say that the k-mBDHIP problem is (t, ϵ) hard if for any t time probabilistic algorithm $\mathcal{A}$, the advantage $\text{Adv}_{\mathcal{A}}\,^{k-mBDHIP} < \epsilon$.

The q-Computation Diffie-Hellman Inverse problem (q-CDHIP): Given an additive group $\mathbb{G}_1$ and a multiplicative group $\mathbb{G}_2$, all with prime order p and $(q + 1)$ tuples $(G, sG, s^2G, ..., s^qG)$, computing $(1/s)P$ is the q-Computation Diffie-Hellman Inverse problem.

The q-Bilinear Diffie-Hellman Inversion problem (q-BDHIP): Given an additive group $\mathbb{G}_1$ and a multiplicative group $\mathbb{G}_2$, all with prime order p and $(q+1)$ tuples $(G, sG, s^2G, ..., s^qG)$, computing $\hat{e}(G, G)^{1/s} \in \mathbb{G}_2$ is the q-Bilinear Diffie-Hellman Inversion problem.

2.3 Identity Based Online/Offline Encryption Schemes(IBOOE)

An identity based online/offline encryption scheme consists of the following algorithms.

Setup(1^κ): Given a security parameter κ, the Private Key Generator(PKG) generates a master private key msk and public parameters $Params$. $Params$ is made public while msk is kept secret by the PKG.

Extract(ID): Given an identity ID, the PKG executes this algorithm to generate the private key D_{ID} corresponding to ID and transmits D_{ID} to the user with identity ID via. secure channel.

Off-Encrypt *(Params)*: To generate the offline share of the encryption, this algorithm is executed without the knowledge of message to be encrypted and the receiver of the encryption. The offline ciphertext is represented as ϕ.

On-Encrypt *(m, ID_A, ϕ)*: For encrypting a message m to user with identity ID_A, any sender can run this algorithm to generate the encryption σ of message m. This algorithm uses a new offline ciphertext ϕ and generates the full encryption σ.

Decrypt(σ, ID_A, D_A): For decryption of σ, the receiver ID_A uses his private key D_A and run this algorithm to get back the message m.

Definition 1. *An ID-Based online/offline encryption scheme is said to be indistinguishable against adaptive chosen ciphertext attacks (IND-IBOOE-CCA2) if no polynomially bounded adversary has a non-negligible advantage in the following game.*

Setup: The challenger $\mathcal{C}$ runs the *Setup* algorithm with a security parameter κ and obtains public parameters *Params* and the master private key *msk*. $\mathcal{C}$ sends *Params* to the adversary $\mathcal{A}$ and keeps *msk* secret.

Phase I: The adversary $\mathcal{A}$ performs a polynomially bounded number of queries. These queries may be adaptive, i.e. current query may depend on the answers to the previous queries.

  - **Key extraction queries(Oracle $\mathcal{O}_{Extract}(ID)$):** $\mathcal{A}$ produces an identity ID and receives the private key D_{ID}.
  - **Decryption queries(Oracle $\mathcal{O}_{Decrypt}(\sigma, ID_A)$):** $\mathcal{A}$ produces the receiver identity $ID_{\mathbb{A}}$ and the ciphertext σ. $\mathcal{C}$ generates the private key D_A and sends the result of $Decrypt(\sigma, ID_A, D_A)$ to $\mathcal{A}$. This result will be *"Invalid"* if σ is not a valid ciphertext or the message m if σ is a valid encryption of message m to ID_A.

Challenge: $\mathcal{A}$ chooses two plaintexts, m_0 and m_1 and the receiver identity $ID_{\mathbb{R}}$, on which $\mathcal{A}$ wishes to be challenged. $\mathcal{A}$ should not have queried for the private key corresponding to $ID_{\mathbb{R}}$ in Phase I. $\mathcal{C}$ chooses randomly a bit $b \in \{0,1\}$, computes $\sigma = Encrypt(m_b, ID_{\mathbb{R}})$ and sends it to $\mathcal{A}$.

Phase II: $\mathcal{A}$ is now allowed to get training as in $Phase - I$. During this interaction, $\mathcal{A}$ is not allowed to extract the private key corresponding to $ID_{\mathbb{R}}$. Also, $\mathcal{A}$ cannot query the decryption oracle with $\sigma, ID_{\mathbb{R}}$ as input, i.e. $\mathcal{O}_{Decrypt}(\sigma, ID_{\mathbb{R}})$.

Guess: Finally, $\mathcal{A}$ produces a bit b' and wins the game if $b' = b$.

$\mathcal{A}$'s advantage is defined as $Adv(\mathcal{A})=2 \left| Pr\left[b' = b \right] - 1 \right|$, where $Pr\left[b' = b \right]$ denotes the probability that $b' = b$.

2.4   Identity Based Online/Offline Signcryption

Identity based online/offline signcryption scheme consists of the following algorithms.

Setup(κ): Given a security parameter κ, the Private Key Generator (PKG) generates the systems public parameters *params* and the corresponding master private key *msk* that is kept secret by PKG.

Key Extract(ID_i): Given a user identity ID_i by user U_i, the PKG computes the corresponding private key D_i and sends D_i to U_i via. a secure channel.

OffSigncrypt$(ID_{\mathbb{S}}, D_{\mathbb{S}})$: Given the sender identity $ID_{\mathbb{S}}$ and the private key $D_{\mathbb{S}}$ of $ID_{\mathbb{S}}$, this algorithm outputs an offline signcryption σ'. This is executed by the sender with identity $ID_{\mathbb{S}}$.

OnSigncrypt$(m, ID_{\mathbb{S}}, ID_{\mathbb{R}}, \sigma')$: This algorithm takes as input a message $m \in \mathcal{M}$, the sender identity $ID_{\mathbb{S}}$, the receiver identity $ID_{\mathbb{R}}$ and the offline signcryption σ' by $ID_{\mathbb{S}}$ as input and outputs the signcryption σ. This algorithm is executed by the sender with identity $ID_{\mathbb{S}}$.

Unsigncrypt$(\sigma, ID_{\mathbb{S}}, ID_{\mathbb{R}}, D_{\mathbb{R}})$: This algorithm takes as input the signcryption σ, sender's identity $ID_{\mathbb{S}}$, the receiver identity $ID_{\mathbb{R}}$ and the receiver's private key

$D_{\mathbb{R}}$ as input and produces the plaintext m, if σ is a valid signcryption of m from the sender $ID_{\mathbb{S}}$ to $ID_{\mathbb{R}}$ or "Invalid" otherwise.

Definition 2. *(Confidentiality) An identity based online/offline signcryption (IBOOSC) is indistinguishable against adaptive chosen ciphertext attacks (IND-IBOOSC-CCA2) if there exists no polynomially bounded adversary having non-negligible advantage in the following game:*

Setup Phase: The challenger $\mathcal{C}$ runs the **Setup** algorithm with the security parameter κ as input and sends the system parameters **params** to the adversary $\mathcal{A}$ and keeps the master private key **msk** secret.

Phase-I: $\mathcal{A}$ performs polynomially bounded number of queries to the oracles provided to $\mathcal{A}$ by $\mathcal{C}$. The description of the queries in the first phase are listed below:

- **Key Extract query**: $\mathcal{A}$ produces an identity ID_i and receives the private key D_i corresponding to ID_i.
- **Signcryption query**: $\mathcal{A}$ produces a message m, the sender identity $ID_{\mathbb{S}}$, and the receiver identity $ID_{\mathbb{R}}$ to the challenger $\mathcal{C}$. $\mathcal{C}$ computes $ID_{\mathbb{S}}$'s private key $D_{\mathbb{S}}$ and runs the algorithm **OffSigncrypt**($ID_{\mathbb{S}}$, $D_{\mathbb{S}}$) to obtain an offline signcryption σ'. Finally $\mathcal{C}$ returns $\sigma = $ **OnSigncrypt**($m, ID_{\mathbb{R}}, \sigma'$) to $\mathcal{A}$.
- **Unsigncryption query**: $\mathcal{A}$ produces the signcryption σ, the sender identity $ID_{\mathbb{S}}$, and the receiver identity $ID_{\mathbb{R}}$ to $\mathcal{C}$. $\mathcal{C}$ generates the private key $D_{\mathbb{R}}$ by querying the **Key Extraction oracle**. $\mathcal{C}$ unsigncrypts σ using $D_{\mathbb{R}}$ and returns m if σ is a valid signcryption from $ID_{\mathbb{S}}$ to $ID_{\mathbb{R}}$, else outputs "Invalid".

$\mathcal{A}$ can present its queries adaptively, i.e. every request may depend on the response to the previous queries.

Challenge: $\mathcal{A}$ chooses two plaintexts $\{m_0, m_1\} \in \mathcal{M}$ of equal length and ID_A and ID_B as the sender and receiver identities on which $\mathcal{A}$ wishes to be challenged. The restriction is that $\mathcal{A}$ should not have queried the private key corresponding to ID_B in Phase-I. $\mathcal{C}$ now chooses a bit $\bar{\delta} \in_R \{0, 1\}$ and computes the challenge signcryption σ^* of $m_{\bar{\delta}}$ and sends σ^* to $\mathcal{A}$.

Phase-II: $\mathcal{A}$ performs polynomially bounded number of requests just like the Phase-I, with the restrictions that $\mathcal{A}$ cannot make **Key Extraction query** on ID_B and should not query for unsigncryption query on C^*.

Guess: Finally, $\mathcal{A}$ produces a bit $\bar{\delta}'$ and wins the game if $\bar{\delta}' = \bar{\delta}$. The success probability is defined by:

$$\text{Succ}_{\mathcal{A}}{}^{IND-IBOOSC-CCA2}(\kappa) = \tfrac{1}{2} + \epsilon$$

Here, ϵ is called the advantage for the adversary in the above game.

Definition 3. *(Unforgeability) An identity based online/offline signcryption scheme (IBOOSC) is said to be existentially unforgeable against adaptive chosen messages attacks (EUF-IBOOSC-CMA) if no polynomially bounded adversary has a non-negligible advantage in the following game:*

Setup Phase: The challenger runs the **Setup** algorithm with a security parameter κ and gives the system parameters **params** to the adversary $\mathcal{A}$ and keeps **msk** secret.

Training Phase: $\mathcal{A}$ performs polynomially bounded number of queries as described in Phase-I of **Definition 2**. The queries may be adaptive, i.e. the current query may depend on the previous query responses.

Existential Forgery: Finally, $\mathcal{A}$ produces a new triple $(ID_\mathbb{A}, ID_\mathbb{B}, C^*)$ (i.e. a triple that was not produced by the signcryption oracle), where the private key of $ID_\mathbb{A}$ was not queried in the **training phase**. $\mathcal{A}$ wins the game if the result of the unsigncryption of $(ID_\mathbb{A}, ID_\mathbb{B}, C^*)$ is $\neq$ "Invalid", in other words C^* is a valid signcrypt of some message $m \in \mathcal{M}$.

3 Review and Attack of IBOOE in [9]

In this section we review the identity based online/offline encryption scheme proposed in [9].

3.1 Review of of Liu et al.'s Scheme (L-IBOOE) [9]

Let $\mathbb{G}$ and $\mathbb{G}_T$ be groups of prime order q, and let $\hat{e}{:}\mathbb{G} \times \mathbb{G}_T \to \mathbb{G}_T$ be the bilinear pairing. We use a multiplicative notation for the operation in $\mathbb{G}$ and $\mathbb{G}_T$.

Setup: The PKG selects a generator $P \in \mathbb{G}$ and randomly chooses $s, w \in \mathbb{Z}_q^*$. It sets $P_{pub} = sP$, $P_{pub}' = s^2 P$ and $W = (w+s)^{-1}P$. Define $\mathcal{M}$ to be the message space. Let $n_M = |\mathcal{M}|$. Let $H_1{:}\{0,1\}^* \to \mathbb{Z}_q^*$ $H_2{:}\{0,1\}^* \times \mathbb{G}_T \to \mathbb{Z}_q^*$ and $H_3{:}\{0,1\}^* \to \{0,1\}^{n_M}$ be two cryptographic hash functions. The public parameters $Params$ and master private key msk are given by,

$$Params = \langle \mathbb{G}, \mathbb{G}_T, q, P_{pub}, P_{pub}', W, w, \mathcal{M}, H_1, H_2, H_3 \rangle \ msk = s.$$

Extract(ID):
- $q_{ID} = H_1(ID)$
- $D_{ID} = \dfrac{1}{q_{ID} + s} P.$

Off-Encrypt($Params$):
- $u, x, \alpha, \beta, \gamma, \delta \in_R \mathbb{Z}_q^*$
- $U = W - uP$
- $R = \hat{e}(wP + P_{pub}, P)^x$
- $T_0 = x(w \ \alpha P + (w + \gamma)P_{pub} + P_{pub}')$
- $T_1 = xw\beta P.$
- $T_2 = x\delta P_{pub}.$
- Output the offline ciphertext
  $\phi = \langle u, x, \alpha, \beta, \gamma, \delta, U, R, T_0, T_1, T_2 \rangle.$

On-Encrypt(m, ID_A, ϕ):
- $t_1 = \beta^{-1}(H_1(ID_A) - \alpha) \bmod q$
- $t_2 = \delta^{-1}(H_1(ID_A) - \gamma) \bmod q$
- $t = H_2(m, R)x + u \bmod q$
- $c = H_3(R) \oplus m$
- Output the ciphertext
  $\sigma = \langle U, T_0, T_1, T_2, t, t_1, t_2, c \rangle$

Decrypt(σ, ID_A, D_A):
- $R = \hat{e}(T_0 + t_1 T_1 + t_2 T_2, D_A)$
- $m = c \oplus H_3(R)$
- and if $R^{H_2(m,R)} \overset{?}{=} \hat{e}(tP + U, wP + P_{pub}) \hat{e}(P,P)^{-1}$, output m else output $\bot$

3.2   Attack on Confidentiality

[1]During the confidentiality game, after the completion of Phase-1 of training, the adversary $\mathcal{A}$ picks two messages, (m_0, m_1) of equal length and an identity $ID_{\mathbb{R}}(D_{\mathbb{R}}$ is not known to $\mathcal{A})$, and submits them to $\mathcal{C}$. $\mathcal{C}$ chooses a bit $b \in_R \{0,1\}$, generates the challenge ciphertext $\sigma^* = \langle U, T_0, T_1, T_2, t_1', t_2', t, c \rangle$ of message m_b and gives σ^* to $\mathcal{A}$. Now, we show that $\mathcal{A}$ can cook up another valid ciphertext $\delta = (U^*, T_0^*, T_1^*, T_2^*, t_1^*, t_2^*, t^*, c^*)$ as given below:

- Chooses $r^*, t_1^*, t_2^* \in_R \mathbb{Z}_q^*$.
- Computes $U^* = U - r^* P = W - (u + r^*)P$.
- Chooses $T_1^*, T_2^* \in_R \mathbb{G}$.
- Computes $T_0^* = T_0 - (t_1^* T_1^* + t_2^* T_2^*) + (t_1 T_1 + t_2 T_2) = x(w + s)(q_A + s)P - (t_1^* T_1^* + t_2^* T_2^*)$ (since $T_0 + t_1 T_1 + t_2 T_2 = x(w + s)(q_A + s)P$).
- Computes $t^* = t + r^* \bmod q$
- Sets $c^* = c$
- Now, $\mathcal{A}$ queries the decrypt oracle with δ as input during $Phase - 2$ of training. Here, the relations between σ^* and δ are $R = R^* = \hat{e}(P,P)^{(w+s)x}$ and $c = c^*$. Hence, the decryption of δ will give the message $m_b = c \oplus H_3(R) = c^* \oplus H_3(R^*)$. So, $\mathcal{A}$ can obtain m_b by constructing δ from σ^* and querying the decrypt oracle with δ as input (which is allowed in the security model of [9], i.e. δ is totally different from the challenge ciphertext). The only restriction for $\mathcal{A}$ during Phase - 2 is that $\mathcal{A}$ should not query the decryption of the challenge ciphertext σ^* and the extract of $ID_{\mathbb{R}}$. Also, it should be noted that the check $R^{* H_2(m_b, R^*)} \stackrel{?}{=} \hat{e}(t^* P + U^*, wP + P_{pub}) \, \hat{e}(P,P)^{-1}$ should hold.

Proof of Correctness: The equality of R and R^* can be shown by,

$$
\begin{aligned}
R^* &= \hat{e}(T_0^* + t_1^* T_1^* + t_2^* T_2^*, D_R) \\
&= \hat{e}(x(w + s)(q_R + s)P - (t_1^* T_1^* + t_2^* T_2^*) + t_1^* T_1^* + t_2^* T_2^*, D_R) \\
&= \hat{e}(x(w + s)(q_R + s)P, D_R) \\
&= \hat{e}(x(w + s)(q_R + s)P, \frac{1}{q_R + s}P) \\
&= \hat{e}(x(w + s)P, P) = \hat{e}((w + s)P, xP) = \hat{e}(wP + P_{pub}, P)^x = R
\end{aligned}
$$

Also, the derived ciphertext δ will pass the verification test, which can be shown as,

$$
\begin{aligned}
\hat{e}(t^* P + U^*, wP + P_{pub})\hat{e}(P,P)^{-1} &= \hat{e}((t + r^*)P + U - r^* P, wP + P_{pub})\hat{e}(P,P)^{-1} \\
&= \hat{e}((xH_2(m_b, R^*) + u + r^*)P, wP + P_{pub}) \\
&\quad \hat{e}(W - (u + r^*)P, wP + P_{pub})\hat{e}(P,P)^{-1} \\
&= \hat{e}(xH_2(m_b, R)P + W, wP + P_{pub})\hat{e}(P,P)^{-1} \text{ (Since } R^* = R) \\
&= \hat{e}(xH_2(m_b, R)P, wP + P_{pub})\hat{e}(W, wP + P_{pub})\hat{e}(P,P)^{-1} \\
&= \hat{e}(xH_2(m_b, R)P, wP + P_{pub})\hat{e}(P,P)\hat{e}(P,P)^{-1} \\
&= \hat{e}(wP + P_{pub}, P)^{xH_2(m_b, R)} = R^{H_2(m_b, R)} = R^{* H_2(m_b, R^*)}
\end{aligned}
$$

---

[1] Although the authors of [9] have claimed that an attack was discussed in a private communication, to the best of our knowledge, it is not recorded anywhere. The attack is subtle and non-trivial. We report the same here.

3.3   A Possible Fix for the Weakness in [9]

The security weakness of [9] shown in section 3.2 can be fixed by providing the modifications to the $On - Encrypt$ algorithm and the definition of the hash function H_2 allowing all other algorithms unaltered. The improved On-Encrypt protocol can be given by,

On-Encrypt(m, ID_A, ϕ)

- $t_1 = \beta^{-1}(H_1(ID_A)- \alpha) \bmod q$
- $t_2 = \beta^{-1}(H_1(ID_A)- \gamma) \bmod q$
- $t = H_2(m, U, R, T_0, T_1, T_2, t_1, t_2)x+u \bmod q$
- $c = H_3(R)\oplus m$
- Output the ciphertext $\sigma = \langle U, T_0, T_1, T_2, t, t_1, t_2, c\rangle$

The hash function H_2 is redefined as $H_2 : \{0,1\}^* \times \mathbb{G}_T \times \mathbb{G}^3 \times \mathbb{Z}_q^* \times \mathbb{Z}_q^* \to \mathbb{Z}_q^*$

4   The New IBOOE

In this section we provide a new identity based online/offline encryption scheme (New-IBOOE), which is more efficient than the fixed version of [9].

4.1   The Scheme

Let $\mathbb{G}$ be a cyclic additive group and $\mathbb{G}_T$ be a cyclic multiplicative group. Both the groups have prime order, q and let $\hat{e}{:}\mathbb{G} \times \mathbb{G} \to \mathbb{G}_T$ be the bilinear pairing. The algorithms in the scheme are described below:

Setup: The PKG selects a generator $P \in_R \mathbb{G}$ and randomly chooses $s \in \mathbb{Z}_q^*$. It computes $P_{pub} = sP$ and $\alpha = \hat{e}(P, P)$. Let $\mathcal{M}$ denotes the message space and $n_M = | \mathcal{M} |$. Let $H_1 : \{0,1\}^* \to \mathbb{Z}_q^*$, $H_2 : \{0,1\}^* \times \mathbb{G}_T \times \mathbb{G}^4 \to \mathbb{Z}_q^*$ and $H_3 : \{0,1\}^* \to \{0,1\}^{n_M}$ be three cryptographic hash functions. The public parameters $Params$ and master private key msk are given as:

$$Params= \langle \mathbb{G}, \mathbb{G}_T, q, P_{pub}, \alpha, \mathcal{M}, H_1, H_2, H_3\rangle \text{ and } msk= s.$$

Extract(ID_A):
- $q_A = H_1(ID_A)$
- $D_A = \dfrac{1}{q_A + s}P.$

Off-Encrypt$(Params)$:
- $u, x, a, \hat{b} \in_R \mathbb{Z}_q^*$
- $U = uP$
- $R = \alpha^x$
- $\beta = H_3(R)$
- $T_1 = a^{-1}xP$
- $T_2 = x(\hat{b} + s)P.$
- Outputs the offline ciphertext
  $\phi = \langle u, x, a, \hat{b}, U, R, T_1, T_2, \beta\rangle.$

On-Encrypt(m, ID_A, ϕ):
- $t_1 = a(q_A - \hat{b}) \bmod q$
- $t_2 = H_2(m, R, U, T_1, T_2, t_1)x + u \bmod q$
- $c = \beta \oplus m$
- Outputs the ciphertext
  $\sigma = \langle U, T_1, T_2, t_1, t_2, c\rangle.$

Decrypt(σ, ID_A, D_A):
- $R = \hat{e}(T_2 + t_1 T_1, D_A)$
- $m = c \oplus H_3(R)$
- $h = H_2(m, R, U, T_1, T_2, t_1)$
- If $R^h \overset{?}{=} \hat{e}(t_2 P - U, P)$, output m else output $\perp$

It should be noted that the offline encryption process is carried out before knowing the message m as well as the receiver identity ID_A. These are the attracting features of our scheme. The correctness of the verification of the equation $R^h \overset{?}{=} \hat{e}(t_2 P - U, P)$ done during the decryption process is given below:

$$
\begin{aligned}
\text{LHS} = R^h &= \hat{e}(T_2 + t_1 T_1, D_A)^h \\
&= \hat{e}(x(\hat{b} + s)P + a(q_A - \hat{b})a^{-1} x P, \tfrac{1}{q_A + s} P)^h \\
&= \hat{e}(x\hat{b}P + xsP + q_A x P - \hat{b}xP, \tfrac{1}{q_A + s} P)^h \\
&= \hat{e}(x(s + q_A)P, \tfrac{1}{q_A + s} P)^h \\
&= \hat{e}(xP, P)^h
\end{aligned}
$$

$$
\text{RHS} = \hat{e}(t_2 P - U, P) = \hat{e}((hx + u)P - U, P) = \hat{e}(hxP + uP - U, P) = \hat{e}(xP, P)^h
$$

Since LHS=RHS, the verification of a well formed ciphertext holds.

Theorem 1. *If there exists an adversary $\mathcal{A}$ that breaks the IND-IBOOE-CCA2 security of the New-IBOOE scheme then, there exists an algorithm $\mathcal{C}$ to solve the k-modified Bilinear Diffie Hellman Inversion Problem (k-mBDHIP).*

Please refer the proof of this theorem in the full version of the paper [11].

5   Review and Attack of IBOOSC Schemes

In this section, we recall the identity based online/offline schemes by Sun et al. presented in [14] and [15]. We demonstrate attacks on both these schemes in this section.

5.1   Scheme by Sun et al.[14]

Review of the Scheme: The scheme consists of five algorithms - **Setup, Extract, OffSigncrypt, Onsigncrypt** and **UnSigncrypt**. A secure symmetric key encryption scheme $(\mathcal{E}, \mathcal{D})$ is employed in this scheme where $\mathcal{E}$ and $\mathcal{D}$ are the secure symmetric encryption and decryption algorithms respectively.

Setup: Given security parameters κ, n and $\mathbb{G}_1, \mathbb{G}_2$ of order q and generator P of $\mathbb{G}_1$, PKG picks a random $s \in \mathbb{Z}_q^*$, ands sets $P_{pub} = sP$. Choose cryptographic hash functions $H_0: \{0, 1\}^* \to \mathbb{G}_1$, $H_1: \{0, 1\}^* \times \mathbb{G}_1 \times \mathbb{G}_1 \to \mathbb{Z}_q^*$, $H_2: \mathbb{Z}_q^* \to \{0, 1\}^n$, $H_3: \mathbb{G}_2 \to \mathbb{Z}_q^* \times \mathbb{Z}_q^*$. The system parameters are $\langle P, P_{pub}, H_0, H_1, H_2, H_3 \rangle$. The master secret key is s.

Key Extract: Given an identity ID_i, the algorithm computes the public key as $Q_i = H_0(ID_i)$ and the corresponding private key as $D_i = sH_0(ID_i)$. The private key is returned to the user via a secure channel.

OffSigncrypt: To send a message m to user $U_\mathbb{R}$ with identity $ID_\mathbb{R}$, the sender $U_\mathbb{S}$ with identity $ID_\mathbb{S}$ follows the steps below.

1. Computes $Q_\mathbb{R} = H_0(ID_\mathbb{R})$.
2. Picks random x, y $\in \mathbb{Z}_q^*$, and sets $k = H_3(e(P_{pub}, Q_\mathbb{R})^x)$.

3. Splits k into k_1, k_2 such that $k_1 \in \mathbb{Z}_q^*$ and $k_2 \in \mathbb{Z}_q^*$, then stores them for future use.
4. Using the private key $D_\mathbb{S}$, $U_\mathbb{S}$ outputs the offline signcryption (S, U), where $S = D_\mathbb{S} - x P_{Pub}$, $U = (y - k_1)P$; also stores x, y for future use.

OnSigncrypt: Given a message $m \in \mathbb{Z}_q^*$, and an off-line signcryption (S, U), this algorithm sets $k_3 = H_2(k_2)$ first. The message encryption is done with k_3 and a symmetric-key encryption algorithm $\mathcal{E}$ such as AES. The ciphertext is $c = \mathcal{E}_{k_3}(m)$. Computes $r = H_1(c, S, U)$ and on-line signcryption $\sigma = rx + y$; returns signcryption (c, S, U, σ).

UnSigncrypt: Given a signcryption (c, S, U, σ), the receiver with identity $ID_\mathbb{R}$ does the following:

1. Computes $T = e(-S, Q_\mathbb{R})e(Q_\mathbb{S}, D_\mathbb{R})$.
2. Sets $k = H_3(T)$,then splits k into k_1, k_2.
3. Sets $k_3 = H_2(k_2)$ and decrypts the message $\mathcal{D}_{k_3}(c) = m$. m is valid if $e(\sigma P_{pub} + rS, P) \stackrel{?}{=} e(U + k_1 P + r Q_{ID_A}, P_{pub})$ holds, where $r = H_1(c, S, U)$.

Existential Forgeability of the Scheme: This scheme is not secure against existential forgery. A forger $\mathcal{F}$ can forge a signcryption for an identity whose private key is not queried. This can be done as follows:

- $\mathcal{F}$ sets an identity ID_A as the target identity for which the forged signcryption is to be generated.
- During unforgeability game, a forger is allowed to extract the private key of receiver (used for generating the forgery) according to the model given by Sun et al [14]
- During the Training phase, $\mathcal{F}$ asks for the signcryption of a message m from ID_A to an arbitrary receiver ID_B. Let the response be (c, S, U, σ). On receiving this, $\mathcal{F}$ computes the following
  - Gets the private key of ID_B using a Key_Extract query on ID_B.
  - Computes $T = \hat{e}(-S, Q_B)\hat{e}(Q_A, D_B)$
  - Sets $k = H_3(T)$ and divides k into two parts: k_1 and k_2.
- $\mathcal{F}$ can now modify the above ciphertext (c, S, U, σ) so that it becomes a valid signcryption on some message m' from ID_A to an arbitrary ID_C. For achieving this $\mathcal{F}$ computes following:
  - $T' = \hat{e}(-S, Q_C)\hat{e}(Q_A, D_C)$
  - $k' = H_3(T')$ and it is divided into two parts: k_1' and k_2'
  - $\Delta k = k_1' - k_1$ and $\sigma' = rx + y + \Delta k$
  - Outputs the new signcryption (c, S, U, σ')

This will pass through the verification because

LHS$= \hat{e}(\sigma' P_{pub} + rS, P)$
$\quad = \hat{e}((rx + y + \Delta k)P_{pub} + r(D_A - x P_{pub}), P)$
$\quad = \hat{e}((y + \Delta k)P_{pub} + rs Q_A, P)$

$$= \hat{e}((y + k_1' - k_1)P + rQ_A, sP)$$
$$= \hat{e}((y - k_1)P + k_1'P + rQ_A, P_{pub})$$
$$= \hat{e}(U + k_1'P + rQ_A, P_{pub})$$
$$= \text{RHS}$$

5.2   Generic Scheme by Sun et al. [15]

Review of the Scheme: We review the generic online/offline signcryption scheme by Sun et al. [15] in this section.

Systems Parameter Generation: Let t be a prime power, and $E(\mathbb{F}_t)$ an elliptic curve over finite field $\mathbb{F}_t$. Let $\#E(\mathbb{F}_t)$ be the number of points of $\#E(\mathbb{F}_t)$, and P be a point of $E(\mathbb{F}_t)$ with prime order q where $q|\#E(\mathbb{F}_t)$. $\mathbb{G}_1$ is the subgroup generated by P. $\mathbb{G}_2$ is a finite group of order q. Choose cryptographic hash function $H_1 : \mathbb{G}_2 \rightarrow \{0,1\}^n$. Let $(\mathcal{L}, \mathcal{H})$ be the chameleon hash family, which will be sent to the designated user on request, based on the discrete logarithm assumption and $(\mathcal{G}, \mathcal{S}, \mathcal{V})$ be any identity-based signature scheme. The system parameters are $SP = (\#E(\mathbb{F}_t), t, q, P, \mathbb{G}_1, \mathbb{G}_2, (\mathcal{G}, \mathcal{S}, \mathcal{V}), H_1)$.

Key Extract: Given an identity ID, run the key extract algorithm of the original identity-based signature scheme to obtain the private/public key pair (D_{ID}, Q_{ID}). On input 1^k, the sender runs the key generation algorithm of the trapdoor hash family $(\mathcal{L}, \mathcal{H})$ to obtain the hash/trapdoor key pair $(Y = xP, x)$.

Assume user $U_\mathbb{S}$ with identity $ID_\mathbb{S}$ sends m to user $U_\mathbb{R}$ with identity $ID_\mathbb{R}$. $U_\mathbb{S}$ obtains private key and hash/trapdoor key $\{D_\mathbb{S}, Y, x\}$. $U_\mathbb{R}$ obtains private key $D_\mathbb{R}$. $\{Q_\mathbb{S}, Q_\mathbb{R}\}$ are public to both of them.

OffSigncrypt: Offline signcryption is done as follows:

- Choose at random $(m, r) \in_R \mathcal{M} \times \mathcal{R}$, where $\mathcal{M}$ is a message space and $\mathcal{R}$ is a finite space, and compute the chameleon hash value $h = H_Y(m', r') = m'P + r'Y$.
- Run the signing algorithm $\mathcal{S}$ with the signing key $D_\mathbb{S}$ to sign the hash value h. Let the output be $\sigma = S_{D_\mathbb{S}}(h||H_Y)$, where H_Y is the description of the chameleon hash.
- Choose at random $y \in_R Z_q^*$ and compute $X = yP$ then compute $\omega = e(yP_{pub}, Q_\mathbb{R})$. Finally set $y' = H_1(\omega)$.
- Store the pair (m', r') and y' for future use.

OnSigncrypt: Online signcryption is done as follows:

- For a given message m, retrieve from the memory x^{-1} and the pair (m, r).
- Compute $r = x^{-1}(m' - m) + r' \mod q$.
- The message encryption is done with y' and a symmetric-key encryption algorithm such as AES. The ciphertext is $c = Enc_{y'}(\sigma||ID_\mathbb{S}||m||r||H_Y)$.
- Final ciphertext is (c, X).

Unsigncrypt: Given ciphertext (c, X), unsigncryption is done as follows:

- Compute $\omega = e(X, d_{ID_B})$ and $y' = H_1(\omega)$.
- Decrypt c as $\sigma||ID_\mathbb{S}||m||r||H_Y = Dec_{y'}(c)$.
- Compute $h = H_Y(m, r) = mP + rY$.
- Verify that σ is indeed a signature of the value $h||H_Y$ with respect to the verification key $Q_\mathbb{S}$.

Attack on the Scheme: In the scheme proposed by Sun et al. [15], there is no binding between the encryption and the signature. Therefore, a signcryption on a message m from ID_A to ID_B can be changed to a valid signcryption on the same message m from ID_A to ID_C. This can be done as follows:

- Get the signcryption of message m from the sender ID_A to receiver ID_B and decrypt it using the secret key D_B of ID_B to get $\sigma||ID_A||m||r||H_Y$.
- Choose $\eta \in_R Z_q^*$ and compute $\omega^* = \hat{e}(P_{pub}, Q_C)^\eta$ and set $X^* = \eta P$ and $y^* = H_1(\omega)$.
- Compute $c^* = Enc_{y^*}(\sigma||ID_A||m||r||H_Y)$
- Output the signcryption as (c^*, X^*)

Note that Q_C is the public key of the user with identity ID_C whose private key is not known. The new signcryption (c^*, X^*) is a valid signcryption from ID_A to ID_C.

6   The New IBOOSC

In this section, we present a provably secure identity based online/offline sign-cryption scheme. It should be noted that the scheme presented in this section is more efficient than the naive combination of online/offline identity based signature and online/offline identity based encryption because, we have considered the case where the receiver identity is not known during the offline phase and more over it is explicit that just combining a signature scheme and an encryption scheme is not signcryption but signcryption should involve cheap computation than the naive combination. The size of the ciphertext and the computations done during the unsigncryption process are bulky than normal signcryption but we consider only the computation complexity of the online signcryption algorithm where we have only modular addition, multiplication and bit-wise exclusive-OR operations. This is considered as the highlight of any online/offline primitive. The IBOOSC scheme consists of the following algorithms:

Setup(1^κ): Given the security parameter 1^κ as input, PKG chooses two groups $\mathbb{G}_1$, $\mathbb{G}_2$ of prime order q, a bilinear map $\hat{e}$: $\mathbb{G}_1 \times \mathbb{G}_1 \rightarrow \mathbb{G}_2$ and a generator $P \in_R \mathbb{G}_1$. The PKG chooses $s \in_R Z_q^*$ and sets master secret key $msk = s$ and also sets master public key $P_{pub} = sP$. PKG then computes $\alpha = \hat{e}(P, P)$ and defines five cryptographic hash functions:

- H_1: $\{0,1\}^* \rightarrow \mathbb{G}_1$.
- H_2: $\mathbb{G}_1 \times \mathbb{G}_1 \times \mathbb{G}_1 \times \{0,1\}^{n_1} \times \{0,1\}^* \rightarrow Z_q^*$.
- H_3: $\{0,1\}^{n_1} \times \{0,1\}^* \times \mathbb{G}_1 \{0,1\}^* \rightarrow Z_q^*$.
- H_4: $\mathbb{G}_2 \rightarrow \{0,1\}^{n_1+n_m}$. where n_m is the message size n_1 is the number of random bits concatenated to message.
- H_5: $\{0,1\}^{n_m} \times \mathbb{G}_2 \times \{0,1\}^{n_1} \times Z_q^* \times Z_q^* \times \{0,1\}^{n_1+n_m} \times \{0,1\}^* \times \{0,1\}^* \rightarrow Z_q^*$.

The public parameters $Params$ of the system are set to be $Params = \langle \mathbb{G}_1, \mathbb{G}_2, \hat{e}, P, R, P_{pub}, H_1, H_2, H_3, H_4, H_5, \alpha \rangle$.

Key Extract(ID_i): On input of identity ID_i of user U_i, the private key D_i is computed as $D_i = (\frac{1}{q_i+s})P)$, where $q_i = H_1(ID_i)$. D_i is given to user by PKG via. secure channel.

Off-Signcrypt($ID_\mathbb{S}$, $D_\mathbb{S}$): This algorithm is run by the sender $U_\mathbb{S}$ with identity $ID_\mathbb{S}$ for sending any message to any receiver. Note that the sender carries out these computations without the knowledge message and receiver information.

1. Selects $\delta \in_R \{0,1\}^{n_1}$ and $b, x, y, z, r \in_R \mathbb{Z}_q^*$.
2. Computes $U_1 = \alpha^r \in \mathbb{G}_2$, $U_2 = yP \in \mathbb{G}_1$ and $U_3 = zP \in \mathbb{G}_1$.
3. Computes $V = (r + h_2)D_\mathbb{S} \in \mathbb{G}_1$, where $h_2 = H_2(U_1, U_2, U_3, \delta, ID_\mathbb{S})$.
4. Computes $a = H_3(\delta, V, ID_\mathbb{S})$.
5. Computes $C_1 = a^{-1}xP$, $C_2 = x(b+s)P$.
6. Sets $k = H_4(\omega = \alpha^x)$.

Outputs the offline signcryption $\sigma' = \langle C_1, C_2, V, U_1, U_2 \rangle$, while $\sigma_{secret} = \langle k, \omega, a, b, y, z \rangle$ are kept as secret for future use in online phase and they are not made public. Note here that the output of the $Off-Signcrypt$ algorithm can be used only once to generate an online signcryption.

Remark: It should be noted that above offline signcryption σ' does not require the knowledge of the message or the receiver.

On-Signcrypt(m, $ID_\mathbb{S}$, $ID_\mathbb{R}$, σ', σ_{secret}): This algorithm is run by the sender, once the message $m \in \mathcal{M}$ and the receiver identity $ID_\mathbb{R}$ are available and makes use of the offline signature $\sigma' = \langle C_1, C_2, V, U_1, U_2 \rangle$, along with the stored values $\sigma_{secret} = \langle k, \omega, a, b, y, z \rangle$.

1. Compute $C_3 = a(q_\mathbb{R} - b) \bmod q$.
2. Compute $C_4 = (m\|\delta) \oplus k$.
3. Compute $v = yh + z \bmod q$ where $h = H_5(m, \omega, \delta, h_2, C_3, C_4, ID_\mathbb{S}, ID_\mathbb{R})$.
4. Outputs the signcryption $\sigma = \langle \{C_i\}_{i=1\,to\,4}, U_1, U_2, U_3, V, v \rangle$.

Remark: Here, the $On-Signcrypt$ phase includes only one hash computation.

Unsigncrypt(σ, $ID_\mathbb{S}$, $ID_\mathbb{R}$, $D_\mathbb{R}$): When the receiver $U_\mathbb{R}$ with identity $ID_\mathbb{R}$ is provided with the signcryption $\langle \sigma, U_\mathbb{S}, U_\mathbb{R} \rangle$ uses the following steps to unsigncrypt the signcryption $\sigma = \langle \{C_i\}_{i=1\,to\,4}, U_1, U_2, U_3, V, v \rangle$ from $ID_\mathbb{R}$:

1. Computes $\omega' = \hat{e}(C_3C_1 + C_2, D_\mathbb{R})$ and $k' = H_3(\omega')$.
2. $(m'\|\delta') = C_4 \oplus k'$.
3. Computes $h_2' = H_2(U_1, U_2, U_3, \delta', ID_\mathbb{S})$ and $h' = H_5(m', \omega', \delta', h_2', C_3, C_4, ID_\mathbb{S}, ID_\mathbb{R})$.
4. Verify $h'U_2 + U_3 \overset{?}{=} vP$, $\hat{e}(P, C_1)^{H_3(\delta', V, ID_\mathbb{S})} \overset{?}{=} \omega'$ and $\hat{e}(V, (q_\mathbb{S}+s)P)\alpha^{-h_2'} \overset{?}{=} U_1$
5. If all the checks in the above step holds, then output the message m', else output "*Invalid*".

Correctness: We show the correctness of the unsigncryption algorithm here.

$$\begin{aligned}
\omega' = \hat{e}(C_3C_1 + C_2, D_\mathbb{R}) &= \hat{e}((q_\mathbb{R} - b)xp + x(b+s)P, \tfrac{1}{q_\mathbb{R}+s}P) \\
&= \hat{e}((q_\mathbb{R} + s)xP, \tfrac{1}{q_\mathbb{R}+s}P) \\
&= \hat{e}(xP, P) = \hat{e}(P, P)^x = \alpha^x = \omega
\end{aligned}$$

The correctness of the verification tests $U_2 h' + U_3 \stackrel{?}{=} vP$, $\hat{e}(P, C_1)^{H_3(\delta', V, ID_{\mathbb{S}})} \stackrel{?}{=}$ ω' and $\hat{e}(V, (q_{\mathbb{S}} + s)P)\alpha^{-h'} \stackrel{?}{=} U_1$ is shown below:

Correctness of $U_2 h' + U_3 \stackrel{?}{=} vP$

$$h' U_3 + U_1 = h'(yP) + rP = (h'y + r)P = vP$$

Correctness of $\hat{e}(P, C_1)^{H_3(\delta', V, ID_{\mathbb{S}})} \stackrel{?}{=} \omega'$

$$\hat{e}(P, C_1)^{H_3(\delta', V, ID_{\mathbb{S}})} = \hat{e}(P, a^{-1}xP)^a = \hat{e}(P, P)^x = \omega' = \omega$$

Correctness of $\hat{e}(V, (q_{\mathbb{S}} + s)P)\alpha^{-h'} \stackrel{?}{=} U_1$

$$
\begin{aligned}
\hat{e}(V, (q_{\mathbb{S}} + s)P)\alpha^{-h'_2} &= \hat{e}((r + h_2)D_{\mathbb{S}}, (q_{\mathbb{S}} + s)P)\hat{e}(P, P)^{-h'_2} \\
&= \hat{e}\left((r + h_2)\frac{1}{q_{\mathbb{S}} + s}P, (q_{\mathbb{S}} + s)P\right)\hat{e}(P, P)^{-h'_2} \\
&= \hat{e}(P, P)^{r + h_2}\hat{e}(P, P)^{-h'_2} = \hat{e}(P, P)^r = U_1
\end{aligned}
$$

7   Security Analysis of Our IBOOSC

In the new identity based online/offline signcryption scheme proposed above, we are not directly signing the message, instead two randomness are signed which are acting as the public keys for signing the message using a one-time schnorr signature[10].

Theorem 2. *If there exists an attacker $\mathcal{A}$ that can break the IND-IBOOSC-CCA2 security (confidentiality) of IBOOSC, then there exists an algorithm $\mathcal{C}$ that is capable of solving the q-SDHIP.*

Please refer the proof of this theorem in the full version of the paper [12].

Theorem 3. *If there exists an attacker $\mathcal{A}$ who can break the EUF-IBOOSC-CMA security of IBOOSC, then there exists an algorithm $\mathcal{C}$ that is capable of solving the q-CDHIP.*

Please refer the proof of this theorem in the full version of the paper [12].

Conclusion

Identity based encryption schemes wherein the encryption is carried out in two phases namely, offline and online phase according to the complexity of the operations performed is known to be identity based online/offline encryption scheme. The subtle issue in designing an identity based online/offline encryption scheme is to split the operations into heavy weight (for offline phase) and light weight (for online phase) without knowing the message and receiver. [9] gives a solution for this problem in the random oracle model. In this paper, we have pointed out that the scheme in [9] is not CCA secure. We have proposed a possible fix for the same and have also given a more efficient identity based online/offline encryption scheme. We have formally proved the security of the new scheme in the random oracle model. The complexity figure of our scheme is given below:

Table 1. Comparison of Complexity

Scheme	Encrypt					Decrypt				
	Offline			Online		BP	SPM	EXP	M	Ex
	BP	SPM	EXP	M	Ex					
Improved L-IBOOE (Sec. 3.3)	1	7	1	3	1	3	4	1	-	1
New-IBOOE	-	4	1	2	1	2	2	1	-	1

*SPM - Scalar Point Multiplication, BP - Bilinear Pairing, EXP -
Exponentiation in $\mathbb{G}_T$, M - Modular Computation in $\mathbb{Z}_q^*$, Ex - Exclusive OR*

We have also showed security weaknesses in two existing identity based on-line/offline signcryption schemes[14,15]. Also, we proposed a provably secure identity based online/offline signcryption scheme which does not require the knowledge of the message and receiver. We proved the security of our scheme in the random oracle model. Since two existing identity based online/offline sign-cryption schemes are showed to be flawed in one way or the other we compare our scheme only with [8]. The IBOOSC scheme presented in this paper has efficiency gain in the online signcryption phase and unsigncryption with one less modular arithmetic and one less hashing, and has one less pairing during respectively when compared with [8]

Table 2. Comparison of Complexity

Scheme	Signcrypt						Unsigncrypt				
	Offline			Online			BP	SPM	EXP	M	Ex
	BP	SPM	EXP	M	Ex	HF					
[8]	-	6	1	3	1	3	3	4	-	-	1
IBOOSC	-	6	2	2	1	2	2	5	-	-	1

*SPM - Scalar Point Multiplication, BP - Bilinear Pairing, EXP -
Exponentiation in $\mathbb{G}_T$, M - Modular Computation in $\mathbb{Z}_q^*$, Ex - Exclusive OR,
HF - Hash Computation*

References

1. An, J.H., Dodis, Y., Rabin, T.: On the Security of Joint Signature and Encryption. In: Knudsen, L.R. (ed.) EUROCRYPT 2002. LNCS, vol. 2332, pp. 83–107. Springer, Heidelberg (2002)
2. Boneh, D., Boyen, X.: Efficient Selective-ID Secure Identity-Based Encryption Without Random Oracles. In: Cachin, C., Camenisch, J.L. (eds.) EUROCRYPT 2004. LNCS, vol. 3027, pp. 223–238. Springer, Heidelberg (2004)
3. Chow, S.S.M., Liu, J.K., Zhou, J.: Identity-based online/offline key encapsulation and encryption. Cryptology ePrint Archive, Report 2010/194 (2010)
4. Dutta, R., Barua, R., Sarkar, P.: Pairing-based cryptographic protocols: A survey. In: Cryptology ePrint Archive, Report 2004/064 (2004)

5. Even, S., Goldreich, O., Micali, S.: On-line/off-line digital signatures. Journal of Cryptology 9(1) (1996)
6. Gentry, C.: Practical Identity-Based Encryption Without Random Oracles. In: Vaudenay, S. (ed.) EUROCRYPT 2006. LNCS, vol. 4004, pp. 445–464. Springer, Heidelberg (2006)
7. Guo, F., Mu, Y., Chen, Z.: Identity-Based Online/Offline Encryption. In: Tsudik, G. (ed.) FC 2008. LNCS, vol. 5143, pp. 247–261. Springer, Heidelberg (2008)
8. Liu, J.K., Baek, J., Zhou, J.: Online/Offline identity-based signcryption revisited. In: Lai, X., Yung, M., Lin, D. (eds.) Inscrypt 2010. LNCS, vol. 6584, pp. 36–51. Springer, Heidelberg (2011), http://eprint.iacr.org/
9. Liu, J.K., Zhou, J.: An Efficient Identity-Based Online/Offline Encryption Scheme. In: Abdalla, M., Pointcheval, D., Fouque, P.-A., Vergnaud, D. (eds.) ACNS 2009. LNCS, vol. 5536, pp. 156–167. Springer, Heidelberg (2009)
10. Schnorr, C.-P.: Efficient signature generation by smart cards. J. Cryptology 4(3) (1991)
11. Sharmila Deva Selvi, S., Sree Vivek, S., Pandu Rangan, C.: Identity based online/offline encryption scheme. Cryptology ePrint Archive, Report 2010/178 (2010)
12. Sharmila Deva Selvi, S., Sree Vivek,S., Pandu Rangan, C.: Identity based online/offline signcryption scheme. Cryptology ePrint Archive, Report 2010/376 (2010)
13. Shamir, A., Tauman, Y.: Improved Online/Offline Signature Schemes. In: Kilian, J. (ed.) CRYPTO 2001. LNCS, vol. 2139, pp. 355–367. Springer, Heidelberg (2001)
14. Sun, D., Huang, X., Mu, Y., Susilo, W.: Identity-based on-line/off-line signcryption. In: Cao, J., Li, M., Wu, M.-Y., Chen, J. (eds.) NPC 2008. LNCS, vol. 5245, pp. 34–41. Springer, Heidelberg (2008)
15. Sun, D., Mu, Y., Susilo, W.: A generic construction of identity-based online/offline signcryption. In: ISPA, pp. 707–712. IEEE, Los Alamitos (2008)
16. Zhang, F., Mu, Y., Susilo, W.: Reducing security overhead for mobile networks. In: AINA 2005: Proceedings of the 19th International Conference on Advanced Information Networking and Applications, pp. 398–403. IEEE Computer Society, Los Alamitos (2005)
17. Zheng, Y.: Digital Signcryption or How to Achieve Cost (Signature & Encryption) << Cost(Signature) + Cost(Encryption). In: Kaliski Jr., B.S. (ed.) CRYPTO 1997. LNCS, vol. 1294, pp. 165–179. Springer, Heidelberg (1997)

"Rank Correction": A New Side-Channel Approach for Secret Key Recovery

Maxime Nassar[1,2], Youssef Souissi[1], Sylvain Guilley[1], and Jean-Luc Danger[1]

[1] Institut TELECOM / TELECOM ParisTech, CNRS LTCI (UMR 5141)
[2] Bull TrustWay
`firstname.lastname@telecom-paristech.fr`

Abstract. In this paper we present the "Rank Corrector"(RC), an empirical approach aiming at enhancing most Side Channel Attack (SCA). We show that during an SCA on a cryptographic algorithm like the Data Encryption Standard (DES), the rank of the secret key displays a specific behaviour with regards to other hypotheses. Hence the Rank Corrector algorithm is devised, in order to improve existing SCAs by exploiting such behaviours. With a profiling phase on a clone device, we precisely evaluate the set of parameters that ensure the adaptability of RC to a large range of cryptographic systems, and the possibility to discriminate the secret key from other hypotheses in an efficient manner. The main principle of RC is to detect and discard the false keys hypotheses when analysing the ranking evolution. This results in improving the rank of the secret key, thus accelerating the attack. The efficiency of our algorithm is assessed by performing a Differential Power Analysis (DPA) with and without the rank corrector. We observe a gain of at least 15% on the "Measurements To Disclosure" (MTD) criteria.

Keywords: Side-channel analysis, distinguishers, success rate, guessing entropy, rank correction.

1 Introduction

Side-channel analysis (SCA) is a technique to recover secrets concealed in embedded systems. They exploit unintentional physical leakage, such as the power consumption or the radiated magnetic field. Since the initial publication of the differential power analysis in 1998, the theoretical tools to conduct SCAs have been much refined. Notably, through adequate evaluation frameworks (typically that of F.-X. Standaert et al. [17]), the attacks have been formally described in two independent steps.

1. A partitioning of the side-channel observations, which depends on the scenario (known/chosen plaintext/ciphertext), on the algorithm (to explore the internal rounds by guessing manageable parts of the secret), and on the implementation (whether it is software or hardware, pipelined or unrolled, protected or not, etc.)

M. Joye et al. (Eds.): InfoSecHiComNet 2011, LNCS 7011, pp. 128–143, 2011.

2. A distinguisher that selects the most relevant partitionings, amongst all the secret hypotheses. The distinguisher is basically a statistical tool, that aims at putting forward any bias. They can be for instance a difference of means [10], a covariance [6], a correlation (linear [2] or rank-based [9]), a mutual information [4] or a variance [16, 12].

Some studies suggest that all distinguishers are equivalent asymptotically [13] (*i.e.* they are sound), and that they only differ by statistical artifacts that are data-dependent. However, in concrete operational cases, the goal is clearly to find some ways to accelerate the attack, taking into account that the scarce resource is the number of measurements. Some papers compare distinguishers, and conclude about their difference of efficiency [16]. Interesting results [5] show that some distinguishers are better for the first order success rate and that others are better for the guessing entropy. Nonetheless, few papers have tried to devise generic methods to improve existing attacks.

In this article, we will present such a scheme: the *rank corrector*, an algorithm which aims at enhancing existing attacks, independently of the distinguisher or the architecture.

The rest of the paper is organized as follows. Sec. 2 presents the background of the study. The principle of the *rank corrector*, as well as its algorithm are detailed in Sec. 3, then, experimental results, illustrated by first order success rate and guessing entropy are given in sec. 4. Finally, Sec. 5 concludes the paper and opens some perspectives. A comparison with other profiling-based attacks is given in appendix A.

2   Background Knowledge

2.1   Rank-Based SCAs

As stated in Sec. 1, the main difference regarding most SCAs relies on the measurements partitioning process and the used distinguisher. Otherwise they usually run iteratively and a new ranking of all secret hypotheses is created at each iteration. Then, when the first ranked hypothesis is stable for a certain amount of iterations, it is returned by the SCA software. The attack is successful when it is, indeed, the actual secret.

In this article, we focus on SCA targeting cryptographic devices embedded with algorithms like the Data Encryption Standard (DES) or the Advanced Encryption Standard (AES), which usually aims at recovering a secret key. Although various biases and noises are introduced by implementations, architectures, and especially measurements acquisition tools, we will show that the rank of the secret key displays a specific behaviour with regards to other hypotheses. This article is based on the study of such behaviours, and explains how to exploit them in order to enhance existing SCAs.

2.2   Notations

In the rest of this article, we will use the following notations:

- RC is the *rank corrector*.
- SK is the secret key.
- PK, the predicted key, is the key hypothesis which has the best rank for the current iteration. The value of PK is updated for each new observation.
- PK_i denotes the predicted key at iteration i.
- FK represents a false key hypothesis (all but the secret key).
- R_k, $R_{k,i}$ are respectively the ranks of key hypothesis k for the current iteration and iteration i.
- S_{init} is the iteration number corresponding to the beginning of stability for a given PK.
- *Trace* denotes a power or electro-magnetic measurement.
- MTD, or Measurement To Disclosure, is the total number of traces needed to successfully perform the attack.

2.3 Key Rank Behaviours

In theory, for a great number of observations, SK should always be ranked first, as we are doing the correct partitioning of traces for each iteration. This is not the case for FKs which should have an unstable (random) rank. However, actual attacks are usually performed with a limited number of measurements, or aim, at least, to be successful using as few of them as possible. Therefore, we studied the behaviours of the ranks of both the secret key and false key hypotheses, by performing numerous DPAs and CPAs on four different architectures of DES and three of AES, implemented Altera Stratix-II and Xilinx Virtex-II FPGAs. The goal of this study was to find an empirical method taking advantage of the distinctive behaviours between SK and the FKs.

First of all, we observed that R_{SK} is always roughly decreasing until it reaches first position, considering that the best rank is 0. Fig. 1 shows examples of such behaviour during a Differential Power Analysis (DPA) on 6 bits of the first S-Box of a DES coprocessor (a) and a Correlation Power Analysis (CPA) on 8 bits of the first S-Box of an AES 256(b), both implemented on FPGA. While in Fig. 1(a) R_{SK} decreases almost monotonically, in Fig. 1(b) it oscillates much more while doing so. Then, in both cases, R_{SK} clearly fluctuates within a short range of the first positions before definitely stabilising. This behaviour is observed most of the time, however, in rare cases, R_{SK} can stabilise as soon as it reaches the first position, without fluctuating.

Regarding false keys, we observed that, as the number of processed traces increases, they clearly tend to display more random behaviours. Fig. 2 shows two examples of false key rank evolution during the same DPA as Fig. 1(a). On the one hand, the leftmost one ($FK1$) is almost random and never ranks first, thus will not be treated as a potential secret key. This type of behaviour is easily differentiable from SK. On the another hand, the rank of the rightmost key ($FK2$) does reach the first position at some point and could therefore be concurrent to SK. However, with the increasing iteration number, R_{FK2} clearly raises, which would not be the case for SK.

In conclusion, our study shows that it should indeed be possible to differentiate between SK and the FKs based on the observation of their ranking. As a matter of fact, R_{SK} is roughly decreasing and then usually fluctuates between a few positions before stabilising, whereas the $R_{FK}s$, when they reach the first rank, usually become random a few iterations later.

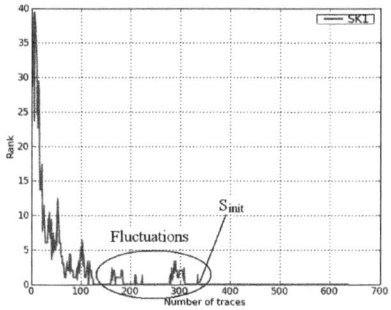

(a) Rank of SK during a DPA on DES

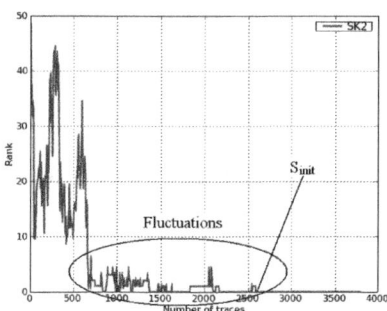

(b) Rank of SK during a CPA on AES

Fig. 1. Examples of rank behaviours for the secret key

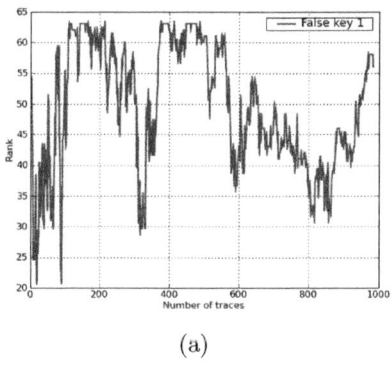

(a)

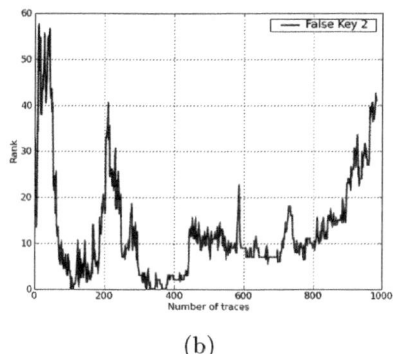

(b)

Fig. 2. Examples of rank behaviours for false keys

3 Rank Corrector: Principle

3.1 Application Field

The main feature of the rank corrector is to be as generic as possible. It can therefore be applied to a wide range of attacks. Indeed, an attack scheme only needs to meet three requirements to be compatible, with our software:

1. It has to be iterative (for instance DPA iterates on a number of power consumption measurements).

2. A ranking of all key hypotheses must be produced at each iteration.
3. The SCA software must decide on the secret key by observing the stability of the first ranked hypothesis.

Up to now, the usual criterion employed to decide on SK is, indeed, the stability of the rank. For example, in the first edition of DPA contest [18], a stability of 100 traces had to be achieved in order to validate the attacks, performed on an unprotected DES cryptoprocessor. Moreover, most of the passive SCAs, usually based on the exploitation of power consumption or electromagnetic measurements, present an iterative behaviour as, at some point, they process those traces one after the other.

Thereby, the rank corrector can be used to enhance a very large number of attacks, like DPA, CPA or Mutual Information Attack (MIA).

3.2   Basic Principle

The rank corrector (RC) is a **generic**[1] custom-made algorithm, which aims at exploiting the key behaviours described in Sec. 2.3 in order to significantly reduce the number of traces needed to achieve a successful SCA.

As a matter of fact, it studies in real-time, the evolution of an iterative ranking (for instance the one produced by a DPA software), in order to virtually reassign previous rank positions to the current PK, depending on past and current rankings. The detailed algorithm is described in Sec. 3.4. It is totally independent of the attack, given that it verifies the requirements described in section 3.1. Indeed, it only modifies, on the fly, the stability of the target SCA, while creating a new ranking in parallel (for the sake of displaying the results).

Eventually, RC can be seen as a plug-in, designed to enhance most existing SCAs.

Now suppose that we are performing a DPA on one sub-key of a cryptographic device implementing an algorithm like DES or AES, and that it will be successful, meaning that SK will eventually be ranked first and reach the given stability. Before stabilizing, R_{SK} should be roughly decreasing (as stated in Sec.2.3). Then most of the time, after reaching the first position ($rank = 0$), it will fluctuate within a short range, and then stabilize, from S_{init} to MTD.

In this case, RC will detect those fluctuations in the proximity of the stabilisation, remove them and increase the stability counter by an equal amount (G) of traces. Thereby, G represents the gain of RC with regards to a simple DPA. Fig. 3 illustrates this scenario, by showing a zoom of the evolution of the R_{SK} displayed in Fig. 1(a), with and without the *rank corrector*. As we can see in this example, without RC the stability starts after 340 traces, whereas with RC, it does after only 240 traces. Thus we have a gain of 100 traces.

---

[1] We insist that our methodology does not consist in trying to tune an attack on a given acquisition campaign so that it retrieves the key as fast as possible, as in [11]. Instead, we attempt to pre-characterize a set of parameters from a training campaign, and to use this prior knowledge subsequently in a positive view to speed up forthcoming attacks.

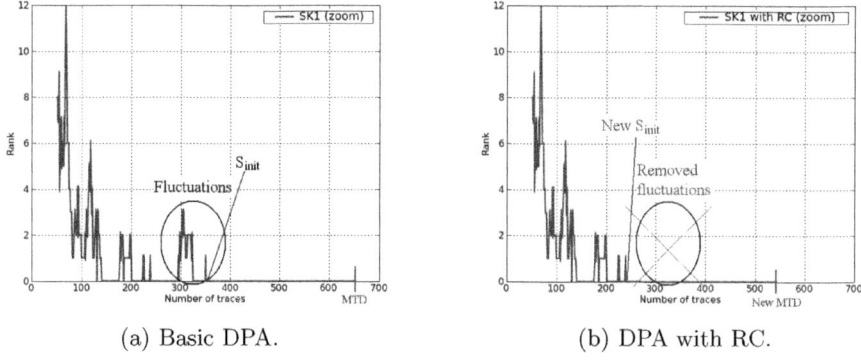

(a) Basic DPA.   (b) DPA with RC.

Fig. 3. Rank of SK during a DPA, with and without RC

The main idea of RC is to locate and disqualify FKs that are ranked first during the fluctuations of SK. Therefore, it proceeds as follows:

1. When a PK has been stable for certain amount of traces STH (stability threshold), starting at S_{init}, it is considered as a potential SK, as shown in Fig. 4(a).
2. Then RC scans a small range of traces before S_{init} (called *correction range*) searching for fluctuations of the current PK (let's call it CPK). If they exceed a certain limit R_{max}, CPK is disqualified and will no longer be a candidate for SK.
3. In the other case, RC will check the ranks, at the current iteration, of all other PKs present in the correction range and discard all those that show a rank exceeding R_{max}. Then the rank of SK, within the correction range, is modified by removing the discarded keys.

Moreover, RC operates by using increasing values of STH. Each time the stability of PK reaches given values STH_n (with $n \in \mathbb{N}^*$), RC is launched. This threshold mechanism was chosen for two reasons. On one hand it allows RC to easily discard any PK that isn't stable for at least STH_1 , and only take into consideration the potential SKs. Moreover, for each new threshold, the correction range (i.e. the potential gain) increases, as shown in Fig. 4(b) which is coherent with the fact that the more stable a PK is, the more likely it is to be SK. On another hand, it keeps the computation time of the attack close to the original one as RC is only called a few times.

3.3 RC Parameters and Their Evaluation

In order to be as generic as possible, RC was designed as a **parametric** algorithm. It is thereby based on two main parameters, that allow RC to adapt to

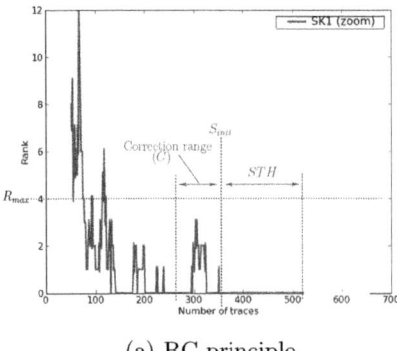
(a) RC principle.

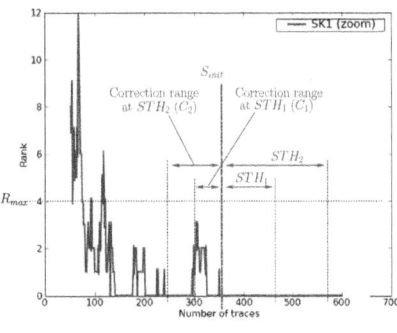
(b) RC threshold mechanism.

Fig. 4. Illustration of RC principle

almost any attack, independently of any bias introduced by either the architecture, the implementation, or the acquisition technique:

1. S is the minimum stability required to ensure that the attack will always decide on the actual secret key (SK).
2. R_{max} is the maximum fluctuation range of SK before the stabilization (i.e. between the first time SK attains the first position, and its stabilization).

These two parameters must be correctly evaluated for RC to work properly. For instance choosing S too small, could easily lead any SCA to decide on a false key, and using RC in this context would clearly increase the probability of doing so.

For this purpose, we use a clone device, and undergo a profiling phase, computing multiple attacks for different SK. For each key and each attack, we record the evolution of the ranks of SK (R_{SK}) and every FK, in order to determine the best R_{max} and S. Indeed, the more representative these two parameters are of SK (and not of any FK), the more efficient RC will be, as it will be able to disregard more FKs, and almost only consider the actual SK as a correction target.

Thanks to this profiling, we are then able to ensure that RC will not lead to finding a false key.

Aside from R_{max} and S, RC takes into account a few other secondary parameters: while these parameters do influence the maximum gain of RC, they do not have a major impact on the overall results. Therefore, and in order to simplify the notations, they will be fixed, in the rest of this article, to the values we used during our experiments.

1. n: the number of thresholds, $n \in 1, 2, 3$.
2. STH_n: the $n-th$ stability threshold, $STH_n = (n * S)/4$.
3. C_n: the $n-th$ correction range, $C_n = STH_n/2$.

Those empirical values were deduced from thorough studies on several crypto-graphic devices. Naturally, they may not be optimal for all SCAs and all implementations, and a finer study should be carried out, using the clone device, before every specific attack.

3.4 Description of the Algorithm

Algo. 1 gives a detailed description of RC. When launched, it starts by searching for an occurrence of the current PK (CPK), in the first rank of the C_n iterations before S_{init} (the current iteration number being $CIT = S_{init} + STH_n$). The search starts at $S_{init} - C_n$ down to $S_{init} - 1$ (step 2 and 3 of our algorithm). Finding CPK at iteration IT, means that R_{CPK} did actually reach first position and fluctuate before stabilizing, meaning it is, as such, open to correction by RC (step 4).

All PKs between S_{init} and IT are then checked in the reverse order (from S_{init} to IT), and reassigned to CPK when possible (step 5). This way, whenever a rank that should not be corrected is found, RC is stopped. Several scenarios can then occur: the trivial one is when $PK_j = CPK$, with $j \in S_{init}$ to IT (though it is never true for $j = S_{init} - 1$). In this case, RC directly increases the stability by one iteration. When $PK_j \neq CPK$ (step 9), RC will look at $R_{CPK,j}$. If $R_{CPK,j} < R_{max}$ (i.e. $R_{CPK,j}$ is near the first position), that means CPK is a possible candidate to be SK (step 10). RC then checks if $R_{PK_j,CIT} \geq R_{max}$, and if this second condition is verified, PK_j is disqualified as a potential SK, and removed from the ranking (step 12 and 13). This check is mandatory, as, for the first thresholds, CPK could be a false key, in which case the real SK is likely to be one of the PK_j, with $j < S_{init}$. This step is repeated until $CPK = PK_j$ or a PK_j that cannot be disqualified ($R_{PK_j,CIT} < R_{max}$) is found. Indeed, when $R_{PK_j,CIT} < R_{max}$ our algorithm considers PK_j to be a possible SK and thus no correction is made. Then, if $CPK = PK_j$, the stability is once again increased (step 15). As a matter of fact we suppose, based on the observations of Sec. 2.3, and the profiled value of R_{max} that R_{SK} will never go past R_{max} once it has been ranked first. Thus any PK that goes past R_{max} is definitively discarded.

These steps are repeated for each threshold, and each time the number of traces that might be corrected increases. As a matter of fact, the more stable a PK is, the more likely it is to be SK. Moreover, a FK that was not corrected at the first threshold, (for instance because it was ranked second), will usually not be in the same position at the second threshold, and will then be replaced by PK.

Consequently, the maximum gain of RC can be computed as shown in eq. 1:

$$GAIN_{max} = \sum_{n=1}^{3} \frac{STH_n}{2} \equiv \sum_{n=1}^{3} \frac{n*S}{8} \qquad (1)$$

3.5 Example

Fig. 5 illustrates the evolution of key ranks during an SCA using RC, when the stability of a given key reaches the first threshold. K represents our secret key,

Algorithm 1. RC detailed algorithm.

1: **for** *each threshold* STH_n $(n \in 1, 2, 3)$ **do**
2:    **for** *iteration* **in** $S_{init} - C_n$ **to** S_{init} **do**
3:       Search for an occurrence of the current CPK.
4:       **if** CPK is found at *iteration* = IT **then**
5:          **for** j **in** S_{init} **to** IT **do**
6:             Check the value of PK_j
7:             **if** $PK_j = CPK$ **then**
8:                increase stability by 1
9:             **else**
10:                **if** $R_{CPK,j} < R_{max}$ **then**
11:                   **while** $CPK \neq PK_j$ **and** $R_{PK_j, CIT} \geq R_{max}$ **do**
12:                      Remove PK_j from the ranking
13:                   **if** $CPK = PK_j$ **then**
14:                      increase stability by 1
15:                   **else**
16:                      Exit.
17:       **else**
18:          Exit.
19: **return** stability

and S_{init} the iteration number marking the beginning of its stability, while K_0, K_1 and K_2 are three false keys. The process of RC can be described in three steps:

1. The rank of K (R_K) reaches the first threshold (i.e. a stability of $STH_1 = S/4$ traces), thus RC searches for K in the PKs of the $S/8$ prior traces. It is found at iteration IT, implying that R_K did actually reach rank 0 and fluctuate before stabilizing.
2. Two different PKs, K_1 and K_2 are found respectively at iteration $S_{init} - 1$ and $S_{init} - 3$. For those iterations R_K is compared to R_{max}. As $R_K \geq R_{max}$ is true in both cases, RC enters the next step of the algorithm and checks the ranks of K_1 and K_2 at the current iteration $CIT = S_{init} + S/4$.
3. $R_{K_2, CIT}$ is greater than R_{max}, so K_2 is discarded. Then, K which was ranked second, becomes the new PK of iteration $S_{init} - 1$ and the stability is increased. K is already ranked first at iteration $S_{init} - 2$ so the stability is once again increased. $R_{K_1, CIT}$, on another hand, does not verify the condition, meaning it is a possible candidate for SK, and RC is therefore stopped.

In this example RC produced a gain of 2 traces after the first threshold, and S_{init} is thereby updated as shown in Fig. 5.

3.6 Optimization

Although most of the time SK does fluctuate before stabilizing, there are rare cases where it permanently stabilizes as soon as it reaches the first position (this occurred in less than 4% of all the attacks we performed during our study). In

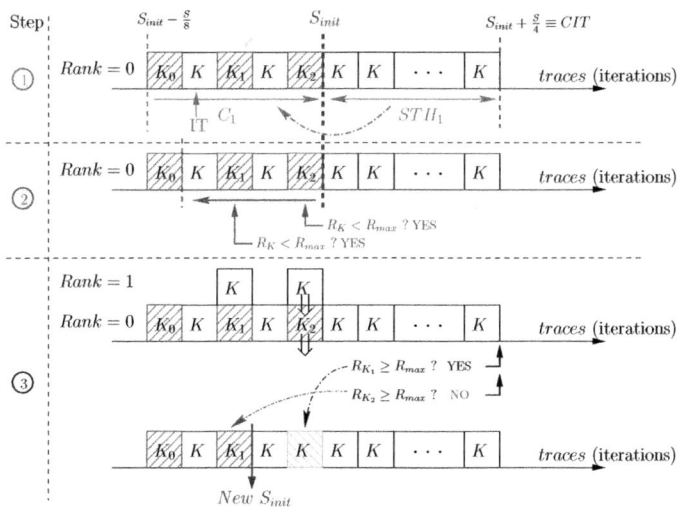

Fig. 5. Illustration of an SCA using RC, at the first threshold

this case, the gain should be null. In order to decrease the probability of having such a gain, we take advantage of the fact that R_{SK} is likely to be $< R_{max}$ just before stabilizing. Thus RC will search for occurrences of SK in those ranks, before the stabilization, and try to disqualify the corresponding PKs, in order to reassign SK to the first rank. This new search range, called $C2_n$, is another secondary parameter (like n and C_n), and will also be fixed in the rest of this article to our experimental value: $C2_n = STH_n/4$ (see Sec. 3.3).

Algo. 1 is then complemented as follows: step 18 is replaced by algo. 2. Then when CPK is not present in the first search range (step 17 of algo. 1) RC will check if $R_{CPK} < R_{max}$ for a smaller range of iterations: from $S_{init}-C2_n$ to S_{init}. The following process is similar to the former one, if all PKs can be disqualified $(R_{PK_k,CIT} \geq R_{max})$, CPK becomes PK_k and the stability is increased.

Algorithm 2. RC optimization.

1: **if** CPK is not found **then**
2:    **for** k in S_{init} to $S_{init} - I2_n$ **do**
3:       **if** $R_{CPK} < R_{max}$ **then**
4:          **while** $CPK \neq PK_j$ and $R_{PK_j,CIT} \geq R_{max}$ **do**
5:             Remove PK_j from the ranking
6:          **if** $CPK = PK_j$ **then**
7:             increase stability by 1
8:       **else**
9:          Exit

Obviously SK will not always display such a behaviour, and there will thus be cases where the gain is null. A more thorough study of these situations could certainly result in an improvement of our algorithm, but is out of the scope of this article.

4   Experimental Results

Our experiments were conducted on Stratix-II FPGAs, soldered on two SASEBO-B boards provided by the RCIS [8] (one for the actual attack an one for the clone device). The target cryptoprocessor implemented in those devices is an unprotected DES. Power consumption measurements were acquired, using a *differential probe* plugged to the positive rail of the FPGA core power supply through a 1 Ω shunt resistor, coupled with a *54855 Infiniium oscilloscope* from Agilent Technologies [1].

First of all, we estimated the parameters (S and R_{max}) with a profiling phase on the first FPGA. Using three different keys, we performed 100 attacks for each one. Eventually, $S = 110$ and $R_{max} = 5$ were deduced as the optimal values for these parameters.

Then, we acquired 50000 traces in order to perform several DPAs on the real device, with and without using the *rank corrector*.

In order to better assess the efficiency of our algorithm, we use two evaluation metrics introduced by Standaert et al. [17]. On one hand, the first-order success rate (Fig. 6) expresses the probability that, given a pool of traces, the attack's best guess is the correct key. On the other hand, the guessing entropy (Fig. 7) measures the position of the correct key in a list of key hypotheses ranked by a distinguisher.

The improvement brought by our scheme is clearly visible on the curve of the success rate in Fig. 6. For instance a success rate of 80% is reached with less than 90 traces with RC, when the basic DPA needs more than 110 traces to do so.

While the guessing entropy is also always lower with RC than without, the gap between the two is definitely thinner than for the success rate. This is explained by the fact that the correction takes place when the rank of SK is lower than 5, so when computing the mean of ranks on a large number of attacks, it doesn't have a great impact on the final results.

Moreover, after 300 complete attacks on random pool of traces, we obtain a mean gain of 43.7 traces. Considering that the basic DPA requires 250 to 300 traces to complete the attack, as shown in Fig. 6, we conclude that using RC results in a gain of $\sim 15\%$ in terms of MTD.

5   Conclusion and Perspectives

In this paper the "rank corrector" method which aims at enhancing any kind of SCA attack, has been presented and evaluated. The principle based on the distinguishable evolution of the ranking between the secret key and any false key has been observed on different SCAs. Two parameters which are the threshold of stability and the maximum range are necessary for the RC to work efficiently. When these parameters are well profiled a gain of at least 15% in terms of MTD can be expected with regards to the classical DPA. As perspectives to enhance the RC it should be interesting to consider the evolution of the values obtained by the SCA to refine the rank evolution. The RC also needs more experimental validation on many kinds of SCAs and target devices even if the ranking behaviour seems identical between different attacks. A theoretical approach based on a study of the probability distribution evolution is also foreseen to prove and improve the efficiency of the method.

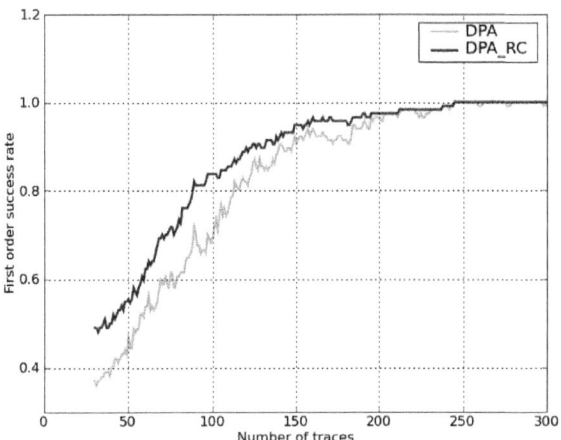

Fig. 6. First order success rate for DPA with and without RC

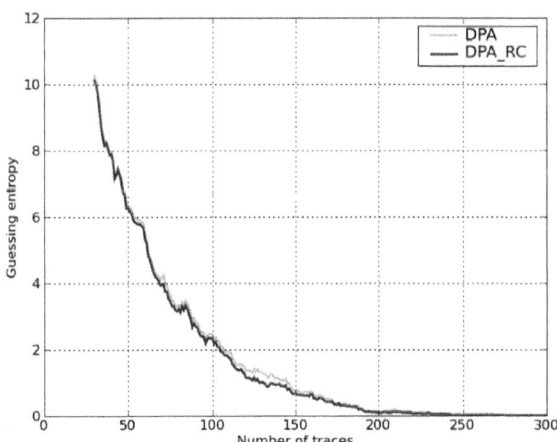

Fig. 7. Guessing entropy for DPA with and without RC

References

1. Agilent Technologies, http://www.agilent.com/
2. Brier, É., Clavier, C., Olivier, F.: Correlation Power Analysis with a Leakage Model. In: Joye, M., Quisquater, J.-J. (eds.) CHES 2004. LNCS, vol. 3156, pp. 16–29. Springer, Heidelberg (2004)
3. Chari, S., Rao, J.R., Rohatgi, P.: Template attacks. In: Kaliski Jr., B.S., Koç, Ç.K., Paar, C. (eds.) CHES 2002. LNCS, vol. 2523, pp. 13–28. Springer, Heidelberg (2003)
4. Gierlichs, B., Batina, L., Tuyls, P., Preneel, B.: Mutual information analysis. In: Oswald, E., Rohatgi, P. (eds.) CHES 2008. LNCS, vol. 5154, pp. 426–442. Springer, Heidelberg (2008)
5. Gierlichs, B., De Mulder, E., Preneel, B., Verbauwhede, I.: Empirical comparison of side channel analysis distinguishers on DES in hardware. In: IEEE (ed.) ECCTD. European Conference on Circuit Theory and Design, Antalya, Turkey, August 23-27, pp. 391–394 (2009)
6. Guilley, S., Sauvage, L., Danger, J.-L., Selmane, N., Pacalet, R.: Silicon-level solutions to counteract passive and active attacks. In: FDTC, 5th Workshop on Fault Detection and Tolerance in Cryptography, pp. 3–17. IEEE-CS, Washington DC, USA (2008)
7. Homma, N., Nagashima, S., Imai, Y., Aoki, T., Satoh, A.: High-Resolution Side-Channel Attack Using Phase-Based Waveform Matching. In: Goubin, L., Matsui, M. (eds.) CHES 2006. LNCS, vol. 4249, pp. 187–200. Springer, Heidelberg (2006)
8. Japanese RCIS-AIST, http://www.rcis.aist.go.jp/special/SASEBO/index-en.html
9. Karsmakers, P., Gierlichs, B., Pelckmans, K., Cock, K.D., Suykens, J., Preneel, B., Moor, B.D.: Side channel attacks on cryptographic devices as a classification problem. COSIC technical report
10. Kocher, P.C., Jaffe, J., Jun, B.: Differential Power Analysis. In: Wiener, M. (ed.) CRYPTO 1999. LNCS, vol. 1666, pp. 388–397. Springer, Heidelberg (1999)
11. Lomné, V., Dehbaoui, A., Maurine, P., Torres, L., Robert, M.: Differential Power Analysis enhancement with statistical preprocessing. In: IEEE (ed.) DATE, March 8-12 (2010)
12. Maghrebi, H., Danger, J.-L., Flament, F., Guilley, S.: Evaluation of Countermeasures Implementation Based on Boolean Masking to Thwart First and Second Order Side-Channel Attacks. In: SCS, November 6-8, pp. 1–6. IEEE, Los Alamitos (2009)
13. Mangard, S., Oswald, E., Standaert, F.-X.: One for All - All for One: Unifying Standard DPA Attacks. Cryptology ePrint Archive, Report 2009/449 (2009)
14. Schindler, W.: Advanced stochastic methods in side channel analysis on block ciphers in the presence of masking. Journal of Mathematical Cryptology 2(3), 291–310 (2008); ISSN (Online) 1862-2984, ISSN (Print) 1862-2976, doi:10.1515/JMC.2008.013
15. Schindler, W., Lemke, K., Paar, C.: A Stochastic Model for Differential Side Channel Cryptanalysis. In: Rao, J.R., Sunar, B. (eds.) CHES 2005. LNCS, vol. 3659, pp. 30–46. Springer, Heidelberg (2005)
16. Standaert, F.-X., Gierlichs, B., Verbauwhede, I.: Partition vs. Comparison Side-Channel Distinguishers: An Empirical Evaluation of Statistical Tests for Univariate Side-Channel Attacks against Two Unprotected CMOS Devices. In: Lee, P.J., Cheon, J.H. (eds.) ICISC 2008. LNCS, vol. 5461, pp. 253–267. Springer, Heidelberg (2009)

17. Standaert, F.-X., Malkin, T.G., Yung, M.: A Unified Framework for the Analysis of Side-Channel Key Recovery Attacks. In: Joux, A. (ed.) EUROCRYPT 2009. LNCS, vol. 5479, pp. 443–461. Springer, Heidelberg (2009)
18. TELECOM ParisTech SEN research group. DPA Contest 1st edn. (2008–2009, http://www.DPAcontest.org/

A   Comparison of the Rank Corrector with Other Profiling Attacks

The rank corrector technique shares characteristics with the profiling attacks, such as template attacks [3]. This section clarifies the common points and the differences between the two types of attacks, and explains in which context the proposed attack methodology empowers an attacker when template attacks would be infeasible or impossible.

A.1   Assumptions on the Profiling Stage

Exactly as template attacks, the proposed methodology applies to the cases when it is wanted to break devices very fast, in "production mode". Template attacks require as a preliminary stage to characterize exhaustively a clone device, that is furthermore "open". This means that the device can be programmed with arbitrary secrets. Once programmed with a key, the device is exercised and some of its side-channels are recorded. The observation under this key leads to the construction of a template (typically consisting in the average and the covariance of the observations when the noise is Gaussian). It is noted in [15] that it can be sufficient to program the device with only one known key, in order to build all the templates. This case requires the templates not to be indexed by the key value, but instead by a sensitive variable (such as the distance between two states within the algorithm) that depends on the key. Then, in the attack phase, the distance with this key is retrieved by an exhaustive matching against all pre-built templates. Such an attack nevertheless requires that the EIS hypothesis[2] holds, which is very often the case in practice (at least no flagrant counter-example has been published so far). In a very similar idea, the stochastic approach [15,14] also considers a partial construction of an approximated model, but still requires the attacker to know the key for the purpose of this step; this condition is a mandatory requirement for the basis characterization of the stochastic approach.

The rank corrector does not demand that the attacker know the value of one key on a clone device. Instead, it only requires that a clone be available and attackable. On this device, the key is extracted by any suitable non-profiled side-channel attack. Then, various behaviours about the attack convergence (those

---

[2] The "Equal Images under the same Sub-key" (EIS) hypothesis assumes that in case the round sub-key k is merged with the plaintext m by a bitwise exclusive-or (XOR) and that the rest of the computation depends only on $m \oplus k$, then the device would leak exactly the same if the key was $k' = k \oplus \delta$ (for an arbitrary δ) and the messages were also translated by δ [15].

discussed in Sec. 3.3) are gathered, and serve as a basis to forge portable indicators of the attack unfolding. These parameters make up the basic substrate for subsequent attacks speed up. Thus, as opposed to template attacks, for which the attacker is expected to know at least one key, this methodology can be conducted blindly w.r.t. the secret. Therefore, in practice, the clone device can be bought from the normal market, as opposed to traditional profiling-based attacks that require an insider ships out an "engineering sample" (normally concealed carefully in strictly access-controlled facilities).

A.2   Templates Portability

In the cases where the attacker indeed manages to get an open clone device, another factor has to be taken into account when comparing the rank-corrector with the traditional template attacks. The templates (or the projection basis involved in stochastic analysis) should be characterized on a clone device, with a similar test environment. Now, the portability of templates is an open issue in the literature.

We indeed show that the waveforms shapes differ from one "training" campaign that has been carried out a long time ago and the "matching" campaign. For the sake of illustration, we compare three campaigns, denoted A, B and C.

1. **Campaign A:** 80 000 measurements garnered in year 2006 at nominal voltage (1.2 V) serve to build the templates,
2. **Campaign B:** 50 000 measurements garnered in year 2010 at nominal voltage (1.2 V) on the same ASIC are used for the matching,
3. **Campaign C:** 50 000 measurements garnered in year 2010 at reduced voltage (1.0 V) on the same ASIC are also used.

All campaigns have been averaged sixteen times by the oscilloscope to filter out as much environmental noise as possible. The goal of the campaign C is to provide with a comparison of two campaigns (B and C) that were carried out close in time, but with slightly different experimental conditions. Here, the variation comes from the supply power.

We observe first of all that campaign A is not in phase with campaigns B and C. The figure 8 typically emphasizes the timing mismatch between A, on the one hand, and B & C on the other hand. This figure is zoomed on the first round of encryption.

Now, if we apply the phase-only correlation (aka POC [7]) resynchronization technique, we end up with a global resynchronization of the curves. The result is depicted in Fig. 9.

Moreover, the amplitudes are not the same. This could be fixed by scaling vertically the curves. Eventually, we observe in Fig. 9 that the waves are different. We also compare the templates in the PCA subspaces. Without surprise, the principal directions are also desynchronized. Using the similar POC resynchronization method as previously done on the average raw traces, we get a time offset correction. After this time shift, the eigenvectors are in phase, as depicted in Fig. 10.

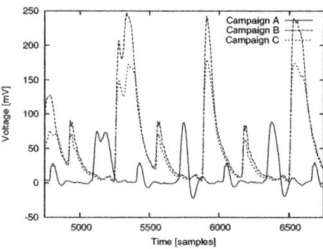

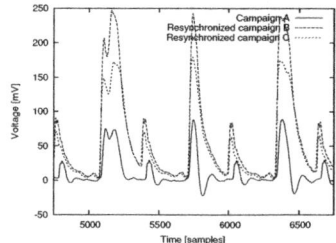

Fig. 8. Comparison of the average of campaigns A, B and C

Fig. 9. Comparison of the average of resynchronized campaigns A, B and C

The eigenvector shapes also differ. Therefore, the success rate of the attack is diminished. At the opposite, the rank-corrector considers global attack parameters, and it is thus free from the local modifications (for instance the waveforms). Although it is likely that some preprocessing on both the training and the matching campaigns manage to ensure a most successful success rate, these are so far to be considered advanced and are unstudied. In this paper, we argue that the rank corrector parameters are global parameters that are little affected by the acquisition conditions, even if they are differing. Thus, their portability (in theory and in practice) is trivially true. This means that we have put forward a systematic and algorithm independent methodologies to speed up the attacks. Still better, if a template profiling stage is feasible, then it is even possible to combine a template attack with the rank-corrector attack accelerator.

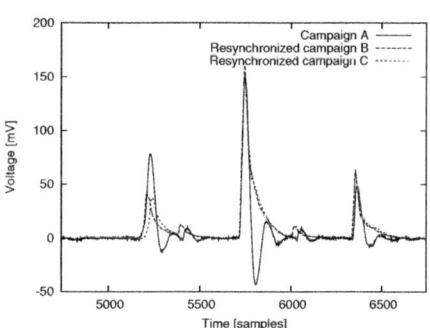

Fig. 10. Comparison of resynchronized first eigenvectors for A,B and C campaigns passed through PCA

A Cache Trace Attack on CAMELLIA

Rishabh Poddar, Amit Datta, and Chester Rebeiro

Department of Computer Science and Engineering,
Indian Institute of Technology, Kharagpur, India
{rishavp,adatta,chester}@cse.iitkgp.ernet.in

Abstract. CAMELLIA is a 128 bit block cipher certified for its security by NESSIE and CRYPTREC. Yet an implementation of CAMELLIA can easily fall prey to cache attacks. In this paper we present an attack on CAMELLIA, which utilizes cache access patterns along with the differential properties of CAMELLIA's s-boxes. The attack, when implemented on a PowerPC microprocessor having a 32 byte cache line size requires power traces from 2^{16} different encryptions. Further, the work shows that this trace requirement reduces to 2^{11} if a 64 byte cache line is used.

1 Introduction

With the development of newer and better encryption schemes, it has become increasingly difficult to find flaws in the algorithm and therefore the schemes are more secure. However, implementations of the encryption algorithms are highly susceptible to being attacked. Attacks that target implementations are known as *side channel attacks*, and were discovered by Paul Kocher in 1996 [10]. These attacks take advantage of the information that gets leaked during the cipher's execution. The channels for leakage are generally power consumption, timing for execution, and electro-magnetic radiation.

Cache attacks are a class of side-channel attacks that glean secret information from the behavior of the processor's cache memory. These attacks utilize the fact that a cache miss has a different power and timing profile compared to a cache hit. Cache attacks were first prophesied by Kelsey et al. in [9]. A theoretical model of a cache attack was then constructed by Page in [12]. In [17] and [18], the first cache attacks were successfully demonstrated. The ciphers targeted were MISTY1, DES, and 3-DES. Since the arrival of AES, it has been the favorite choice among side-channel attackers. There were several variants of cache attacks that were demonstrated on AES [1,3,4,5,6,7,8,11,16]. All attacks on AES can be classified into three depending on the channel used to collect information. These channels are power consumption traces, spy processes, and timing information. In scenarios where the attacker has direct access to the encryption device, monitoring power consumption traces is the best strategy in order to minimize the interactions with the device. These attacks, which came to be known as *cache trace attacks*, was the method used to attack AES in [1,4,7,8].

M. Joye et al. (Eds.): InfoSecHiComNet 2011, LNCS 7011, pp. 144–156, 2011.

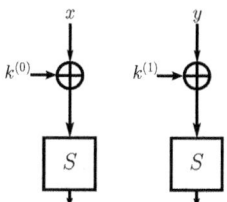

Fig. 1. S-box Table Accesses

One strategy common to all cache attacks is to split the large secret key of the cipher into a number of small key parts (for example the 128 bit key of AES is split into 16 bytes). During the attack, each of these key parts is obtained independently and then combined to obtain the entire key. In a Substitution-Permutation Network (SPN) structure like AES, all 16 bytes of the key are used in the first round itself. Attacking just the first round is simple because it is easy for the adversary to have control of the round inputs. In Feistel ciphers however, retrieving the entire 128 bit key often requires attacking more than one round. This is much more difficult because as the depth of the attack (in terms of the round being attacked) increases, it becomes increasingly difficult for the attacker to control the round inputs. In [13] for example, an attack was demonstrated on the generalized Feistel cipher CLEFIA [15], where obtaining the entire 128 byte key required attacking three rounds of the cipher. As seen in [13], the attack on the first round is very simple compared to the second round, while the third is the most complex.

In this paper we propose a cache trace attack on the 128-bit block cipher CAMELLIA [2]. CAMELLIA like CLEFIA is based on the Feistel structure. Therefore our attack follows a similar strategy as the attack on CLEFIA described in [13]. CAMELLIA however has the classical Feistel structure, while CLEFIA uses a type-2 generalized Feistel structure [19]. In a type-2 generalized Feistel structure, the adversary can control round inputs up to the 4th round. In the classical Feistel structure, however, only the second round inputs can be controlled. Further, retrieving the 128 bit CLEFIA key required attacking only 3 rounds. On the other hand, for CAMELLIA, 4 rounds need to be attacked. These reasons make an attack on CAMELLIA a bigger challenge and hence motivates the work in this paper.

The outline of the paper is as follows: the next section introduces cache attacks and gives a brief summary of CAMELLIA. Section 3 present the attack procedure. Section 4 discusses how the attack was practically mounted. The final section has the conclusions and future directions.

2 Preliminaries

In this section we first present the principle behind cache attacks and then give a brief description of the CAMELLIA structure.

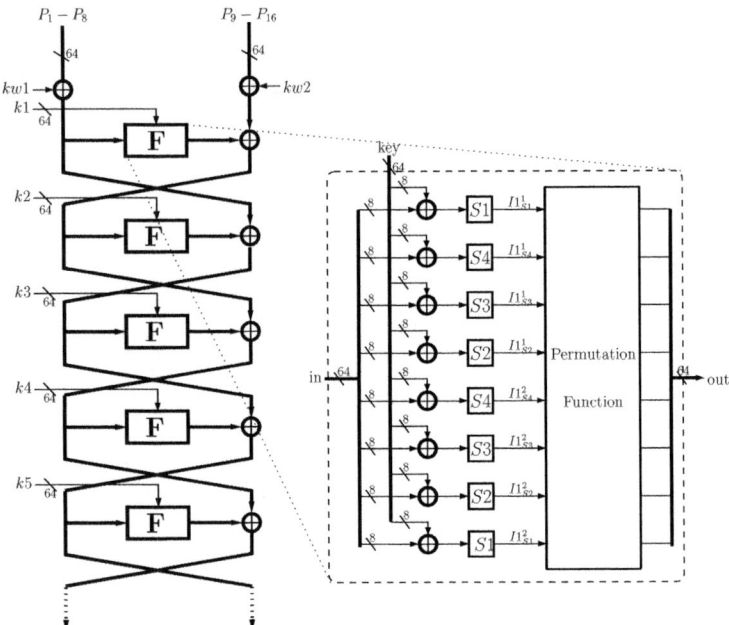

Fig. 2. Partial Structure of CAMELLIA

2.1   Principle of Cache Attacks

All cache attacks target structures in the block cipher such as in Figure 1. The figure shows two accesses to table S with indices $(x \oplus k^{(0)})$ and $(y \oplus k^{(1)})$. When a cache hit occurs the following relation holds, leading to leakage of information about the ex-or of the keys.

$$\langle k^{(0)} \oplus k^{(1)} \rangle = \langle x \oplus y \rangle \tag{1}$$

We note that due to the affects of the cache line, only the most significant bits can be equated, therefore $\langle \cdot \rangle$ refers to only these most significant bits. If the size of $k^{(0)}$ and $k^{(1)}$ is l bits, and there are 2^{δ} elements that share a cache line, then only the most significant $b = l - \delta$ bits satisfy the above equation. Similarly, when a cache miss occurs, the following inequality holds.

$$\langle k^{(0)} \oplus k^{(1)} \rangle \neq \langle x \oplus y \rangle \tag{2}$$

2.2   The CAMELLIA Structure

CAMELLIA is the 128-bit block cipher that was jointly developed by Mitsubishi and NTT in 2000. Since this cipher has been made available under a royalty-free license, it has been certified for use by the European Union and Japan. It has also become part of the OpenSSL Project, and incorporated in Mozilla's Network Security Services (NSS modules). Support for CAMELLIA has been added to several security libraries as well as Mozilla's popular web-browser, Firefox 3.

CAMELLIA has been so designed that an encryption can be done using either a 128-bit, a 192-bit or a 256-bit key. We have tested our attack on a 128-bit implementation. However the techniques described can be extended to other key lengths.

The $128-$bit block cipher CAMELLIA [2] has a Feistel structure as shown in Figure 2. The 16 bytes plaintext input $P_1 \cdots P_{16}$ is grouped in two words of 8 bytes each. There are 18 rounds in all, broken up into groups of 6 each. After the 6th and the 12th rounds, there are two FL/FL^{-1} function layers. In each round, there is an F-function, which is a combination of key addition, substitution and diffusion. The substitution is done by using four s-boxes, whereas the diffusion is implemented as follows:

$$
\begin{pmatrix} z_1 \\ z_2 \\ . \\ . \\ z_8 \end{pmatrix} \longmapsto \begin{pmatrix} z_1' \\ z_2' \\ . \\ . \\ z_8' \end{pmatrix} = M \cdot \begin{pmatrix} z_1 \\ z_2 \\ . \\ . \\ z_8 \end{pmatrix}
$$

where,

$$
M = \begin{pmatrix}
1 & 0 & 1 & 1 & 0 & 1 & 1 & 1 \\
1 & 1 & 0 & 1 & 1 & 0 & 1 & 1 \\
1 & 1 & 1 & 0 & 1 & 1 & 0 & 1 \\
0 & 1 & 1 & 1 & 1 & 1 & 1 & 0 \\
1 & 1 & 0 & 0 & 0 & 1 & 1 & 1 \\
0 & 1 & 1 & 0 & 1 & 0 & 1 & 1 \\
0 & 0 & 1 & 1 & 1 & 1 & 0 & 1 \\
1 & 0 & 0 & 1 & 1 & 1 & 1 & 0
\end{pmatrix}
$$

Each round has an addition of a round key. The ith round uses the round key k_i. Each of these round keys are of 64 bits. Additionally, whitening keys kw_1 and kw_2 are applied at the start of encryption, while kw_3 and kw_4 are applied at the end of encryption.

The implementation of CAMELLIA attacked in this paper consists of one 256 byte table which implements each s-box. The next part of the section discusses the basic principle behind cache attacks.

3   The Attack on CAMELLIA

We depict the first two rounds of CAMELLIA's Feistel structure to describe the principle behind the proposed attack (Figure 3).

The input $\mathbf{x}$ consists of 8 concatenated bytes $(x_1|x_2|x_3|x_4|x_5|x_6|x_7|x_8)$ and is known as the *differential introducing input*. The input $\mathbf{y}$ consists of the bytes $(y_1|y_2|y_3|y_4|y_5|y_6|y_7|x_8)$ and is known as the *restoring input*. The F in the figure is CAMELLIA's F function (see Figure 2). For a particular fixed value of $\mathbf{x}$, we vary the bytes of $\mathbf{y}$ until we obtain cache hits in all s-box tables in the second

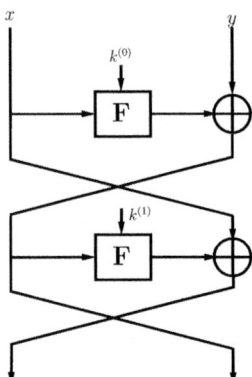

Fig. 3. First two rounds of CAMELLIA

round F function. We call this the *collision setup* phase. At the end of the setup, the following equations holds for $1 \leq i \leq 8$ if a cache hit is obtained.

$$\langle x_i \oplus k_i^{(0)} \rangle = \langle y_i \oplus k_i^{(1)} \oplus F(x, k^{(0)})_i \rangle \tag{3}$$

Similarly, the following inequalities hold if a cache miss is obtained.

$$\langle x_i \oplus k_i^{(0)} \rangle \neq \langle y_i \oplus k_i^{(1)} \oplus F(x, k^{(0)})_i \rangle \tag{4}$$

We now displace the input byte x_1 by $d_{x_1} \neq 0$, keeping the rest of the bytes of $\mathbf{x}$ unchanged. After the s-box operation, the displacement is diffused to the output bytes of the F function. As a result, some or all of the cache hits in the second round are lost. We now modify the bytes of $\mathbf{y}$ to restore cache hits in the second round, and once again obtain the collision state. This is called the *restoring phase*. Let $\mathbf{y}' = (y_1'|y_2'|y_3'|y_4'|y_5'|y_6'|y_7'|y_8')$ be the new value of $\mathbf{y}$ after the modification. Therefore, the differences in the output of the F function are $d_{y_i} = y_i \oplus y_i'$.

From the difference distribution table for the s-box, one can derive the set of possible output differentials corresponding to the input differential d_{x_1}. Let this set be called $\mathcal{D}$. For every output differential $d_o \in \mathcal{D}$, we compute the matrix product $M \cdot (d_o, 0, 0, 0, 0, 0, 0, 0)^T$. This is used to obtain the differentials $(d_{z_1}, d_{z_1}, d_{z_2}, d_{z_3}, d_{z_4}, d_{z_5}, d_{z_6}, d_{z_7}, d_{z_8})^T$. For the correct s-box output differential d_o, $\langle d_{z_i} \rangle = \langle d_{y_i} \rangle$ for $1 \leq i \leq 8$. We exploit this to obtain the set of possible keys (S) for the key byte $k_1^{(0)}$. The number of candidate keys can be reduced by repeating the attack several times and taking the intersection between the sets. If r repetitions are done, then,

$$\text{Expected number of candidate keys after } r \text{ repetitions} = \frac{|S|^r}{256^{r-1}} \tag{5}$$

In a similar way, displacements introduced at $x_2, x_3, \ldots, x_8$, would lead to leakages in $k_2^{(0)}, k_3^{(0)}, \ldots, k_8^{(0)}$ respectively. The technique used to generate the candidate keys is given by Algorithm 1, provided the collisions have been set up. The next part of the section describes the full attack on CAMELLIA. The proposed attack first determines $k_1 \oplus kw_1$, then $k_2 \oplus kw_2$, followed by $k_3 \oplus kw_1$, and finally $k_4 \oplus kw_2$ (see Figure 2). This information is used to reverse the key scheduling algorithm to obtain the entire key.

Algorithm 1. find : Finding Key Byte $k_i^{(0)}$ assuming collisions have been setup

---

Input: $i \in \{1, 2, \ldots, 8\}$, the differential introducing input x and restoring input y
Output: $S(k_i^{(0)})$: Candidate Key Set for $k_i^{(0)}$

1 **begin**
2 $\quad$ $S(k_i^{(0)}) \leftarrow \{\}$
3 $\quad$ $x_i \leftarrow x_i \oplus d_{x_i}$
4 $\quad$ *Restore collisions* : Find $y_1', y_2', \ldots, y_8'$ which causes collisions in the accesses of the 2nd round
5 $\quad$ $\mathcal{D} \leftarrow$ output difference set corresponding to the input difference d_{x_i}
6 $\quad$ **foreach** $d_o \in D$ **do**
7 $\quad\quad$ $(d_{z1}, d_{z2}, d_{z3}, d_{z4}, d_{z5}, d_{z6}, d_{z7}, d_{z8})^T \leftarrow M \cdot (d_o, 0, 0, 0, 0, 0, 0, 0)^T$
8 $\quad\quad$ **if** $(\langle d_{z1} \rangle = \langle y_1 \oplus y_1' \rangle$ *and* $\langle d_{z2} \rangle = \langle y_2 \oplus y_2' \rangle$ *and* $\langle d_{z3} \rangle = \langle y_3 \oplus y_3' \rangle$ *and* $\langle d_{z4} \rangle = \langle y_4 \oplus y_4' \rangle$ *and* $\langle d_{z5} \rangle = \langle y_5 \oplus y_5' \rangle$ *and* $\langle d_{z6} \rangle = \langle y_6 \oplus y_6' \rangle$ *and* $\langle d_{z7} \rangle = \langle y_7 \oplus y_7' \rangle$ *and* $\langle d_{z8} \rangle = \langle y_8 \oplus y_8' \rangle)$ **then**
9 $\quad\quad\quad$ $S(k_i^{(0)}) \leftarrow S(k_i^{(0)}) \cup \{d_o\}$
10 $\quad\quad$ **end**
11 $\quad$ **end**
12 **end**

3.1   Determining $k_1 \oplus kw_1$

Let the 16 bytes of the input plaintext be $(P_1|P_2|\cdots|P_{16})$. We consider the memory accesses to the first and second round F functions. The structure is similar to Figure 3 with the 8 leftmost bytes $P_1, P_2, \cdots P_8$ as the differential introducing input, and the 8 rightmost bytes $P_9, P_{10}, \cdots P_{16}$ as the restoring input. In CAMELLIA, each s-box is used twice per round. Therefore, a resulting cache hit in the second round would be due to collisions with either of these accesses. Let $I\alpha_{S\beta}^i$ be the index to the ith access to table $S\beta$ in round α (see Figure 2). Thus, a collision in $I2_{S1}^1$ could be with either or both of $I1_{S1}^1$ and $I1_{S1}^2$. To eliminate this ambiguity, we ensure that all accesses in the first round are themselves colliding. That is for $S1$,

$$\langle I1_{S1}^1 \rangle = \langle I1_{S1}^2 \rangle$$

Similarly, for $S2$, $S3$ and $S4$ we have

$$\langle I1_{S2}^1 \rangle = \langle I1_{S2}^2 \rangle$$

$$\langle I1_{S3}^1 \rangle = \langle I1_{S3}^2 \rangle$$

and

$$\langle I1_{S4}^1 \rangle = \langle I1_{S4}^2 \rangle$$

We call such a state the $1-round$ collision state. Algorithm 2 shows how a $1-$round collision state can be obtained in the cipher. Algorithm 3 is then used to determine $k_1 \oplus kw_1$.

Algorithm 2. 1−round collision

Input: P_1, P_2, P_3 and P_4
Output: P_5, P_6, P_7 and P_8
1 **begin**
2   Find P_5 causing a collision in $I1^2_{S1}$
3   Find P_6 causing a collision in $I1^2_{S2}$
4   Find P_7 causing a collision in $I1^2_{S3}$
5   Find P_8 causing a collision in $I1^2_{S4}$
6 **end**

Analysis : From side-channel analysis, it is possible to determine whether a memory access resulted in a cache hit or a miss. Testing for a collision at a particular memory access requires $\frac{256}{C}$ encryptions, where C is the cache line size. However, by using the inequality in Equation 4, it is sufficient to have $\frac{256}{C} - 1$ encryptions in order to find the collision. Algorithm 2 therefore requires $4(\frac{256}{C} - 1)$ encryptions. Setting up the 8 collisions in line 4 of Algorithm 3 requires $8(\frac{256}{C} - 1)$ encryptions. Further, each invocation of the *find* function requires $8(\frac{256}{C} - 1)$ encryptions. Thus in total, finding all the 8 bytes of $k_1 \oplus kw_1$ requires $60(\frac{256}{C} - 1)$ encryptions.

Algorithm 3. Finding candidate keys for $\kappa = k_1 \oplus kw_1$

Output: $S(\kappa_i)$: Candidate Keys for $\kappa = k_1 \oplus kw_1$, where $i \in \{1, 2, \ldots, 8\}$
1 **begin**
2   Randomly select P_1, P_2, P_3 and P_4
3      $(P_5, P_6, P_7, P_8) \leftarrow$ 1−RoundCollision(P_1, P_2, P_3, P_4)
4   *Set up collisions :* Find $P_9, P_{10}, \cdots, P_{16}$ causing collisions in $I2^1_{S1}, I2^1_{S2}, \ldots, I2^2_{S4}$
     respectively
5      $S(\kappa_1) \leftarrow find(1, P_1 \cdots P_8, P_9 \cdots P_{16})$
6      $S(\kappa_2) \leftarrow find(2, P_1 \cdots P_8, P_9 \cdots P_{16})$
7      $S(\kappa_3) \leftarrow find(3, P_1 \cdots P_8, P_9 \cdots P_{16})$
8      $S(\kappa_4) \leftarrow find(4, P_1 \cdots P_8, P_9 \cdots P_{16})$
9      $S(\kappa_5) \leftarrow find(5, P_1 \cdots P_8, P_9 \cdots P_{16})$
10      $S(\kappa_6) \leftarrow find(6, P_1 \cdots P_8, P_9 \cdots P_{16})$
11      $S(\kappa_7) \leftarrow find(7, P_1 \cdots P_8, P_9 \cdots P_{16})$
12      $S(\kappa_8) \leftarrow find(8, P_1 \cdots P_8, P_9 \cdots P_{16})$
13 **end**

For a 64 byte cache line, 228 encryptions are required to obtain a set of 64 candidates per key on average. On average repeating the attack 4 times would result in a single key. Therefore in total 912 encryptions are required. Similarly for a 32 byte cache line, 532 encryptions are required to obtain a candidate key set. Filtering out the wrong keys would require a total of 1596 encryptions.

3.2 Determining $k_2 \oplus kw_2$

We consider the F functions in the second and third rounds to determine candidates for $k_2 \oplus kw_2$, with $P_9 \cdots P_{16}$ as the differential introducing inputs, and $P_1 \cdots P_8$ as the restoring inputs. As in the first stage of the attack, ambiguities about collisions may arise when cache hits are forced in the third round F function. Therefore, the cipher is put in a 2−*round colliding state*. In a 2−*round colliding state*, all accesses except the first are in collision for each table, i.e.,

$$\langle I1^1_{S1}\rangle = \langle I1^2_{S1}\rangle = \langle I2^1_{S1}\rangle = \langle I2^2_{S1}\rangle$$

$$\langle I1^1_{S2}\rangle = \langle I1^2_{S2}\rangle = \langle I2^1_{S2}\rangle = \langle I2^2_{S2}\rangle$$

$$\langle I1^1_{S3}\rangle = \langle I1^2_{S3}\rangle = \langle I2^1_{S3}\rangle = \langle I2^2_{S3}\rangle$$

$$\langle I1^1_{S4}\rangle = \langle I1^2_{S4}\rangle = \langle I2^1_{S4}\rangle = \langle I2^2_{S4}\rangle$$

We note that the results obtained in the previous stage of the attack (i.e. determining $k_1 \oplus kw_1$) may be used to put the cipher in the $2-round\ colliding\ state$. Hence, no additional encryptions are required.

To prevent further ambiguities in the third round accesses to a table, the inputs must be controlled in a manner that causes no hits to be lost in all previous accesses made to that table, i.e. the $2-round\ colliding\ state$ remains intact. This is accomplished as follows.

The restoring inputs for this stage of the attack are formed by $P_1 \cdots P_8$ ex-ored with the outputs of the second round F (see Figure 2). These values may be controlled by displacements made in the values of $P_1 \cdots P_8$ ensuring that collisions are not lost in the first two rounds. For example, suppose a hit is desired in $I3^1_{S1}$. This is done by controlling P_1. However changing P_1 may result in loss of collision in $I1^2_{S1}$. Further, the change in P_1 would affect several outputs of the first round F function due to the diffusion. This might disturb the collisions in the second round. To avoid this loss in the $2-round$ colliding state, the previously determined value of $k_1 \oplus kw_1$ is used. Using this, P_8 can be set to ensure collision in $I1^2_{S1}$ persists. The determined key is also used to compute the outputs of the first round F. The values of $P_9 \cdots P_{16}$ are now ex-ored with these outputs, so that the effect of the disturbance on the second round accesses is annulled. Thus, the $2-round$ colliding state persists.

This principle can similarly be applied to determine candidates for all the bytes of $k_2 \oplus kw_2$. Algorithm 4 describes the steps for the attack. An important point to note is the modification that needs to be made in the $restore\ collisions$ phase of Algorithm $find$. This step must now be performed in keeping with the discussion in the previous paragraph.

Algorithm 4. Finding candidate keys for $\kappa = k_2 \oplus kw_2$

Input: $P_1 \cdots P_{16}$, so that a $2-round\ colliding\ state$ has been set up
Output: $S(\kappa_i)$: Candidate Keys for $\kappa = k_2 \oplus kw_2$, where $i \in \{1,2,\ldots,8\}$
1 begin
2       $Set\ up\ collisions$: Find $P_1, P_2, \cdots, P_8$ causing collisions in $I3^1_{S1}, I3^1_{S2}, \ldots, I3^2_{S4}$ respectively
3       $S(\kappa_1) \leftarrow find(1, P_9 \cdots P_{16}, P_1 \cdots P_8)$
4       $S(\kappa_2) \leftarrow find(2, P_9 \cdots P_{16}, P_1 \cdots P_8)$
5       $S(\kappa_3) \leftarrow find(3, P_9 \cdots P_{16}, P_1 \cdots P_8)$
6       $S(\kappa_4) \leftarrow find(4, P_9 \cdots P_{16}, P_1 \cdots P_8)$
7       $S(\kappa_5) \leftarrow find(5, P_9 \cdots P_{16}, P_1 \cdots P_8)$
8       $S(\kappa_6) \leftarrow find(6, P_9 \cdots P_{16}, P_1 \cdots P_8)$
9       $S(\kappa_7) \leftarrow find(7, P_9 \cdots P_{16}, P_1 \cdots P_8)$
10      $S(\kappa_8) \leftarrow find(8, P_9 \cdots P_{16}, P_1 \cdots P_8)$
11 end

Analysis : Obtaining collisions in all eight accesses in the third round requires $8(\frac{256}{C} - 1)$ encryptions. Once this is done, deducing each key byte requires $8(\frac{256}{C} - 1)$ encryptions. Since there are 8 unknown key bytes, a total of $65(\frac{256}{C} - 1)$ encryptions is needed to obtain the candidate key set. With a 64$-$byte cache line, this attack step should be repeated 4 times to isolate a single key. This requires 768 encryptions. Similarly with a 32$-$byte cache line, and 3 iterations of the attack step, a single key is isolated in 1365 encryptions.

3.3   Determining $k_3 \oplus kw_1$ and $k_4 \oplus kw_2$

To determine candidates for $k_3 \oplus kw_1$, we consider the F functions in the third and fourth rounds, with $P_1 \cdots P_8$ as the differential introducing inputs, and $P_9 \cdots P_{16}$ as the restoring inputs. The cipher should be ideally put in a 3$-round$ *colliding state* before mounting the attack. However, achieving such a state is more difficult than obtaining a 2$-round$ *colliding state*. To circumvent this difficulty, we initially put the cipher in a *partial* 3$-round$ *colliding state* using the following technique, for the third stage of the attack.

We first obtain a 2$-round$ *colliding state*. The values of $P_9 \cdots P_{16}$ are subsequently ex-ored by small amounts less than the cache line size. Since these displacements are small, accesses in the second round continue to collide with the same cache lines, and no hits are lost. These small displacements, however, would become random changes affecting all outputs of the second round F. Thus, for suitable values of these displacements, collisions may be established in particular accesses of our choice in the third round (creating a *partial* 3$-round$ *colliding state*), without losing any hits in the first 2 rounds. The state is thus a *partial* colliding state because not all third round accesses are hits. The colliding accesses are chosen as follows.

Suppose the byte of the key to be determined is ex-ored with a byte of the differential introducing input ($P_1 \cdots P_8$) that accesses table $S\beta$ in the third round F (see Figure 2). Then both accesses to $S\beta$ must be established as hits. Evidently, once this state has been obtained, for $\beta = 1$,

$$\langle I1_{S1}^1 \rangle = \langle I1_{S1}^2 \rangle = \langle I2_{S1}^1 \rangle = \langle I2_{S1}^2 \rangle = \langle I3_{S1}^1 \rangle = \langle I3_{S1}^2 \rangle$$

while for $\beta \neq 1$, $\langle I3_{S\beta}^1 \rangle$ and $\langle I3_{S\beta}^2 \rangle$ may or may not be equal to $\langle I1_{S\beta}^1 \rangle = \langle I1_{S\beta}^2 \rangle = \langle I2_{S\beta}^1 \rangle = \langle I2_{S\beta}^2 \rangle$. This does not affect the results of the attack in any way.

The restoring inputs are controlled following the principle described in section 3.2 using bytes $P_9 \cdots P_{16}$. However, this might lead to ambiguities in the fourth round memory accesses. For example, a cache hit in $I4_{S1}^1$ can be forced by small displacements in one or more of $P_9 \cdots P_{16}$. Since these displacements are small, no collisions will be lost in the second round accesses to $S1$. However, changing these bytes may cause hits to be lost in the third round $S1$ accesses. Thus a collision in $I4_{S1}^1$ may be a result of the desirable cache hit with $I1_{S1}^1$, $I1_{S1}^2$, $I2_{S1}^1$ and $I2_{S1}^2$, or due to undesirable cache hits with $I3_{S1}^1$ and $I3_{S1}^2$.

Thus, for a table $S\beta$, a collision in the fourth round is the result of a desirable cache hit with a probability $\frac{1}{n+1}$, where n is the number of misses in the third round accesses to the table. Since 2 accesses are made to each table per round, this probability is at least $\frac{1}{3}$, and sufficient confidence in the correctness of the collision is obtained if the test is repeated 3 times.

In the fourth stage of the attack, candidates for $k_4 \oplus kw_2$ are obtained by considering the F functions in the fourth and fifth rounds, with $P_9 \cdots P_{16}$ as the differential introducing inputs, and $P_1 \cdots P_8$ as the restoring inputs. Ideally, the cipher should be initially put in at least a *partial 4−round colliding state* before mounting the attack on the fourth round. However, such a state cannot be easily obtained without losing collisions in the accesses of the previous rounds. Moreover, attempting small displacements in the values of $P_9 \cdots P_{16}$ will entail a lot more encryptions to obtain a *partial 4−round colliding state*, as opposed to a *partial 3−round colliding state*. Therefore, we proceed to mount the attack with the cipher in a *partial 3−round colliding state* as obtained earlier.

Collisions in the fourth round may be established at the expense of hits in the third round. For a table $S\beta$, this implies that hits obtained in the fourth round may either be due to desirable collisions with accesses in the first 2 rounds, or due to undesirable collisions with any access resulting in a miss in the third round. That is, for table $S1$,

$$\langle I1_{S1}^1 \rangle = \langle I1_{S1}^2 \rangle = \langle I2_{S1}^1 \rangle = \langle I2_{S1}^2 \rangle$$

are desirable collisions. Accesses $\langle I3_{S1}^1 \rangle$ and $\langle I3_{S1}^2 \rangle$ may or may not be desirable. Thus, for a table $S\beta$, a collision in the fourth round is the result of a desirable cache hit with a probability $\frac{1}{m+1}$, where m is the number of misses in the third round accesses to the table.

Similarly, we may obtain hits in the fifth round with the restoring inputs by small displacements of $P_9 \cdots P_{16}$ at the expense of the third and fourth round hits. The probability of a correct hit is thus $\frac{1}{n+1}$, where n is the total number of misses in the third and fourth round accesses. Therefore, the entire method results in a success with probability $\frac{1}{(m+1)(n+1)}$. Since in the worst case, $m = 2$ and $n = 4$, this probability is at least $\frac{1}{(2+1)(4+1)} = \frac{1}{15}$, and the test should be repeated 15 times on an average, to obtain sufficient confidence in the result.

Analysis : Once a *2−round colliding state* has been obtained, we need to enforce hits in 2 accesses in the third round to get a *partial 3−round colliding state*. Since an access to a table may occupy any of 4 cache lines for $C = 64$ and 8 cache lines for $C = 32$, we get the required cache hit with a probability $\frac{1}{4}$ on 64 byte cache lines and $\frac{1}{8}$ on 32 byte cache lines after one encryption.

For the third stage of the attack, once a *partial 3−round colliding state* has been created, collisions are obtained in the fourth round with a minimum probability of $\frac{1}{3}$. Thus, an attack in the third stage is successful with a probability $\frac{1}{3\times4} = \frac{1}{12}$ for $C = 64$ and $\frac{1}{3\times8} = \frac{1}{24}$ for $C = 32$. Thus for $C = 64$, 12 encryptions are required to extract key candidates for one byte of the key. Since the key comprises 8 bytes, the expected number of encryptions is $12 \times 8 = 96$. This has to be repeated at-least 8 times to isolate a unique key, making a total requirement of 768 encryptions. Similarly, for $C = 32$, a total of 1536 encryptions are required.

For the fourth stage, the attack is successful with a minimum probability $\frac{1}{15}$. Since we need to obtain a *partial 3−round colliding state* before mounting the attack, the minimum probability of success is $\frac{1}{15 \times 4} = \frac{1}{60}$ for $C = 64$. Thus, 60 encryptions are required on an average to extract one byte of the key. The expected number of encryptions for extracting the entire key is $60 \times 8 \times 8 = 3480$ when $C = 64$ and 7680 encryptions are needed when $C = 32$.

3.4   Obtaining the Secret Key

The third and fourth stages of the attack on the cipher leak the values of $k_3 \oplus kw_1$ and $k_4 \oplus kw_2$ respectively. From the CAMELLIA key schedule for a 128-bit key, we know that

$$k_3 \oplus kw_1 = (K_L \oplus (K_L \lll 15))_L$$

$$k_4 \oplus kw_2 = (K_L \oplus (K_L \lll 15))_R$$

Thus, from the attack on the first 4 rounds, we can obtain the value $C = (K_L \oplus (K_L \lll 15))$. This information is sufficient to derive the value of K_L, which is the required secret 128-bit key. Algorithm 5 shows how the candidates for the secret key can be extracted. Using the algorithm, we get at most 2 candidates for K_L. For the sake of convenience, the 128-bit values have been represented as arrays of dimension 128.

Algorithm 5. Finding candidates for the secret key K_L

Input: $C[] = (K_L \oplus (K_L \lll 15))$
Output: $S(K)$: Candidate key set for the secret key K_L
1 begin
2 | $S \leftarrow \{\}$
3 | $K[] \leftarrow \{0\}$
4 | for $lsb \in \{0, 1\}$ do
5 | | $K[0] \leftarrow lsb$
6 | | $j \leftarrow 0$
7 | | for $i \in \{0, 1, \ldots, 127\}$ do
8 | | | if $j \geq 128$ then
9 | | | | $j \leftarrow j\%128$
10 | | | end
11 | | | $K[(j - 15)\%128] \leftarrow K[j] \oplus C[j]$
12 | | end
13 | | $S \leftarrow S \cup \{K\}$
14 | end
15 | return S
16 end

---

4   Practically Mounting the Attack

To test the attack we used a similar setup as in [13] with CAMELLIA's reference code[1] modified to use 4 tables. The attack consists of two phases, the online and the offline phase, which are repeated for each step of the attack. The online phase dealt with obtaining the required power traces from the board. The attack

---
[1] http://info.isl.ntt.co.jp/crypt/eng/camellia/source.html

targeted the cache of the PowerPC present in the Xilinx FPGA in the SASEBO board [14]. The PowerPC cache has a 32 byte cache line and a size of $16KB$. During the offline phase, the traces are first analyzed in Matlab to retrieve the cache access patterns. This is then fed to the analysis program, which guesses the secret key. For the 32 byte cache line, the number of encryptions required to be made is 12177.

5   Conclusions and Future Directions

The paper presents a cache trace attack on the 128 bit block cipher CAMEL-LIA. The attack first finds the keys used in rounds 1 to 4 and then uses the key scheduling algorithm of CAMELLIA to retrieve the entire secret key. On a PowerPC processor, having a $32-$byte cache line size, this requires monitoring of around 2^{16} power traces. On a processor using the more standard 64 byte cache line, the number of power traces required are 2^{11}.

A comparison of the proposed attack on CAMELLIA with cache trace attacks on AES exemplifies the difficulty in attacking Feistel ciphers. As a future work various cipher structures can be analyzed for their robustness against cache attacks. This analysis would play a pivotal role in constructing a cipher inherently secure against cache attacks.

References

 1. Acıiçmez, O., Koç, Ç.K.: Trace-Driven Cache Attacks on AES (Short Paper). In: Ning, P., Qing, S., Li, N. (eds.) ICICS 2006. LNCS, vol. 4307, pp. 112–121. Springer, Heidelberg (2006)
 2. Aoki, K., Ichikawa, T., Kanda, M., Matsui, M., Moriai, S., Nakajima, J., Tokita, T.: Specifications of Camellia – a 128-bit Block Cipher (2001)
 3. Bernstein, D.J.: Cache-timing Attacks on AES. Tech. rep. (2005)
 4. Bertoni, G., Zaccaria, V., Breveglieri, L., Monchiero, M., Palermo, G.: AES Power Attack Based on Induced Cache Miss and Countermeasure. In: ITCC (1), pp. 586–591. IEEE Computer Society, Los Alamitos (2005)
 5. Bonneau, J., Mironov, I.: Cache Collision Timing Attacks Against AES. In: Goubin, L., Matsui, M. (eds.) CHES 2006. LNCS, vol. 4249, pp. 201–215. Springer, Heidelberg (2006)
 6. Canteaut, A., Lauradoux, C., Seznec, A.: Understanding Cache Attacks. Research Report RR-5881, INRIA (2006), http://hal.inria.fr/inria-00071387/en/
 7. Fournier, J.J.A., Tunstall, M.: Cache Based Power Analysis Attacks on AES. In: Batten, L.M., Safavi-Naini, R. (eds.) ACISP 2006. LNCS, vol. 4058, pp. 17–28. Springer, Heidelberg (2006)
 8. Gallais, J.-F., Kizhvatov, I., Tunstall, M.: Improved Trace-Driven Cache-Collision Attacks against Embedded AES Implementations. In: Chung, Y., Yung, M. (eds.) WISA 2010. LNCS, vol. 6513, pp. 243–257. Springer, Heidelberg (2011)
 9. Kelsey, J., Schneier, B., Wagner, D., Hall, C.: Side Channel Cryptanalysis of Product Ciphers. J. Comput. Secur. 8(2,3), 141–158 (2000)
10. Kocher, P.C.: Timing Attacks on Implementations of Diffie-Hellman, RSA, DSS, and Other Systems. In: Koblitz, N. (ed.) CRYPTO 1996. LNCS, vol. 1109, pp. 104–113. Springer, Heidelberg (1996)

11. Osvik, D.A., Shamir, A., Tromer, E.: Cache Attacks and Countermeasures: The Case of AES. In: Pointcheval, D. (ed.) CT-RSA 2006. LNCS, vol. 3860, pp. 1–20. Springer, Heidelberg (2006)
12. Page, D.: Theoretical Use of Cache Memory as a Cryptanalytic Side-Channel (2002)
13. Rebeiro, C., Mukhopadhyay, D.: Cryptanalysis of CLEFIA Using Differential Methods with Cache Trace Patterns. In: Kiayias, A. (ed.) CT-RSA 2011. LNCS, vol. 6558, pp. 89–103. Springer, Heidelberg (2011)
14. Research Center for Information Security National Institute of Advanced Industrial Science and Technology: Side-channel Attack Standard Evaluation Board Specification (Version 1.0) (2007)
15. Sony Corporation: The 128-bit Blockcipher CLEFIA : Algorithm Specification (2007)
16. Tromer, E., Osvik, D.A., Shamir, A.: Efficient Cache Attacks on AES, and Countermeasures. Journal of Cryptology 23(2), 37–71 (2010)
17. Tsunoo, Y., Saito, T., Suzaki, T., Shigeri, M., Miyauchi, H.: Cryptanalysis of DES Implemented on Computers with Cache. In: Walter, C.D., Koç, Ç.K., Paar, C. (eds.) CHES 2003. LNCS, vol. 2779, pp. 62–76. Springer, Heidelberg (2003)
18. Tsunoo, Y., Tsujihara, E., Minematsu, K., Miyauchi, H.: Cryptanalysis of Block Ciphers Implemented on Computers with Cache. In: International Symposium on Information Theory and Its Applications, pp. 803–806 (2002)
19. Zheng, Y., Matsumoto, T., Imai, H.: On the Construction of Block Ciphers Provably Secure and Not Relying on Any Unproved Hypotheses. In: Brassard, G. (ed.) CRYPTO 1989. LNCS, vol. 435, pp. 461–480. Springer, Heidelberg (1990)

An Improvement of Linearization-Based Algebraic Attacks

Satrajit Ghosh and Abhijit Das

Department of Computer Science and Engineering
Indian Institute of Technology Kharagpur, India
{satrajit,abhij}@cse.iitkgp.ernet.in

Abstract. In an algebraic attack on a cipher, one expresses the encryption function as a system (usually overdefined) of multivariate polynomial equations in the bits of the plaintext, the ciphertext and the key, and subsequently solves the system for the unknown key bits from the knowledge of one or more plaintext/ciphertext pairs. The standard eXtended Linearization algorithm (XL) expands the initial system of equations by monomial multiplications. The expanded system is treated as a linear system in the monomials. For most block ciphers (like the Advanced Encryption Standard (AES)), the size of the linearized system turns out to be very large, and consequently, the complexity to solve the system often exceeds the complexity of brute-force search. In this paper, we propose a heuristic strategy XL_SGE to reduce the number of linearized equations. This reduction is achieved by applying structured Gaussian elimination before each stage of monomial multiplication. Experimentation on small random systems indicates that XL_SGE has the potential to improve the performance of the XL algorithm in terms of the size of the final solvable system. This performance gain is exhibited by our heuristic also in the case of a toy version of AES.

Keywords: Block cipher, AES, multivariate polynomial equation, algebraic attack, linearization, XL, sparse linear system, structured Gaussian elimination.

1 Introduction

The security of many cryptosystems is based on the difficulty of solving large systems of nonlinear multivariate polynomial equations [1]. The main idea of algebraic cryptanalysis is to express the encryption transform of a cipher as an overdefined system of multivariate polynomial equations in the bits of the plaintext, the ciphertext and the key. Algebraic cryptanalysis deals with different ways of solving the multivariate system from known plaintext/ciphertext pairs. Techniques based upon Gröbner-basis computation (like Faugère's F_4 and F_5 algorithms [2,3]) usually take exponential (or more) time in the size of the system, and so are practically infeasible. Kipnis and Shamir [4] introduce an alternative elimination technique called *relinearization* which is expected to run

M. Joye et al. (Eds.): InfoSecHiComNet 2011, LNCS 7011, pp. 157–167, 2011.

in subexponential time. Several variants of this relinearization technique have been proposed in the literature (like XL [5], XSL [6] and MutantXL [7]). A third elimination technique proposed by Bard et al. [8] makes use of SAT solvers.

There are practical examples of algebraic attacks on stream ciphers, block ciphers and public-key cryptosystems. In 1999, Kipnis and Shamir cryptanalyze the HFE public-key cryptosystem by their relinearization technique [4]. In 2000, Courtois et al. [5] propose the XL algorithm (eXtended Linearization). Its modification named XSL (eXtended Sparse Linearization) is proposed by Courtois and Pieprzyk [6] in 2002. In 2007, Courtois and Bard [9] cryptanalyze six rounds of DES from only one known plaintext/ciphertext pair using SAT solvers. In 2008, Courtois et al. [10] use slide-algebraic attack to cryptanalyze the KeeLoq block cipher using SAT solvers, with a complexity equivalent to about 2^{53} KeeLoq encryptions (with 2^{16} known pairs). In 2009, Courtois et al. [11] describe a full-key recovery attack on the Hitag2 stream cipher. The Master's thesis of Vörös [12] lists practical algebraic attacks on some other stream ciphers.

Although algebraic attacks have a few success stories, the general time complexity of these attacks is prohibitively high. The main problem of applying algebraic attacks to the case of block ciphers is that the size of the final solvable system becomes unmanageably huge. As a result, the attack complexity exceeds the complexity of brute-force search. For example, in the case of 128-bit AES, a direct application of XL produces a solvable system for $D = 18$ [6], but the size of the solvable system is very large (about 2^{110}). As a result, the complexity to solve that system (more than 2^{220} with sparse system solvers) exceeds the complexity of brute-force search (at most 2^{128} encryptions). To bring down the complexity of algebraic attacks on block ciphers, one possibility is to reduce the size of the final system so that the system can be generated and solved efficiently. Since the linearized equations generated by XL are usually sparse, special sparse system-solving algorithms may be exploited in the context of XL.

Our Contribution: In this paper, we propose a new heuristic to improve the XL method by reducing the size of the final linearized system. The heuristic uses the structured Gaussian elimination (SGE) algorithm [13] to reduce the growth of the number of variables during the expansion stage of XL. It also helps by decreasing the number of linearly dependent equations. SGE sometimes exhibits excessive reduction in the system size (a phenomenon called *avalanche effect*) which adversely affects the application of SGE in tandem with XL. We control the avalanche effect by tuning a heuristic parameter. Experiments carried out on small systems and toy ciphers indicate that our heuristic holds the promise of bringing down the complexity of XL.

In short, the basic novelty of our work is the application of sparse system-solving techniques in the *expansion phase* of the standard XL algorithm. Two main improvements of the XL algorithm, already available in the literature, are XSL [6] and MutantXL [7]. Both of these are capable of generating smaller linearized systems compared to XL. However, neither of these seems to be practical for solving real-life ciphers like 128-bit AES. Our heuristic too does not immediately lead to a practical cryptanalytic method for AES (or, for that matter, for any other real-life cipher). It is instead proposed as another improvement of XL with the hope that it may throw some insight in research pertaining to algebraic attacks. Indeed, most of the current algebraic attack techniques are essentially heuristic in nature, and many of them lack solid analytic foundations. Our method too seems promising only from the positive results we obtained from our experimental experience with it. As a final remark, we mention that XL_SGE is, by design, not competing with XSL or MutantXL. On the contrary, it can be used to boost the performance of these XL variants in the same way as it aids XL. Currently, we have experimented with XL only.

The rest of the paper is organized as follows. Section 2 provides some basic background on algebraic attacks over AES-like block ciphers. In particular, it describes the XL algorithm. Moreover, we briefly discuss the structured Gaussian elimination procedure in this section. In Sections 3, we propose our algorithm XL_SGE. In Section 4, we supply our experimental results, and compare the performance of XL_SGE with that of XL. We conclude the paper in Section 5 after highlighting scopes for further research in this direction.

2   Background

In this section, we briefly describe algebraic attacks and the structured Gaussian elimination procedure.

2.1   Algebraic Attack on AES-Like Ciphers

In August 2000, the block cipher Rijndael [14] was selected as the Advanced Encryption Standard (AES). Rijndael is a key-iterated block cipher with a strong algebraic structure. AES can be represented as algebraically closed equations over $GF(2^8)$ [6]. It can also be represented as a system of multivariate *quadratic* equations over $GF(2)$ with plaintext, ciphertext and key bits as variables.

The *MQ problem* is the problem of solving systems of multivariate quadratic equations. The MQ problem is NP-Hard for a general field [15]. Solving a system of quadratic equations over any *finite* field is NP-Complete [12] (since over a finite field, one can verify a correct solution in polynomial time). In general, no polynomial-time algorithm is known to solve the MQ problem. However, for overdefined systems of multivariate quadratic equations (Number of equations $\gg$ Number of variables), there exist algorithms which can run in polynomial time under certain conditions [4,5].

An algebraic attack consists of two basic steps: (1) Equation generation, and (2) Solving the system of equations. These steps are briefly described below.

Equation Generation
Usually, a block cipher consists of a linear part and a nonlinear part. The nonlinear part is due to the presence of S-Boxes in the cipher. Constructing equations for the linear part is trivial. To construct the equations for the nonlinear part of the cipher, one follows two different approaches. First, the structure of the

S-Boxes is exploited to generate equations. Second, one uses the null-space equations for the S-Boxes. For our experiments, we have used a scaled-down version of AES (Baby Rijndael) as described in [15]. Baby Rijndael has the same algebraic structure as AES. The block size and the key size of baby Rijndael are 16 bits. The linear layer of baby Rijndael yields linear equations, whereas the S-Boxes produce quadratic equations. Using the inverse function used in the S-Box of baby Rijndael, one obtains 11 quadratic equations per S-Box. Computing the null space for each S-Box yields 21 linearly independent equations. For details on how the equations are generated, we refer the reader to [15].

Solving the System of Equations
The usual method to solve overdefined multivariate systems of equations is to use Gröbner-basis algorithms. The fastest of such algorithms are F_4 and F_5 proposed by Faugère [2,3]. The XL (eXtended Linearization) algorithm was proposed as an efficient alternative [5]. For a system of m quadratic equations with n variables, the algorithm is expected to run in polynomial time with an exponent $O(1/\sqrt{\epsilon})$, if $m \geq \epsilon n^2$, $0 < \epsilon \leq 1/2$. In general, the XL algorithm is expected to run in subexponential time. A third approach based upon SAT solvers is also proposed in the literature [8] to solve systems of multivariate algebraic equations.

2.2   eXtended Linearization (XL)

The XL algorithm is effective when the number of equations exceeds the number of variables. The main idea is to increase the number of initial equations by adding new algebraically dependent equations which are linearly independent of the initial system. This system expansion is carried out using multiplications by monomials of limited degrees.

   The XL algorithm accepts as input the initial system of equations $\mathbb{A}$ (which has at least one solution), and a degree bound $D \in \mathbb{N}$. The steps of the algorithm are described now.

1. **Multiply:** Generate the new system $\mathbb{A}'$:

$$\mathbb{A}' = \bigcup_{0 \leq k \leq D - d_{max}} X^k \mathbb{A},$$

   where X^k stands for the set of all monomials of degree k, and d_{max} is the maximum degree of the initial system of equations.
2. **Linearize:** Consider each monomial in the variables x_i of degree $\leq D$ as a new variable, and perform Gaussian elimination on the system $\mathbb{A}'$. The ordering of the monomials must be such that all the terms containing single variables (like x_1) are eliminated last.
3. **Solve:** Assume that Step 2 yields at least one univariate polynomial equation in some variable x_1. Solve this equation over the underlying finite field using a standard root-finding algorithm.
4. **Repeat:** Simplify the equations, and repeat the process to find the values of the other variables.

2.3   Structured Gaussian Elimination

Structured Gaussian Elimination (SGE) is an algorithm used to reduce the dimension of a sparse matrix by eliminating some of its rows and columns [13]. SGE exploits the special structure of the matrices arising from integer-factorization and discrete-logarithm algorithms. It is applicable for sparse matrices where the columns can be divided into two types: heavy-weight and light-weight. It is a heuristic procedure that tends to preserve the sparsity of the light columns.

SGE repeats the following steps until no further reduction is possible.

1. Delete columns of weight 0 and 1.
2. Delete rows of weight 0 and 1.
3. Delete rows of weight 1 in the light part. After Step 2 and Step 3, update column weights.
4. Delete redundant rows.

3   eXtended Linearization with Structured Gaussian Elimination (XL_SGE)

3.1   Motivation

The problem with the XL algorithm is that the size of the system increases drastically with the increase in the degree bound D used in the algorithm. Many linearly dependent equations are generated during the expansion process (Step 1) in XL. The equations generated by the XL algorithm are generally very sparse. Moreover, we have observed, from the statistics of the system obtained in XL (for $D = 2$), that the columns of the generated system can be distinguished as heavy-weight and light-weight. Depending on these observations, we propose a new heuristic (XL_SGE) to reduce the number of linearized equations in XL. According to the heuristic, the generated intermediate systems are reduced using structured Gaussian elimination (SGE). The reduced systems are multiplied with monomials to get systems of higher algebraic degrees.

The XL_SGE algorithm reduces the sizes of the intermediate systems of equations in XL using the first three steps of structured Gaussian elimination. It does not use the apparently irrelevant fourth step of SGE. The main motivation behind proposing XL_SGE is size reduction. Besides this, XL_SGE is expected to exhibit some side effects, some of which can be exploited to our advantage. For example, partial elimination of variables before each stage of monomial multiplication may result in the generation of fewer linearized variables (higher-degree monomials). This, in turn, is capable of reducing the rank deficit. As a result, we may even expect a smaller degree bound D than XL for arriving at a solvable system. One should, however, avoid the avalanche effect of SGE, which results in a slow growth of the linearized system, demanding larger values of D than needed in XL.

3.2   XL_SGE Algorithm

The XL_SGE algorithm accepts as input the initial system of equations (consisting of linear equations and quadratic equations) $\mathbb{A}$ (which has at least one solution), and a degree bound $D \in \mathbb{N}$. The basic steps of the XL_SGE expansion procedure are as follows.

1. Expand the initial system of equations $\mathbb{A}$ up to degree $d = 2$ using XL to obtain a linearized system $\mathbb{A}'$.
2. Apply structured Gaussian elimination (SGE) on $\mathbb{A}'$ to obtain a reduced system of equations $\mathbb{A}''$ of degree d.
3. Multiply the reduced system $\mathbb{A}''$ with monomials of degree 1, append the generated equations to $\mathbb{A}''$, and rename this appended system as $\mathbb{A}'$. $\mathbb{A}'$ now contains equations of degrees up to $d + 1$.
4. If the degree of the system of equations $\mathbb{A}'$ is D, end the process. Otherwise, go to Step 2.

If we get a full-rank system (or a close-to-full-rank system) for a particular D, we solve that system. Otherwise, we increase the degree bound D, and run XL_SGE again to obtain a system of smaller rank deficit. This process is repeated until the rank deficit becomes zero or goes below a tolerable limit.

We have observed that sometimes due to avalanche effect, most of the equations are removed in the SGE stage. Consequently, XL_SGE suffers from a slow growth in the size of the linearized system with the increase in the degree bound D, and the rank deficit in XL_SGE decreases much more slowly with D than in XL. To reduce this avalanche effect, we use a parameter K in Step 2 of the XL_SGE algorithm. Suppose that the j-th column has weight 1 with the non-zero entry appearing in the i-th row. Only if this row contains at least K non-zero entries, the i-th row and the j-th column are removed. The value of K is heuristically chosen depending upon the weight distribution of the rows.

An optional preprocessing of $\mathbb{A}$ offers a possibility of initial reduction in the system size. As mentioned during the description of baby Rijndael, we get both linear and quadratic equations from the encryption rounds. If we substitute the linear equations in appropriate quadratic equations, we can eliminate some of the variables, and remove all the linear equations from the initial system $\mathbb{A}$. The reduced system consisting only of quadratic equations is expanded. Although the number of non-zero terms in each quadratic equation increases because of these substitutions, the effects of this increase can be appropriately handled. However, whether this initial reduction helps at all is not clear from our experiments.

4   Experimental Results

We have tried the heuristic (XL_SGE) on small random sparse quadratic systems, and have found that the heuristic significantly improves the performance of the XL algorithm in most cases, in terms of the size of the final system. The results obtained for some small random systems are shown in Table 1. This table corresponds to $K = 0$, that is, the avalanche effect for SGE is not handled in these experiments. The initial system size $x \times y$ indicates x quadratic equations in y variables. On the other hand, the final system size $x \times y$ indicates x linearized equations in y monomials. For both XL and XL_SGE, we report the final system size. Notice that we apply SGE *before* each stage of monomial multiplication. This, in turn, implies that the final systems in XL_SGE, reported in all the tables below, are again expected to reduce in size if another round of SGE is applied to them. Indeed, it is a standard practice to apply SGE to any large sparse system before solving it. The final systems available from XL would also experience size reduction upon application of a round of SGE. For both XL and XL_SGE, the sizes reported in the tables correspond to those systems before that external application of SGE which may be used to solve the systems.

Table 1. Comparison of XL with XL_SGE (with $K = 0$) for random systems

Size of Initial System	D in XL_SGE	System Size after XL_SGE	Rank Deficit	D in XL	System Size after XL	Rank Deficit
10×6	3	67×27	0	3	149×42	0
15×8	3	231×87	0	3	276×93	0
20×10	3	427×156	0	3	500×172	0
20×10	6	3959×655	0	5	7445×638	0
20×12	7	2809×917	11	7	98611×3302	0
20×12	7	5006×1547	10	7	114863×3302	0
20×12	3	714×271	0	3	795×299	0
22×12	3	708×209	0	4	5464×794	0
22×12	3	897×263	0	4	6478×794	0
24×13	3	1029×375	0	3	1137×378	0
24×14	3	1085×449	0	5	44476×3473	0

From the experimental results, it is clear that for the same degree bound (D), the size of the final system obtained from XL_SGE is in most cases much smaller than the size of the final system obtained from XL. There are instances where larger degree bounds D are needed by XL_SGE (than XL) for obtaining a full-rank system, but the size reduction is always a positive feature of XL_SGE. The performance of the XL_SGE algorithm hugely depends on the structure of the initial system of equations. We have observed that if the initial system of equations enjoys the following two properties, XL_SGE performs significantly better than XL.

1. Number of equations $\gg$ Number of variables
2. Number of equations $\ll$ Number of one-degree terms + Number of two-degree terms

There are cases where XL performs better than XL_SGE. In some cases, XL generates a full-rank system, whereas XL_SGE fails to generate a full-rank system. Consider the example of Row 5 of Table 1. In this case, we get a full-rank system for $D = 7$ using XL. For the same D, the rank deficit in case of XL_SGE is 11. However, the size of the final system in case of XL is much larger, that is, a slightly increased rank deficit for XL_SGE is more than compensated by a dramatic reduction in the system size. Interestingly, for the same initial system, we obtain a system of size 502×253 and rank deficit 2 using XL_SGE for $D = 3$ (using XL with $D = 3$, the system size is 639×296 with rank deficit 10).

The performance of XL_SGE also depends on the proportion of linear equations and quadratic equations present in the initial system. For some systems, we get a full-rank system after few iterations of XL_SGE (say, for $D = 3$). So the size of the final system is small in those cases. For some other systems of the same initial size, we get full-rank systems after more number of iterations of XL_SGE (say, for $D = 6$). In those cases, the size of the final system is large. Consider the examples of Row 3 and Row 4 of Table 1. In both cases, the sizes of the initial systems are the same. The initial system of the third row contains 4 linear equations and 16 quadratic equations. The initial system of the fourth row contains 2 linear equations and 18 quadratic equations. In the case of Row 3, XL_SGE gives a full-rank system of size 427×156 for $D = 3$, whereas for Row 4, we get a full-rank system of size 3959×655 for $D = 6$.

The main problem with XL_SGE is the avalanche effect suffered by the SGE stage. If any intermediate generated system of XL_SGE experiences avalanche effect, no further increment in the size of the system is possible. In that case, XL_SGE fails to generate a full-rank system, no matter how large the degree bound D is. In some cases, little reduction takes place (depends on the structure of the initial system) with XL_SGE. In those cases, the performances of XL_SGE and XL are similar.

Table 2. Comparison of XL with XL_SGE (with $K \geq 0$) for random systems

Size of Initial System	D in XL_SGE	K in XL_SGE	System Size after XL_SGE	Rank Deficit	D in XL	System Size after XL	Rank Deficit
22×12	3	4	513×292	0	3	534×298	0
23×13	4	4	2863×1073	0	5	11219×2379	0
24×13	3	0	726×377	0	3	726×377	0
24×15	4	0	6400×1940	0	4	6451×1940	0
24×16	4	7	6311×2516	0	4	6587×2516	0
24×16	4	5	6513×2516	0	4	6527×2516	0
25×17	4	6	8609×3213	0	4	8609×3213	0
25×18	5	6	34027×12615	0	5	36825×12615	0

Table 2 lists results on some small random systems with the avalanche effect taken into account. For a given D, we have tuned the parameter K in the sequence $0, 1, 2, \ldots$ until we obtain a value of K for which the rank deficit of the expanded system is zero. In all our experiments, we could locate suitable values for K (although there is no theoretical guarantee that such a K must exist). These results once again illustrate the superiority of XL_SGE over XL in terms of the size of the final solvable system.

Table 3 describes the variation of the performance of the XL_SGE expansion procedure with the parameter K for a random initial system of size 25×18. This is the same system reported in the last row of Table 2. In general, for small values of K, the size reduction in SGE may be too high, that is, the avalanche effect may set in. This may lead XL_SGE to obtain higher rank deficits compared to XL for the same degree bound D. On the other hand, if K is too large, SGE fails to reduce the intermediate system sizes, and consequently, the performance of XL_SGE becomes identical to that of XL. A good value of K can be experimentally chosen for a given input system.

Table 3. Dependence of the performance of XL_SGE on the parameter K

K	$D = 3$		$D = 4$		$D = 5$	
	System Size	Rank Deficit	System Size	Rank Deficit	System Size	Rank Deficit
0	922×975	271	6015×4047	294	28070×12615	131
5	958×976	244	6357×4047	132	30043×12615	38
6	1032×982	192	7043×4047	19	34027×12615	0
8	1050×983	179	7214×4047	10	35014×12615	0
10	1086×987	154	7556×4047	4	36988×12615	0

Depending on the initial structure of the system, some modifications of the XL_SGE algorithm may improve the performance of the algorithm. The exact nature of this dependence is not clear yet. To see whether XL_SGE works well on the systems generated by AES-like block ciphers, we have generated systems of equations for the toy version of AES (Baby Rijndael) as described in Section 2.1. On this system, XL_SGE exhibits slightly better performance than XL. The results are shown in Table 4.

Table 4. Comparison of XL with XL_SGE for baby Rijndael for $D = 3$

Number of Rounds	Size of Initial System	K in XL_SGE	System Size after XL_SGE	Rank Deficit	System Size after XL	Rank Deficit
1	232×64	0	142945×43745	0	178892×43745	0
2	448×112	3	634810×233633	24	642423×234225	48
3	664×160	7	1755432×682273	576	1768628×682401	576

We have also reduced the initial system (according to the last paragraph of Section 3) of baby Rijndael for one round, and get a system of 192 quadratic equations in 24 variables. After expanding that system using XL_SGE, we get a final system of size 97447×12919 for $D = 4$ with rank deficit 36. On the other hand, XL gives a final system of size 97943×12919 with rank deficit 36 for the same D. It, therefore, remains uncertain whether the preprocessing of the initial system (that is, absorbing the linear equations in the quadratic equations) produces any noticeable benefits at all.

The programs for generating equations and expanding equations using XL and XL_SGE were written in the C programming language. The PARI/GP package was used to carry out some intermediate calculations needed to generate equations. The mathematical package Sage (Version 4.4.2) was used to calculate the rank of sparse matrices available from XL and XL_SGE.

5   Conclusion

The main problem with algebraic attacks on block ciphers is that the solvable system size becomes large, and so the complexity to solve the system often exceeds the complexity of brute-force search. XL generates too many linearly dependent equations while expanding the initial system of equations. The number of variables also grows rapidly during the expansion stage of XL. Our proposed heuristic XL_SGE uses structured Gaussian elimination in order to improve the performance of XL by reducing the growth of variables and of linearly dependent equations in the expansion stage of the XL algorithm. Experiments reveal that XL_SGE performs better than XL in many cases for random systems and also for a toy version of AES.

We end this paper after highlighting some directions for future research.

– It is not yet clear on which factors the performance of XL_SGE depends. A theoretical analysis of XL_SGE is required, and accordingly modifications of our present algorithm are called for to make it more versatile and effective. As an example, the nature of dependency of the performance of XL_SGE on the choice of the heuristic parameter K needs to be analytically investigated.
– Columns of weight two can be eliminated in the SGE phase without increasing the number of non-zero entries in the matrix. However, elimination of columns of weight three or more cannot be so gracefully handled.
– Partial monomial multiplication during the expansion phase can effectively reduce the size (both the number of variables and the number of equations) of the final solvable system. Moreover, after each application of SGE, all columns have weight at least two. Complete monomial multiplication on this system can never generate columns of weight zero or one. Partial monomial multiplication can potentially solve this problem, but possibly at the cost of degradation in the rank profile with increasing D.
– Another important area of investigation is to use SGE in conjunction with the variants of XL (like XSL and MutantXL) already proposed in the literature. Comparisons with other algebraic-attack algorithms (like F_4, F_5, SAT-solver techniques) are also worth studying.

References

1. Shannon, C.E.: Communication theory of secrecy systems. Bell System Technical Journal 28, 657–715 (1949)
2. Faugère, J.C.: A new efficient algorithm for computing Gröbner basis (F_4). Journal of Pure and Applied Algebra 139(1), 61–88 (1999)
3. Faugère, J.C.: A new efficient algorithm for computing Gröbner basis without reduction to zero (F_5). In: ISSAC 2002, pp. 75–83 (2002)

4. Kipnis, A., Shamir, A.: Cryptanalysis of the HFE public key cryptosystem by relinearization. In: Wiener, M. (ed.) CRYPTO 1999. LNCS, vol. 1666, pp. 19–30. Springer, Heidelberg (1999)
5. Courtois, N.T., Klimov, A.B., Patarin, J., Shamir, A.: Efficient algorithms for solving overdefined systems of multivariate polynomial equations. In: Preneel, B. (ed.) EUROCRYPT 2000. LNCS, vol. 1807, pp. 392–407. Springer, Heidelberg (2000)
6. Courtois, N., Pieprzyk, J.: Cryptanalysis of block ciphers with overdefined systems of equations. In: Zheng, Y. (ed.) ASIACRYPT 2002. LNCS, vol. 2501, pp. 267–287. Springer, Heidelberg (2002)
7. Ding, J., Buchmann, J., Mohamed, M., Moahmed, W., Weinmann, R.: Mutantxl. In: SCC, pp. 16–22 (2008)
8. Bard, G., Courtois, N., Jefferson, C.: Solution of sparse polynomial systems over GF(2) via sat-solvers. In: ECRYPT workshop Tools for Cryptanalysis (2007)
9. Courtois, N., Bard, G.V.: Algebraic cryptanalysis of the data encryption standard. In: IMA Int. Conf., pp. 152–169 (2007)
10. Courtois, N., Bard, G.V., Wagner, D.: Algebraic and slide attacks on keeLoq. In: Nyberg, K. (ed.) FSE 2008. LNCS, vol. 5086, pp. 97–115. Springer, Heidelberg (2008)
11. Courtois, N., O'Neil, S., Quisquater, J.J.: Practical algebraic attacks on the hitag2 stream cipher. In: Samarati, P., Yung, M., Martinelli, F., Ardagna, C.A. (eds.) ISC 2009. LNCS, vol. 5735, pp. 167–176. Springer, Heidelberg (2009)
12. Vörös, M.: Algebraic attack on stream ciphers. Master's thesis, Comenius University, Faculty of Mathematics, Physics and Informatics, Department of Computer Science (2007)
13. LaMacchia, B.A., Odlyzko, A.M.: Solving large sparse linear systems over finite fields. In: Menezes, A., Vanstone, S.A. (eds.) CRYPTO 1990. LNCS, vol. 537, pp. 109–133. Springer, Heidelberg (1991)
14. Daemen, J., Rijmen, V.: Rijndael for AES. In: AES Candidate Conference, pp. 343–348 (2000)
15. Kleiman, E.: The XL and XSL attacks on Baby Rijndael. Master's thesis, Iowa State University, Department of Mathematics (2005)

Generalized Avalanche Test for Stream Cipher Analysis

P.R. Mishra, Indivar Gupta, and N.R. Pillai

SAG , DRDO, Metcalfe House Complex, Delhi-110054, India
{pr_mishra,indivargupta,nrpillai}@sag.drdo.in

Abstract. In this paper we consider tests for avalanche effect in Key sequence generators. In avalanche effect, small changes in input result in large changes in the output. We adapt the Strict Avalanche Criterion (SAC) randomness test proposed by Castro et al in 2005 in their paper in *Mathematics and Computers in Simulation* to obtain an avalanche test for Key sequence generators. We then propose a Generalized avalanche criterion (GAC) test which includes strict avalanche criterion and other known avalanche criteria. We apply the known avalanche criteria on a toy example and demonstrate that GAC is able to detect a bigger set of related keys as compared to other existing criteria. GAC may prove a useful criterion for analysis of Key sequence generators.

Keywords: Avalanche Criteria, Hamming Distance, Strict Avalanche Criteria, Correlation, block cipher, stream cipher and security evaluation.

1 Introduction

To resist cryptanalysis, it is desirable that small changes in the input settings lead to large changes in the output. This makes it difficult to apply Hill climbing or gradient descent approaches for key search. The property of small changes in inputs triggering large changes in output has been known as avalanche criteria (AC)/Strict Avalanche Criteria (SAC) [2,7] and is a desired property to check for during security evaluation of any cipher. Different mathematical formulations of this criterion have been given in different contexts eg block ciphers, boolean functions, hash algorithms etc. In the case of a block cipher, a small change in either the plaintext or the key should produce a significant change in the ciphertext [5]. Similarly, SAC for Boolean functions has been proposed in [2]. Different generalizations of SAC for boolean functions were analyzed in [3,4]. In stream ciphers, the underlying pseudo-random generator should exhibit good avalanche effect with respect to its key. In this article, we consider avalanche criteria for stream ciphers.

The most common definition of *Avalanche Criteria (AC)* found in the literature is based on the amount of change in the output sequence when the key is changed by one bit [1,5,7]. Mathematically, a mapping F taking a fixed length input to an n-bit output satisfies avalanche criteria if

$$\forall x \mid \forall y \text{ such that } H_{wt}(y) = 1, \quad H_{dist}(F(x), F(x \oplus y)) \approx n/2, \tag{1}$$

M. Joye et al. (Eds.): InfoSecHiComNet 2011, LNCS 7011, pp. 168–180, 2011.

Where y are chosen in a such way that the Hamming weight $(H_{wt}(y))$ is equal to 1 and H_{dist} denotes Hamming distance. Since it is infeasible to apply the test for all possible keys in the key space, the test is applied for randomly chosen subset from the key space. If avalanche property is satisfied for all the keys in the subset, then one assumes that generator might be satisfying avalanche criteria. For an m-bit key, this involves $m + 1$ runs of the key sequence generator and m Hamming distance computations of n-bit sequences. A useful (but impractical) generalization would be to remove condition on Hamming weight of y. The definition would become – F should satisfy the condition $H(F(x), F(x \oplus y)) \approx n/2$ for arbitrary $x, y \in K$, K being the key space. This would be a test for related keys. This criterion requires the calculation of Hamming distances for any two pairs of distinct keys in the key space. It can be easily seen that for a key length m, 2^m runs of key sequence generator and $\binom{2^m}{2}$ computations of Hamming distance between two n-bit sequences are to be made. This generalization is impractical as to apply it even for a single key, one has to compare it with all the other keys in the entire key space.

In this article, we suggest a method with $m + 1$ runs of key sequence generator and $\binom{m}{2}$ sequence comparisons which subsumes the 1-bit change test and at the same time checks for existence of related keys which are different only in k consecutive bit positions.[1] The conventional SAC test in comparison takes $m + 1$ runs and m sequence comparisons.

An interesting generalization of SAC was proposed by Castro et al. They interpreted the Hamming distances between $F(x)$ and $F(x \oplus y)$ as a random variable and stated that it should follow the Binomial distribution $B(1/2, n)$ [1]. We will refer to their test as SAC-CAS. For applying the test on key sequence generator, the sequence is interpreted as a sequence of n-bit blocks ($n \in \{8, 16, 32, 64, 128\}$) and the distribution of Hamming distances between pairs of adjacent blocks is observed. The closeness of this distribution with $B(1/2, n)$ is measured by means of chi-square goodness-of-fit test and used as avalanche criteria.

The SAC-CAS test as proposed in [1] is more of a randomness test for a single sequence rather than test for avalanche effect in a key sequence generator. We adapt the SAC-CAS test for checking avalanche effect in a key sequence generator.

We briefly summarize the contributions of this paper below.

1. We adapted the procedure of avalanche criterion test by Castro et al [1] to obtain a test for avalanche effect in key sequence generators.
2. We propose a generalization for avalanche criterion: *Generalized Avalanche Criterion (GAC)* and a test based on it. This test checks for the avalanche effect for 1-bit changes in the key. It also detects closeness of sequences generated by pairs of keys where the keys differ in k consecutive bits. Such a generalization has not been studied before, to the best of our knowledge.

---

[1] In the case of block ciphers one can apply this test on the Keyschedule which takes in the user key and produces the expanded key.

3. We demonstrate the effectiveness of GAC for detecting avalanche effect where other methods fail by applying them on a toy stream cipher designed by us.

Organization of our paper is as follows.

In Section 2 we briefly describe the avalanche test given by Castro et al followed by our remarks on the test.

In Section 3 we propose a new generalized avalanche criterion (GAC) for analysis of stream ciphers. A Toy stream cipher (designed for testing purpose only) is presented in Subsection 4.1 and the avalanche criteria tests are compared in Subsection 4.2.

Experimental results and the discussions on the comparative performance are given. We conclude the paper with Section 5.

2   Castro et al Strict Avalanche Criterion Test

Castro et al [1] proposed a new definition for Strict Avalanche Criterion Test (SAC-CAS) for randomness testing. The first improvement suggested was to look at the distribution of the Hamming distances, instead of just checking closeness of Hamming distance to $n/2$. The definition of SAC-CAS suggested was:

$$\forall x \mid \forall y \text{ such that } H_{wt}(y) = 1, \quad H_{dist}(F(x), F(x \oplus y)) \sim \mathbf{B}(\frac{1}{2}, n). \quad (2)$$

Where $\mathbf{B}(\frac{1}{2}, n)$ denotes the Binomial distribution function with parameters $\frac{1}{2}$ and n.

While applying it on Key sequence generators, they converted it into a 'randomness test'. The test is applied on sequences from the generator taken one at a time. The sequence under test is interpreted as a sequence of n-bit words. The value of n can be chosen $8, 16, 32, 64, 128 \cdots$ etc. The distribution of Hamming distance for adjacent words of sequence is taken and compared with $B(1/2, n)$, which is the expected distribution for distances in the case of random sequences. If the observed distribution is close to the expected distribution, the sequence is considered to pass the test.

2.1   Our Observation on SAC-CAS Test

The test as described in [1] checks for randomness property of a sequence. In fact the SAC-CAS test can be described as a poker test [6] on the sequence derived by xoring the given sequence with a shifted (shift of n bits) version of itself.

It is important to note that in SAC-CAS test, the authors have not applied the definition in the sense of an avalanche criterion. They have assumed that the function[2]. F is a transition function that takes bit stream of length n and

---

[2] The definition of F is also such that there will be sequences where it is not well defined. Map is a more appropriate description of F.

produces n bits output. (n can be any value from $8, 16, 32, 64, 128$). They interpret the given sequence as a sequence of n-bit words $w_0, w_1, w_2, w_3, w_4, \cdots$ and F is considered to be the map which takes w_i to w_{i+1}. For measuring avalanche properties of F, instead of checking for $H_{dist}(F(x), F(x \oplus y))$ with $H_{wt}(y) = 1$, they calculate the value of $H_{dist}(w_i, w_{i+1})$ for all i and check if the observed distribution follows the distribution $\mathbf{B}(\frac{1}{2}, n)$. In this case the x is w_{i-1} and the corresponding y is $w_i \oplus w_{i-1}$. Observe that $H_{wt}(y)$ can take any value between 0 to n. That is, the test is not checking for avalanche in the true sense (*small* change in input leading to large change in output).

The second point to be noted is that the test checks for randomness property of a sequence and it is not checking for 'small changes to key setting leading large changes in the key sequence' which is what one means by avalanche criterion for key sequence generators.

2.2   Modified SAC-CAS Test

In this subsection we adapt the SAC-CAS for checking avalanche property of key sequence generators. We will refer to the modified SAC-CAS test as MSAC test. As is clear from our observations in 2.1 that the pairs of inputs to the transition function F described above are not having 'small' differences in input and hence are not capturing the idea of avalanche criterion. Therefore, it becomes imperative to modify their test suitably. Moreover, we also made our criterion a check for the avalanche effect in true sense.

A direct application of the definition given in [1] gives one possible test when $F(x)$ is interpreted as the output of the key sequence generator on initializing with key x. This test will be a generalization of the usual method of expecting the Hamming distance to be close to $N/2$ where N is the length of $F(x)$.

Instead of a simple Hamming distance test for closeness of two sequences, we considered the Hamming distances between corresponding blocks of the sequences and then used the fact that the expected distribution was Binomial distribution. This is explained more precisely in the following paragraphs.

Given a key sequence generator taking m-bit keys an producing say N-bit output, we take F as a black box function which takes m bits as input and produces m_1 n-bit blocks as output (n can be 8,16, 32 .. and $m_1 = N/n$). Let for a given m-bit input x, $F_i(x)$ denote the ith $n-$bit block of the output where $1 \leq i \leq m_1$.

Using the definition that a single bit change in input causes changes in output according to $B(1/2, n)$, we arrive at the following condition for avalanche criterion - for all m-bit vectors y such that $H_{wt}(y) = 1$;

$$\forall 0 \leq i \leq m_1, \; H_{dist}(F_i(x), F_i(x \oplus y)) \sim \mathbf{B}\left(\frac{1}{2}, n\right)$$

Ideally one should run the test for each block separately and in effect check for avalanche property of function F_i. However, to simplify the test, we do not distinguish between the Hamming distances computed at one block location from those computed at another block location. This is same as relaxing the condition that the avalanche is satisfied within each block of output to condition of avalanche being satisfied when all the m_1 blocks are considered together.

For a given y, for j, $0 \leq j \leq n$, we define $freq_y(j) = \#\{i | H_{dist}(F_i(x), F_i(x \oplus y)) = j, i = 1, \ldots, m_1\}$. We use $freq_y(j), j = 0, \ldots, n$ as the observed frequencies for the random variable and check for its closeness to distribution $B(1/2, n)$. For the implementation purpose we have taken $n = 8$.

3   Generalized Avalanche Test

Avalanche test can be generalized in two directions –

1. by relaxing the constraint on Hamming distance of y (interpretation of the condition 'small difference in input')
2. the interpretation of the condition 'large difference in output'

Generalization in the direction (2) has been suggested in [1] where the Hamming distance of output sequences is considered to be following Binomial distribution (instead of the usual definition of Hamming distance should be close to $n/2$). The other direction (1) is relaxing the condition on input differences. If we allow input Hamming distance up to k, then one has to generate $\sum_{i=0..k} \binom{m}{i}$ sequences and perform $\sum_{i=1,\ldots,k} \binom{m}{i}$ Hamming distance computations. For input Hamming distances up to k, the number of sequences to be generated becomes m^k. Generation and storage of the sequences will take both lot of storage and time.

In this section we propose a way of testing avalanche properties of sequence generators which not only checks for the effect of 1-bit changes in the input but also checks for all k-bit changes in input where the k bits are consecutive. We have devised our test in such a way that it has only a small time overhead and no data overhead. We have to generate $m + 1$ sequences which is the same as for standard SAC case with 1-bit input difference. Since Hamming distance computations are not as costly as sequence generation, we have taken the liberty of increasing the number of Hamming distance computations from m to $\binom{m}{2}$.

We assume that the key length is m and the black box function F, takes m bits as input (key) and produces n bit sequence as output. Let us denote the m-bit key by a vector $K = (k_1, \ldots, k_m) \in \mathbb{F}_2^m$ where k_i denotes bit at ith position. We define support of vector as follows:

$$Supp(K) = \{i : k_i \neq 0\}.$$

For a given key $K \in \mathbb{F}_2^m$ We generate $m + 1$ difference vectors (Ys) viz $Y_0, Y_1, \ldots Y_m \in \mathbb{F}_2^m$ with the property that $Supp(Y_i) = \{1, \ldots, i\}$ and $Supp(Y_0) = \phi$ Now we set generalized avalanche criterion as follows.

Let $\mathcal{S} = \{Y_0, Y_1, \ldots, Y_m\}$ then F is said to follow *Generalized Avalanche Criterion (GAC)* if following condition holds:

$$\forall K \in \mathbb{F}_2^m \text{ and } \forall Y, Z \in \mathcal{S}, Y \neq Z \ H_{dist}(F(K \oplus Y), F(K \oplus Z)) \approx \frac{n}{2}. \quad (3)$$

As in the usual SAC tests we apply this test for a randomly chosen subset of Keys. Though this criterion involves $\binom{m}{2}$ computations of Hamming distances, we have to generate only $m + 1$ sequences $F(K \oplus Y_0), F(K \oplus Y_1), .., F(K \oplus Y_m)$ in the pre-computation phase. In this way we have kept the data generation overheads from increasing.

It can be easily seen that the case of single bit Hamming distance in ith input bit is checked for when $Y = Y_i$ and $Z = Y_{i-1}$ (in this case, $H_{dis}(K \oplus Y_i, K \oplus Y_{i-1}) = 1$ for $1 \leq i \leq m$). In a single application of this test, the effect of single bit change is checked for all possible input positions which is what SAC/AC does. In this sense GAC is a generalization of AC/SAC.

4   Advantage of GAC over Other Avalanche Criteria

As GAC covers a wider portion of changes over key space, the probability of detecting related keys increases for the same amount of data generation and a marginal increase in computation. There are sequence generators which escape AC/SAC but do not pass GAC. In this section we present a stream cipher that passes AC but it fails GAC.

A toy stream cipher has been designed to show the comparative advantage of GAC over AC and SAC-CAS. Many other security considerations have not been taken into account while designing it. Authors do not recommend using it for practical purposes. The block diagram of the cipher is given in Figure 1.

4.1   Description of the Toy Cipher

The algorithm takes 92-bit key for its initialization. There are two LFSRs (of lengths 73 and 79) and three 8:1 multiplexers used in this cipher. There are two polynomial banks, each containing 32 polynomials of degree 73 and 79 respectively for providing polynomials for LFSRs. We denote the 92-bit key by $k_1, k_1, ..., k_{92}$. The initialization details are provided in the table below:

Table 1. Key Distribution in Toy Cipher

S.No.	Key bits	Initialization
1	k_1-k_{73}	LFSR-73
2	k_{74}-k_{78}	Polynomial selection for LFSR-73
3	k_{79}-k_{83}	Polynomial selection for LFSR-79
4	k_{84}-k_{86}	Selection bits for multiplexer-1
5	k_{87}-k_{89}	Selection bits for multiplexer-2
6	k_{90}-k_{92}	Selection bits for multiplexer-3

While initializing LFSR-73, k_1 is kept at feedback end. For all selection keys, the key bit with lowest index forms the MSB. If all the bits from k_1 to k_{73} are zero then k_1 is taken to be 1 before initialization. This is done to ensure that LFSR is not initialized to an all zero state.

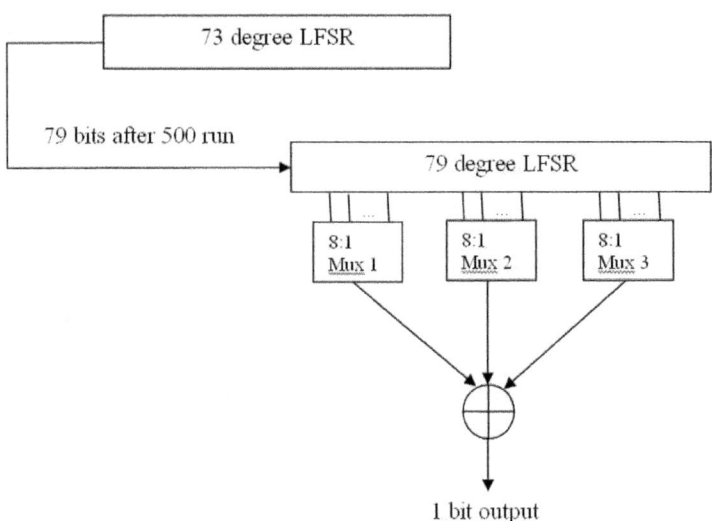

Fig. 1. Toy Stream Cipher

After initialization of LFSR-73, it is run 500 times without taking output. Then 79 output bits are collected to initialize LFSR-79. Once the initialization is completed, LFSR-79 is clocked once and 24 bits are tapped for three 8:1 multiplexers. The details of multiplexers are given in table below:

Table 2. Multiplexer Tap Points

Multiplexer No.	Tap points
1	2,4,8,12,12,18,20,24
2	5,9,17,25,35,17,62,74
3	13,19,35,47,58,60,66,75

The counting starts from 1 at feedback end of the LFSR. The three output bits from three multiplexers are xored to get one bit output of the cipher. For generating the other bits of the sequence, only LFSR-79 is clocked.

4.2   Comparative Studies and Analysis

For comparative studies we implemented all the definitions of strict avalanche criteria on the Toy stream cipher described in the section 4.1.

For the conventional AC, we randomly chose a 92-bit key $K = (k_1, k_2, \ldots, k_{92})$ and generated 92 keys $K_1, \ldots, K_{92}$ with the property that $Supp(K \oplus K_i) = \{i\}$, $i = 1, 2, \ldots, 92$. We then generated 10^6 bit key sequence by the Toy stream cipher corresponding to the original key and the related keys. We calculated the %Hamming Distances and correlation values. We found that %Hamming

Distance values lie near 50% and the correlation values lie near zero which is as per expected. The results are placed in Appendix A.

As SAC-CAS test is more of a sequence randomness test and not a test for avalanche property with respect to key, we compare results from the modified version of SAC-CAS test with the test we propose. We applied the MSAC test (modified SAC-CAS test) for checking key avalanche properties on sequences generated from our Toy cipher. The results are in Appendix B.

For the same key vector we calculated 93 key sequences as described in Section 3 and then applied our GAC test. It has been observed that our GAC detects inherent weakness of the stream cipher indicating the related keys. As, there are $\binom{93}{2}$ correlation values, we have not listed all the values but listed only those values which exceed a threshold of 0.002 i.e., the correlation values lying outside the interval $[-0.002, 0.002]$. These values are listed in Appendix C. It is clear from the result that the key sequence pairs (83,86),(83,89)and (86,89) have correlation 1 i.e., they are identical.[3]

From the results given in Appendices A, B and C, it is clear that GAC is an improvement over existing avalanche criteria. It is possible to combine Castro's idea of Binomial Distribution and χ^2 goodness-of-fit with our GAC. In the results here we have shown only raw correlation values here to reflect identical key sequences.

5   Conclusion

We have presented a new avalanche criterion viz., Generalized Avalanche Criterion (GAC). With the same amount of data generation as for a single bit SAC test, the proposed test covers the existing single bit change SAC tests and also checks for related keys which differ in k consecutive positions.

We have constructed a toy cipher to show a class of maps which will pass the regular SAC tests, the SAC-CAS test and MSAC test, but fail our GAC test. Therefore it can be used as a replacement for the existing avalanche criteria.

Acknowledgements. The authors would like to extend their gratitude to Di rector SAG for allowing them to carry out this work. Authors are also grateful to Dr. S S Bedi and Dr. Meena Kumari for technical discussions and valuable suggestions. Finally authors express their sincere thanks to Navneet Gaba for her insightful comments which helped them to improve the quality of the paper.

References

1. Castro, J.C.H., Sierrab, J.M., Sezneca, A., Izquierdoa, A., Ribagordaa, A.: The strict avalanche criterion randomness test. Mathematics and Computers in Simulation 68, 1–7 (2005)

---

[3] All the tests given in the paper have been implemented by the authors in C/C++. Source code can be obtained from the authors.

2. Forre, R.: The strict avalanche criterion: Spectral properties of boolean functions and an extended definition. In: Goldwasser, S. (ed.) CRYPTO 1988. LNCS, vol. 403, pp. 450–468. Springer, Heidelberg (1990)
3. Gupta, K.C., Sarkar, P.: Construction of Perfect Nonlinear and Maximally Nonlinear Multi-output Boolean Functions Satisfying Higher Order Strict Avalanche Criteria. In: Johansson, T., Maitra, S. (eds.) INDOCRYPT 2003. LNCS, vol. 2904, pp. 107–120. Springer, Heidelberg (2003)
4. Hussain, I., Shah, T., Mahmood, H., Afzal, M.: Comparative Analysis of S-boxes Based on Graphical SAC. International Journal of Computer Applications 2(5), 5–8 (2010)
5. Gustafson, H., Dawson, E., Neilsen, L., Caelli, W.: A Computer Package for Measuring the Strength of Encryption Algorithm. Computer and Security 13, 687–697 (1994)
6. Menezes, A.J., van Oorschot, P.C., Vanstone, S.A.: Handbook of Applied Cryptography, p. 182. CRC Press, New York (1997)
7. Webster, A.F., Tavares, S.E.: On the Design of S-boxes. In: Williams, H.C. (ed.) CRYPTO 1985. LNCS, vol. 218, pp. 523–534. Springer, Heidelberg (1986)

A   Test Result of Conventional AC

Number of sequences: 93
Length of each sequence: 1000000

==

SN CorCoef %HD	SN CorCoef %HD	SN CorCoef %HD
1. -1.05e-003 50.05	2.|32. -2.66e-004 50.01	63. +6.66e-004 49.97
-2.02e-003 50.10	3.|33. -1.11e-003 50.06	64. -4.14e-004 50.02
-1.14e-003 50.06	4.|34. -1.11e-003 50.06	65. +5.56e-004 49.97
-6.70e-004 50.03	5.|35. -1.11e-003 50.06	66. +1.17e-003 49.94
-6.72e-004 50.03	6.|36. -1.11e-003 50.06	67. +1.44e-003 49.93
+1.77e-003 49.91	7.|37. -4.18e-004 50.02	68. +1.44e-003 49.93
+1.77e-003 49.91	8.|38. -4.18e-004 50.02	69. -1.32e-004 50.01
+1.77e-003 49.91	9.|39. +1.07e-003 49.95	70. +9.34e-004 49.95
+8.80e-004 49.96	10.|40. +1.06e-003 49.95	71. +9.36e-004 49.95
-9.10e-004 50.05	11.|41. +9.04e-004 49.95	72. -2.80e-005 50.00
-1.74e-003 50.09	12.|42. +8.32e-004 49.96	73. -2.80e-005 50.00
-3.02e-004 50.02	13.|43. +8.32e-004 49.96	74. -1.07e-003 50.05
+2.19e-003 49.89	14.|44. -1.21e-003 50.06	75. +1.64e-004 49.99
-7.10e-004 50.04	15.|45. +2.98e-004 49.99	76. +1.76e-003 49.91
-4.86e-004 50.02	16.|46. +2.96e-004 49.99	77. -3.22e-004 50.02
+4.28e-004 49.98	17.|47. -8.96e-004 50.04	78. +2.30e-004 49.99
-5.02e-004 50.03	18.|48. -1.38e-003 50.07	79. +2.68e-004 49.99
+1.16e-003 49.94	19.|49. -1.38e-003 50.07	80. +1.24e-004 49.99
+1.16e-003 49.94	20.|50. +9.30e-004 49.95	81. +4.78e-004 49.98
+1.15e-003 49.94	21.|51. -4.20e-004 50.02	82. -6.98e-004 50.03
+6.88e-004 49.97	22.|52. +1.46e-004 49.99	83. +3.40e-004 49.98
+1.34e-003 49.93	23.|53. -4.80e-005 50.00	84. +8.04e-004 49.96
+1.34e-003 49.93	24.|54. +4.70e-004 49.98	85. -1.29e-003 50.06
+1.67e-003 49.92	25.|55. +1.00e-005 50.00	86. -2.56e-004 50.01
-5.88e-004 50.03	26.|56. +1.20e-005 50.00	87. -1.18e-003 50.06
-5.86e-004 50.03	27.|57. +1.17e-003 49.94	88. -1.52e-003 50.08
-1.28e-003 50.06	28.|58. +1.20e-005 50.00	89. +1.38e-003 49.93
-7.04e-004 50.04	29.|59. +1.00e-005 50.00	90. +3.12e-004 49.98
+1.57e-003 49.92	30.|60. +8.00e-006 50.00	91. +8.66e-004 49.96
+1.57e-003 49.92	31.|61. -1.45e-003 50.07	92. -5.42e-004 50.03
-2.66e-004 50.01	|62. +6.64e-004 49.97	

==

Max. +2.19e-003 50.10
Min. -2.02e-003 49.89

==

CorCoeff=Correlation Coefficient
%HD=%Hamming Distance

B   MSAC Test Result

Sequence size (in bytes): 125000
Number of sequences: 93

Chi square value= 3.138240743. Passed at 1% los.
Chi square value= 21.205184743. Failed at 1% los.
Chi square value= 3.982119143. Passed at 1% los.
Chi square value= 4.300912286. Passed at 1% los.
Chi square value= 2.838120971. Passed at 1% los.
Chi square value= 9.755295829. Passed at 1% los.
Chi square value= 4.779102000. Passed at 1% los.
Chi square value= 5.368223829. Passed at 1% los.
Chi square value= 10.126934686. Passed at 1% los.
Chi square value= 3.094804857. Passed at 1% los.
Chi square value= 16.933371257. Passed at 1% los.
Chi square value= 5.774294686. Passed at 1% los.
Chi square value= 15.533395029. Passed at 1% los.
Chi square value= 6.792567600. Passed at 1% los.
Chi square value= 8.337220400. Passed at 1% los.
Chi square value= 6.784393886. Passed at 1% los.
Chi square value= 9.150035029. Passed at 1% los.
Chi square value= 8.912814457. Passed at 1% los.
Chi square value= 8.416123257. Passed at 1% los.
Chi square value= 6.235877314. Passed at 1% los.
Chi square value= 8.145363029. Passed at 1% los.
Chi square value= 11.602774686. Passed at 1% los.
Chi square value= 7.544487143. Passed at 1% los.
Chi square value= 7.229863143. Passed at 1% los.
Chi square value= 3.945595257. Passed at 1% los.
Chi square value= 6.167565543. Passed at 1% los.
Chi square value= 5.816414000. Passed at 1% los.
Chi square value= 1.076361886. Passed at 1% los.
Chi square value= 19.761410571. Passed at 1% los.
Chi square value= 10.694596400. Passed at 1% los.
Chi square value= 4.073357543. Passed at 1% los.
Chi square value= 4.955156857. Passed at 1% los.
Chi square value= 5.546571714. Passed at 1% los.
Chi square value= 4.904823600. Passed at 1% los.
Chi square value= 15.194472971. Passed at 1% los.
Chi square value= 12.338628400. Passed at 1% los.
Chi square value= 7.468948857. Passed at 1% los.
Chi square value= 2.536790686. Passed at 1% los.
Chi square value= 10.148764171. Passed at 1% los.
Chi square value= 5.664909543. Passed at 1% los.
Chi square value= 5.675273886. Passed at 1% los.
Chi square value= 4.361430686. Passed at 1% los.
Chi square value= 8.671315029. Passed at 1% los.
Chi square value= 3.144073886. Passed at 1% los.
Chi square value= 7.249246000. Passed at 1% los.

```
Chi square value= 17.977584286. Passed at 1% los.
Chi square value= 6.296461543. Passed at 1% los.
Chi square value= 13.848403029. Passed at 1% los.
Chi square value= 7.986957543. Passed at 1% los.
Chi square value= 10.664955257. Passed at 1% los.
Chi square value= 3.295775829. Passed at 1% los.
Chi square value= 9.858405314. Passed at 1% los.
Chi square value= 5.268676400. Passed at 1% los.
Chi square value= 2.994317543. Passed at 1% los.
Chi square value= 1.524307029. Passed at 1% los.
Chi square value= 5.586149314. Passed at 1% los.
Chi square value= 2.970560743. Passed at 1% los.
Chi square value= 5.887991600. Passed at 1% los.
Chi square value= 6.787195257. Passed at 1% los.
Chi square value= 5.512827257. Passed at 1% los.
Chi square value= 8.279177886. Passed at 1% los.
Chi square value= 7.921128971. Passed at 1% los.
Chi square value= 7.744726686. Passed at 1% los.
Chi square value= 8.658463829. Passed at 1% los.
Chi square value= 4.465640971. Passed at 1% los.
Chi square value= 11.652950686. Passed at 1% los.
Chi square value= 3.938866114. Passed at 1% los.
Chi square value= 5.481284400. Passed at 1% los.
Chi square value= 3.293544971. Passed at 1% los.
Chi square value= 7.122372400. Passed at 1% los.
Chi square value= 3.750987714. Passed at 1% los.
Chi square value= 12.817728743. Passed at 1% los.
Chi square value= 5.280891257. Passed at 1% los.
Chi square value= 5.881858571. Passed at 1% los.
Chi square value= 16.454164857. Passed at 1% los.
Chi square value= 11.366208743. Passed at 1% los.
Chi square value= 3.982821314. Passed at 1% los.
Chi square value= 4.505887829. Passed at 1% los.
Chi square value= 3.192055600. Passed at 1% los.
Chi square value= 5.939769429. Passed at 1% los.
Chi square value= 5.007717314. Passed at 1% los.
Chi square value= 4.356563029. Passed at 1% los.
Chi square value= 4.606748171. Passed at 1% los.
Chi square value= 1.854931029. Passed at 1% los.
Chi square value= 6.852160743. Passed at 1% los.
Chi square value= 4.105902457. Passed at 1% los.
Chi square value= 3.168211029. Passed at 1% los.
Chi square value= 3.433683029. Passed at 1% los.
Chi square value= 5.027941314. Passed at 1% los.
Chi square value= 6.780447829. Passed at 1% los.
Chi square value= 7.340180857. Passed at 1% los.
Chi square value= 8.088863829. Passed at 1% los.
```

C   Test Result of GAC

Key Pair	Cor. Value	Key Pair	Cor. Value	Key Pair	Cor. Value
(1,3)	0.002828	(21,33)	0.00348	(43,52)	-0.00253
(4,75)	-0.002502	(21,34)	0.003128	(43,62)	-0.002816
(5,12)	-0.00259	(22,29)	0.002534	(45,87)	0.002594
(5,80)	-0.003064	(22,34)	0.00348	(57,72)	-0.002864
(6,8)	-0.002894	(22,35)	0.003128	(58,68)	-0.00278
(6,80)	-0.002516	(25,26)	-0.002528	(58,88)	0.002746
(7,38)	-0.00294	(26,50)	0.003264	(59,69)	-0.002782
(7,69)	-0.003004	(28,87)	0.002736	(60,68)	0.002554
(8,39)	-0.00294	(30,90)	-0.002888	(64,91)	0.003428
(9,28)	-0.002754	(31,42)	0.003052	(66,85)	0.002636
(12,52)	-0.002902	(33,46)	-0.002726	(69,73)	-0.003042
(12,70)	0.002592	(34,47)	-0.002726	(82,84)	0.002712
(17,41)	0.002666	(34,83)	-0.003372	(83,86)	1
(18,34)	0.00266	(34,86)	-0.003372	(83,89)	1
(18,35)	0.003008	(34,89)	-0.003372	(86,89)	1
(19,36)	0.00301	(36,45)	0.003154	(87,91)	-0.002616
(21,22)	-0.002644	(39,53)	-0.002714		
(21,28)	0.002534	(42,51)	-0.00253		

On Applications of Singular Matrices over Finite Fields in Cryptography

Dhirendra Singh Yadav, Rajendra K. Sharma, and Wagish Shukla

Department of Mathematics
Indian Institute of Technology Delhi
Hauz Khas, New Delhi - 110016, India

Abstract. The main goal of this paper is to exhibit the use of singular matrices over finite fields in cryptography. Using these matrices, we propose a key exchange method in which two users over an insecure channel want to agree upon a secret key to be used in some private key cryptosystem.

Keywords: Finite Fields, Cryptography, Singular Matrices, Sequences.

1 Introduction

The origin of the general theory of finite fields began with the work of Galois [1] while the structure theory of finite prime fields reach back into the 17th and 18th centuries with the work of eminent mathematicians as Euler, Fermat, Legendre, and Lagrange.

Finite fields play a vital role in cryptography. For example, the arithmetic of Advanced Encryption Standard (AES) is done in a special finite field so-called *"Rijndael field"* [9]. Elliptic curve cryptography proposed by Neal Koblitz [2] is an approach to public-key cryptography based on the algebraic structure of elliptic curves over finite fields. Permutation polynomials over finite fields have been used in designing public key cryptosystem and digital signatures [3,4,6]. Finite fields have also been used in many other cryptosystems such as in stream ciphers, and McEliece cryptosystem [11,10,12,13,8].

Suppose a user Alice wants to send a secret message to another user Bob. She decides to represent her plaintext as a long string of elements of finite field $\mathbb{F}_q$. She wants to use a small key as a "seed" to create a sufficiently long key string of elements of $\mathbb{F}_q$ to encrypt the message. Encryption is done by adding this key string to the message string and decryption by subtracting the same key string from the encrypted message string. Now the question arises how to exchange the "seed" which is to be used for encryption by Alice and for decryption by Bob?

We propose a possible solution to the above problem using singular matrices over finite fields. To achieve a viable solution we make use of the linear recurring sequences over finite fields. The mechanism that follows is similar to Shamir's 3-pass protocol but as mentioned before this setup is only to demonstrate how this protocol works. The main objective here is to exhibit the use of

M. Joye et al. (Eds.): InfoSecHiComNet 2011, LNCS 7011, pp. 181–185, 2011.

singular matrices in cryptography. There may be many other possible ways to
implement it.

We first give a brief introduction about linear recurring sequences over finite
fields. Let $\mathbb{F}_q$ be a finite field with q elements and k be a positive integer. A
kth-order *homogeneous linear recurrence relation (HLRR)* is given by

$$s_{n+k} = a_{k-1}s_{n+k-1} + a_{k-2}s_{n+k-2} + \cdots + a_0 s_n \quad \text{for } n = 0, 1, 2 \ldots \quad (1)$$

with initial state vector $\bar{S}_0 = (s_0, s_1, \ldots, s_{k-1}) \in \mathbb{F}_q^k$ and $a_i \in \mathbb{F}_q$ for $0 \le i \le$
$(k-1)$. HLRR given by (1) generates a sequence $s_0, s_1, s_2 \ldots$. This sequence
is called a *kth-order homogeneous linear recurring sequence* (HLRS) over $\mathbb{F}_q$
corresponding to the HLRR (1).

If we associate a $k \times k$ matrix

$$M = \begin{bmatrix} 0 & 0 & 0 & \cdots & 0 & a_0 \\ 1 & 0 & 0 & \cdots & 0 & a_1 \\ 0 & 1 & 0 & \cdots & 0 & a_2 \\ \vdots & \vdots & \vdots & \cdots & \vdots & \vdots \\ 0 & 0 & 0 & \cdots & 1 & a_{k-1} \end{bmatrix}_{k \times k} \quad (2)$$

over $\mathbb{F}_q$, then the nth state vector $\bar{S}_n = (s_n, s_{n+1}, \ldots s_{n+k-1}) \in \mathbb{F}_q^k$ of the sequence is given by

$$\bar{S}_n = \bar{S}_0 M^n \quad \text{for } n = 0, 1, 2, \ldots \quad (3)$$

The polynomial

$$f(x) = x^k - a_{k-1}x^{k-1} - a_{k-2}x^{k-2} - \cdots - a_0 \in \mathbb{F}_q[x]$$

is called the *characteristic polynomial* of the HLRS. Every kth-order HLRS
over $\mathbb{F}_q$ is ultimately periodic with least period bounded by $q^k - 1$ and if its
characteristic polynomial $f(x)$ is a primitive polynomial over $\mathbb{F}_q$ and its initial state vector $\bar{S}_0$ is non-zero then it is periodic with least period $q^k - 1$
(see [10], Ch. 6).

Berlekamp Messey algorithm [7,5] shows that if an HLRS has characteristic polynomial of degree $\le k$ then any $2k$ consecutive terms of the sequence
determine a characteristic polynomial and thus the entire sequence. Therefore
these sequences are not suitable for constructing secure cryptosystems. In spite
of their proven insecurity they are very popular in stream ciphers because their
large least periods. Since our purpose here is to exhibit the protocol, we do not
worry about these facts as they can easily be overcome by using some more
sophisticated sequences such as multi-sequences etc.

2   Exchanging the Seed over Insecure Channel

Alice first chooses a k-th order HLRS over $\mathbb{F}_q$ for a suitable k so that least
period of the HLRS is sufficiently large to encrypt her message. In view of (1),

(2), and (3) it is clear that the matrix M and the initial state vector $\bar{S}_0 = (s_0, s_1, \ldots, s_{k-1}) \in \mathbb{F}_q^k$ can be taken as a "seed" to generate the whole sequence.

Alice then constructs the matrix T of order $k + 1$ by k given by

$$T = \begin{bmatrix} s_0 & s_1 & s_2 & \cdots & s_{k-2} & s_{k-1} \\ 0 & 0 & 0 & \cdots & 0 & a_0 \\ 1 & 0 & 0 & \cdots & 0 & a_1 \\ 0 & 1 & 0 & \cdots & 0 & a_2 \\ \vdots & \vdots & \vdots & \cdots & \vdots & \vdots \\ 0 & 0 & 0 & \cdots & 1 & a_{k-1} \end{bmatrix}_{(k+1) \times k} \tag{4}$$

$$= \begin{bmatrix} \bar{S}_0 \\ \hline M \end{bmatrix}_{(k+1) \times k}$$

Thus the matrix T in (4) contains the "seed" which is sufficient to generate the whole sequence.

Then she chooses a positive integer t and construct a matrix A having t rows and $t + k + 1$ columns over $\mathbb{F}_q$ such that rows of matrix A are linearly dependent i.e. $Rank(A) < t$.

Finally she constructs the square matrix L of order $t + k + 1$ over $\mathbb{F}_q$ as follows

$$L = \left[\begin{array}{c|c} A_{t \times (t+k+1)} & \\ \hline O_{(k+1) \times (t+1)} & T_{(k+1) \times k} \end{array} \right] \tag{5}$$

where $O_{(k+1) \times (t+1)}$ is null matrix.

Since rows of matrix A are linearly dependent so matrix L is non-invertible. Thus the matrix T in (4) which contains the "seed" has been embedded in a singular matrix L. Notice that the design of the matrix L is such that "seed" matrix T can easily be recognized and extracted from L.

After constructing matrix L Alice chooses a random matrix $L_A \in GL(t + k + 1, \mathbb{F}_q)$(i.e. invertible square matrix of order $(t + k + 1)$ over $\mathbb{F}_q$)) and computes $U = L_A L$ and sends it to Bob. After receiving U, Bob chooses some random matrix $L_B \in GL(t + k + 1, \mathbb{F}_q)$ and computes $V = UL_B$ and sends V back to Alice. Alice again computes $W = L_A^{-1} V$ and sends it to Bob and finally Bob computes $X = WL_B^{-1}$.

Following computation shows that matrix X is equal to the matrix L:

$$X = WL_B^{-1} = (L_A^{-1}V)L_B^{-1} = L_A^{-1}(UL_B)L_B^{-1}$$
$$= L_A^{-1}(L_A L)L_B L_B^{-1} = L$$

Thus Bob can extract the "seed" matrix T from the matrix $X(= L)$ and use it to generate the same HLRS to decrypt the message sent by Alice.

3   Security of the Method

In this method information that has been transmitted over insecure channel are the matrices $U(= L_A L)$, $V(= L_A L L_B)$ and $W(= L L_B)$. Breaking this system is equivalent to computing any one of the matrices L_A, L_B, or L using the matrices U, V, and W.

Security of this method depends on the *singularity* of matrix L. Notice that if the matrix L had not been singular then so would have been the matrices U, V and W. And then U, V and W would immediately have produced all three matrices L_A, L_B, and L since $L_B = U^{-1}V$, $L_A = VW^{-1}$ and then $L = L_A^{-1}U = WL_B^{-1}$.

Since the matrix L is singular so are the matrices U, V and W as the product of singular and non-singular matrices is singular. Following are the two viable attacks, an adversary could try to break the system:

1. By factoring any of the matrix U, V, or W, and
2. By observing that $V = UL_B$ or $V = L_A W$ and trying to solve these matrix equations.

First attack leads to factorization of singular matrices as product of a singular and a non-singular matrix over finite fields which we believe is a hard problem and a knowledgeable reader will easily recognize. Though it is not proven but there is not much literature available that deals with the factorization of matrices. There are some known factorization techniques but they work only on some special kind of matrices and produce only specific kind of factors and these are completely irrelevant in our case so we prefer not to refer them here.

For second attack we only discuss the case $V = UL_B$ as the second case is similar in nature. In the case of $V = UL_B$, matrices V and U are known singular matrices and L_B is unknown non-singular matrix.

Suppose $Rank(L) = r$ then $r < (t + k + 1)$ since the matrix L is singular. Using the fact that if A and B are matrices such that product $A.B$ is defined then $Rank(AB) \leq \min\{Rank(A), Rank(B)\}$ we see that

$$\max\{Rank(U), Rank(V), Rank(W)\} \leq r.$$

Solving the matrix equation $V = UL_B$ for L_B leads to $t + k + 1$ system of linear equations of the form $UX = b$. Each of these linear system of equations gives at least q possible solutions for X (depending on the rank of matrix U). By solving these $t + k + 1$ systems, we see that matrix L_B will have at least q^{t+k+1} possible choices which is obviously not practical.

4   Conclusion

We have shown that singular matrices can be used for cryptographic purposes. Security of our proposed method depends on the seemingly difficult problem of factorization of matrices. We are working on some protocols that answer the questions like "why" one may prefer this new method over existing methods like RSA and Diffie-Hellman key exchange, "how" to protect the integrity of the secret, and some other cryptographic issues. Finding new ways to factor matrices is a problem which requires a lot more attention of mathematical community.

Acknowledgments. The authors would like to thank the reviewers for their constructive comments. This work was partly supported by grant no. 09/086 (0749)/2005-EMR-I funded by Council of Scientific and Industrial Research (CSIR), India.

References

1. Galois, E.: Sur La théorie Des Nombres. Bull. Sci. Math. de M. Ferussac 30, 428–435 (1830)
2. Koblitz, N.: Elliptic Curve Cryptosystems. Mathematics of Computation 48, 203–209 (1987)
3. Levine, J., Brawley, J.V.: Some Cryptographic Applications of Permutation Polynomials. Cryptologia 1, 76–92 (1977)
4. Lidl, R., Muller, W.B.: Permutation Polynomials in Rsacryptosystems. In: Advances in Cryptology, pp. 293–301 (1984)
5. Massey, J.L.: Shift-register Synthesis and BCH Decoding. IEEE Trans. Information Theory 15, 122–127 (1969)
6. Schwenk, J., Huber, K.: Public Key Encryption and Digital Signatures Based on Permutation Polynomials. Electronics Letters 34(2), 759–760 (1998)
7. Berlekamp, E.R.: Algebraic Coding Theory. McGraw-Hill, New York (1968)
8. Shparlinski, I.E.: Finite Fields: Theory and Computation. Kluwer Academic Publishers, Dordrecht (1999)
9. Daemen, J., Rijmen, V.: The Design of Rijndael: AES - The Advanced Encryption Standard. Springer, Heidelberg (2002)
10. Lidl, R., Niederreiter, H.: Introduction to Finite Fields and Their Applictions. Cambridge University Press, Cambridge (1994)
11. Koblitz, N.: Algebraic Aspects of Cryptography. Springer, Heidelberg (1999)
12. Lidl, R., Niederreiter, H.: Finite Fields: Encyclopedia of Mathematics and Its Applications. Cambridge University Press, Cambridge (1997)
13. Menezes, A.J., Blake, I.F., Gao, X., Mullin, R.C., Vanstone, S.A.: Applications of Finite Fields. Kluwer Academic Publishers, Dordrecht (1993)

Author Index

Bandyopadhyay, Sambaran 45
Bhunia, Swarup 30
Burman, Sanjay 1

Chakraborty, Rajat Subhra 30, 45

Danger, Jean-Luc 128
Das, Abhijit 157
Datta, Amit 144
Dutta, Ratna 57, 72

Ghosh, Santosh 16
Ghosh, Satrajit 157
Guilley, Sylvain 128
Gupta, Indivar 93, 168

Mishra, Dheerendra 57
Mishra, P.R. 168
Mohandas, Radhesh 3
Mukhopadhyay, Sourav 57

Narasimhan, Seetharam 30
Naskar, Ruchira 45
Nassar, Maxime 128

Padhye, Sahadeo 83
Pais, Alwyn R. 3
Pandu Rangan, C. 111
Pillai, N.R. 168
Poddar, Rishabh 144

Rebeiro, Chester 144
Roychowdhury, Dipanwita 16

Sadalkar, Kunal 3
Saxena, P.K. 93
Schmidt, Jörn-Marc 2
Sharma, Rajendra K. 181
Sharmila Deva Selvi, S. 111
Shukla, Wagish 181
Souissi, Youssef 128
Sree Vivek, S. 111

Tiwari, Namita 83

Yadav, Dhirendra Singh 181

GPSR Compliance

*The European Union's (EU) General Product Safety Regulation (GPSR)
is a set of rules that requires consumer products to be safe and our
obligations to ensure this.*

*If you have any concerns about our products, you can contact us on
ProductSafety@springernature.com*

In case Publisher is established outside the EU, the EU authorized
representative is:

Springer Nature Customer Service Center GmbH
Europaplatz 3
69115 Heidelberg, Germany

Batch number: 09490872

Printed by Printforce, the Netherlands